D0682348

The young officer took his place at the left side of his superior. The sniper's cross hairs lay directly on the general's heart.

Hathcock's mind raced through all his markmanship principles, "Good firm grip, watch the cross hairs, squeeze the trigger, wait for the recoil."

Recoil sent a jolt down his shoulder. He blinked and the general lay flat on his back. Blood gushed from the old officer's chest and his lifeless eyes stared into the sun's whiteness . . .

CHARLES HENDERSON

Marine Sniper

93 Confirmed Kills

SPHERE BOOKS LIMITED

A SPHERE BOOK

ISBN 0 7474 0562 X

Printed and bound in Great Britain by
Collins, Glasgow

Sphere Books Ltd
A Division of
Macdonald & Co (Publishers) Ltd
Orbit House
1 New Fetter Lane
London EC4A 1AR

A member of Maxwell Pergamon Publishing Corporation plc

ACKNOWLEDGMENTS

No author has ever written a book totally alone—somewhere along the line, he had assistance. In most cases, that assistance has been great. This book is no exception.

First, I thank Raymond B. Lech, a fellow author who introduced my work to Sol Stein and then guided me over the first hurdles of being published. I will be eternally grateful to Ray for that.

Thanks to my editor, Bill Fryer, for boiling down more than seven hundred pages of manuscript and leaving the content and focus of Carlos Hathcock's story intact.

And thank you, Sol Stein, for your faith in me as a writer.

Special thanks go to Lt. Col. David Willis, a distinguished marksman and one of the finest Marines I have ever had the pleasure of knowing. He had faith in my integrity and introduced me to Carlos Hathcock. He assured Carlos that I was a man of honor and worthy of his trust. Without that, I am certain that Carlos would never have consented to reveal to me his most private and deeply held personal experiences.

Thanks are not enough for Maj. E. J. Land. He gave me many, many hours of his time, assisted me in my research, and opened his private library to me. But above all, he opened his soul and let me see a very personal part of his life. He told me about it in detail and withheld nothing that I requested.

Also, I cannot forget Sgt. Maj. David Sommers, M. Gunnery Sgt. Ron McAbee, and David Holden, who freely gave bits and pieces of their past to me.

The Historical Division at Headquarters, U.S. Marine Corps, also provided invaluable assistance, especially Ben Frank of the Marine Corps Oral History Branch and Ev Englander of the Marine Corps Historical Center Library.

I thank Lt. Col. Rick Stepien for his assistance, tolerance, and encouragement.

I also say thank you to my family. I occupied their lives with my book for more than a year and a half. I denied them a real family life while I spent all my time, that was otherwise theirs, researching and writing and rewriting.

Last, and most important, I thank Gunnery Sgt. Carlos Hathcock. He refused me nothing: he fed me, gave me his bed, and called me his friend. He shared countless hours with me, opening his heart, telling me the stories now bound in this volume. It is a great honor to know him and a privilege to call him my friend.

For all the snuffies of the Corps, and to the memory of my brother Marines, Tony, Sammy, and Iron Mike

CONTENTS

FOREWORD

To be a nationally recognized shooting champion takes a special kind of individual. To be effective on the battlefield as a sniper requires even more extraordinary qualities.

Gunnery Sergeant Carlos Hathcock is one of those rare individuals who has carved a niche in Marine Corps history by being both.

It takes a special kind of courage to be alone: to be alone with your thoughts; to be alone with your fears; to be alone with your doubts. This courage is not the superficial brand stimulated by the flow of adrenalin. Neither is it the courage that comes from the fear that others may think one a coward.

It is the courage born of honor.

Honor on the battlefield is a sniper's ethic. He shows it by the standards and discipline with which he lives life in combat. By the decency he shows his comrades. And by the rules he adheres to when meeting the enemy.

The sniper does not hate the enemy; he respects him or her as a quarry. Psychologically, the only motives that will sustain the sniper is the knowledge that he is doing a necessary job and the confidence that he is the best person to do it. On the battlefield hate will destroy any man—and a sniper quicker than most.

The sniper is the big-game hunter of the battlefield, and he needs all the skills of the woodsman, marksman, hunter, and poacher. He must possess the field craft to be able to position himself for a killing shot, and he must be able to effectively place a single bullet into his intended target.

Gunnery Sergeant Hathcock was all of these things with a full measure of the silent courage and quiet optimism of a true champion.

The war in Viet Nam was ideally suited to sniper warfare. However, the rules of engagement and a lack of understanding of the sniper's role made his effective employment a constant struggle. The struggle continues.

Sadly, there are few officers in the United States Armed Forces today who understand even the basic rudiments of marksmanship, much less sniping. Thus they cannot possibly understand the potential of this flexible, versatile, and cost efficient fighting asset. Sniping has a history extending from the Renaissance achievements of Leonardo da Vinci who, standing on the walls of besieged Florence, picked off enemy soldiers with a rifle of his own design and of Benvenuto Cellini who, during the siege of Rome in 1527, sniped the enemy commander, the Constable de Bourbon, to the modern era and Hathcock's 93 confirmed kills in Viet Nam, which included high-ranking commanders.

At the beginning of every conflict in this century there has been a slowly dawning realization of the need for snipers, and at the end of every conflict there has been an effort to put that genii back in its bottle. Not only has the officer corps showed little understanding of the support and employment techniques necessary to the successful deployment of the weapons system we call a sniper, but because of weak stomachs, or a desire to conciliate others with weak stomachs, they have attempted to suggest that sniper warfare is morally wrong and unworthy of a role in the United States Armed Forces. The only reply to that must be that it is doubtful if it is either reasonable or moral to import the standards of Hollywood westerns, in which the good guys never shoot first, onto the battlefield.

I'm comfortable in my mind that there is little hope for understanding from the old guard. However, I pray that the young officers of today will read this book with an inquisitive mind. I hope that they will look at the requirements of the modern battlefield and see the great potential of the sniper system. Hopefully, they will see that the success and effectiveness of the sniper is limited only by one's imagination.

There can be little doubt that Gunnery Sergeant Hathcock was effective in his role as a sniper. What is not widely known is that he became the focal point of a staff effort to legitimize sniping.

I was the marksmanship coordinator in the Office of Training at Headquarters, United States Marine Corps, from 1975 through 1977. During this period we staffed a proposal for a permanent table of organization and table of equipment for the sniper unit.

There was a strong effort at this time to delete the sniper program from the Marine Corps. As a result, I conducted a personal lobbying program that extended from the handball courts to the briefing rooms; from the Officer's Club at Quantico to seminars on urban warfare. There, Carlos became the symbol of what could be.

Carlos's story was told again and again. It added credibility to the too often impersonal and unimaginative thought processes used by a major staff. Carlos Hathcock not only sparked but inflamed the imaginations of many who would have removed all traces of sniping from the Marine Corps. His real-life heroics served as a demonstration of what could be accomplished with proper training, equipment, and leadership.

Eventually, through the efforts of many men, a permanent sniper table of organization and table of equipment within every Marine Division was established, and approval was given for what has become the finest school on the art of sniping in the world. Without Hathcock's story and without his courage, perhaps none of this would have come to pass.

E. J. LAND
Major, U.S. Marine Corps (Retired)

PREFACE

This book is based upon the personal recollections of the participants and upon the official Marine Corps records kept at the Marine Corps Historical Center in Washington, D.C. Operational orders, situation reports, and after action reports provide the historical framework for the story *Marine Sniper* tells. As for the actions of the enemy, whatever was not observed by American eyes was reconstructed from the evidence found after battle. And in specific instances spectacular windfalls came my way: the notebook of the "Apache woman," in which she kept a record of her day-to-day movements and observations and in which she reports on her encounters with the American enemy, was recovered after her death and lent me by a Marine who was on Hill 55.

In a few places I have taken the liberty of inventing dialogue for Hathcock's North Vietnamese and Viet Cong opponents. Those are the only elements in the book that cannot be fully justified by a careful examination of the evidence. Everything else has been made factually accurate to the best of my ability.

There is no hunting like the hunting of man, and those who have hunted armed men long enough and liked it, never care for anything else thereafter.

—Ernest Hemingway

1

Duc Pho Shooting Gallery

A GENTLE BREEZE rustled the white feather in the Marine sniper's floppy hat as he watched the land below through the telescopic gun sight. The soft stir of air had swept up the hill from the rice paddies and, just moments earlier, had touched a twelve-year-old Vietnamese boy whose khaki shirt hung loose and wet across his skinny back and who struggled to keep his heavily laden bicycle upright.

It was a mild February afternoon in 1967, and Sgt. Carlos Norman Hathcock II sat cross-legged behind his M-2 .50-caliber machine gun. A year and a half earlier, at Camp Perry, Ohio, the slim, twenty-four-year-old Marine had won the U.S. 1,000-Yard High-Power Rifle Championship. Now he took aim from the southern finger of a solitary peak in South Vietnam.

He squinted as he stared through the eight-power Unertl sniper scope mounted on the top, right-hand corner of the machine gun's receiver. His spotter, a darkly tanned, shirtless Marine staff sergeant named Charles A. Roberts, silently crouched next to him and looked through an M-49 twenty-power spotting scope, watching for the enemy.

The brim of Carlos Hathcock's faded camouflage bush hat sagged over the dull green tube of the telescopic sight as he observed a distant speck wobbling toward him up the dirt road.

Slowly the boy on the bicycle grew larger in Hathcock's

gun sight, and a troubled expression crept across Hathcock's narrow, suntanned face. He saw a number of rifles—four dangling from the handlebars, two on each side, and three more tied sideways beneath the bicycle's seat. A dirty, green haversack hung from the center of the handlebars, bulging fat with hundreds of rifle cartridges packed in bandoleers or loaded in a dozen banana-curved magazines that protruded from beneath the flap of the old canvas pack. This boy was not just another kid on a bike; he was a Viet Cong resupply "mule," carrying arms and ammunition to an enemy patrol. When night fell, that patrol would turn the rifles that this underfed, twelve-year-old boy now struggled to deliver, directly on Hathcock's brother Marines.

Hathcock never wanted to kill men, much less children. He knew, however, that this was no ordinary child. Children in war grow up quickly. And Marines die as fast from bullets fired by twelve-year-old boys as they do from bullets fired by twelve-year-old boys as they do from bullets fired by men.

The bicycle teetered closer and closer. The sniper's grip tightened on the gun's two wooden handles. His thumbs rested firmly on the butterfly-shaped trigger, which was mounted between the handles at the gun's butt. He followed the youth until the boy came abeam him, allowing for a clean, two thousand-yard, broadside shot.

Hathcock moved his scope's cross hairs onto the front wheel and fork of the boy's bike. He pressed his thumbs slowly down on the trigger and sent a heavy (two and-one-half-inch, seven hundred-grain) bullet ripping into the bicycle's framework.

The boy somersaulted over the handlebars and crashed into the orange dust that covered the road. His deadly cargo scattered, and Hathcock smiled. Maybe now this boy would run away and leave the work of death to men.

That hope rapidly vanished. The shaken lad grabbed the nearest automatic rifle and, with a quickness gained from many firefights, jammed a banana-curved magazine into the weapon. Then he raised the gun. Just as he began to shoot, Carlos Hathcock dropped him dead.

A Marine patrol walked down to the road and took the load

of enemy rifles and ammo. Vietnamese farmers who had been working in the nearby rice paddies carried the boy's body away.

As he always did after engaging the enemy, Hathcock jotted down the facts of the incident in a dog-eared, green notebook—his "sniper log"—that he carried in the slanted breast pocket of his camouflage shirt. Later that evening, he would describe the "kill" in a situation report that would be sent to his new officer in charge, Maj. D. E. Wight.

Hathcock didn't need to take notes, however, to keep that experience forever vivid.

He and Roberts looked over the sandbag wall and watched the villagers carry the boy's limp body toward the mud-and-rice-straw huts that stood a few hundred feet away. The broken bike lay unattended on the roadside. It would be gone by morning.

The sniper's dark eyes followed the road back toward the mountain passes—the many corridors of the Ho Chi Minh Trail. No doubt those weapons had been boxed in China and had ridden the rails through Nanning and Ningming, across the North Vietnamese border to Lang Son, Kep, and into Hanoi. There women took them from their boxes and repacked the rifles into smaller lots for their trip southward to the Mu Gia Pass, the main funnel from North Vietnam to the Ho Chi Minh Trail and to South Vietnam's combat zones.

During the United States involvement in the Southeast Asian conflict, American forces divided South Vietnam into three zones of combat. In the far south, Saigon rested in the heart of the III Corps Tactical Zone—the Mekong Delta lowlands; Camau Peninsula (later designated IV Corps); and the hill country north of Bien Hoa Air Base. The II Corps encircled the vast Central Highlands with Dac Son and Da Lat bordering the south and Pleiku and Phu Cat the north.

From the 17th parallel—the cease-fire and demarcation line of July 1954, popularly called the DMZ—to the Central Highlands' northern ridges is I Corps.

In 1966 and '67, I Corps was a tough place for an American fighting man to live. Primarily controlled by Viet Cong and North Vietnamese forces, that combat area's western border blended into Laotian jungles where the Ho Chi Minh Trail's three main arteries flooded arms and freshly trained troops into Vietnam's war.

At the point where the southernmost route of the Ho Chi Minh Trail enters I Corps, the Sihanouk Trail joins it, giving the Viet Cong, or VC, a second supply flow of Soviet- and Chinese-built arms and ammunition, landed into Cambodia via the Gulf of Siam and carried by elephant, by train, and on human backs into Laos for entry into Vietnam.

A few kilometers inland from where the South China Sea washes Vietnam's east coast, at a place called Duc Pho—I Corps' southern-most tip—a high, lone hill overlooks miles of farm fields and hundreds of mud-and-straw huts. Off to the west steep mountains rise and, between the peaks, streams and rivers flow into broad valleys that spread like fingers on an outstretched hand, feeding water to this rich, rice-growing countryside.

From where the Ho Chi Minh and Sihanouk trails meet inside Laos on the Vietnamese border, a lacework of roads, footpaths, and tunnels branch out across the rugged mountains, following ridges and streams across the breadth of Vietnam to the rice lands that Duc Pho's solitary hill overlooks.

On that hill, Carlos Hathcock sat with his spotter* watching this "Indian Country," slowly scanning the miles of terrain spread out before them, and hunting and killing "Charlie"— Charlie the man, Charlie the woman, and Charlie the twelve-year-old boy.

That youngster had ridden a long way, judging from the salt rings that encrusted his shirt. He had peddled and pushed that rifle-laden bike since before daybreak. The sun was just setting now above the rugged peaks of the mountains that make up the high backbone of Vietnam, the Annamite Cordillera. No doubt the rifles had almost reached their destination

---

*A sniper's partner. He is the half of the sniper team who seeks out targets by use of a spotting telescope or powerful binoculars. Once locating a target he will direct the sniper's fire to it, and call his shots as well as recommend sight adjustments. The spotter also provides cover and security fire for the sniper, and takes turns manning the sniper rifle to allow one team member to rest while the other stands watch.

when this Marine sniper had halted their transport and, in the process, killed a child.

He wondered if the men who lay waiting for that delivery had seen their cargo stopped dead by his bullet. To him it was cowardly to send a child to do a soldier's work, and as he leaned back against the sandbags and lit a cigarette, he shook his head. He thought of occasions on which the Viet Cong had wired three- and four-year-old children as booby traps and had blown away the unlucky Marines who stopped and offered the tots chewing gum or chocolate, and of the Marines who had accepted cold sodas from slightly older children. The sodas had been poured into cups filled with tiny shards of broken glass, mixed with chipped ice. It did not take many stories like those before a Marine learned to stay clear of children.

Hathcock stood and dusted the seat of his trousers, and as Roberts departed up the hill, disappearing behind large rocks, he took one final look down the narrow road that led to the mountains and the setting sun. This was his favorite time of day. It had always been special for him, ever since he was a kid staying with his grandmother in the countryside near Little Rock, Arkansas. It seemed long ago now. He wondered what she would have thought about his killing the boy this day. Would she understand that he had no choice?

He looked at the graying sky and wished he could be home. "Tour's almost done, Carlos," he said to himself, trying to kill the pang of homesickness that struck. "Golly, I'll bet Sonny has grown a foot taller by now." In a few months he'd be home to celebrate his twenty-fifth birthday, and eighth year in the Marine Corps, with his wife, Josephine, and his little boy, Carlos Norman Hathcock III.

For now, he closed out another day on his hilltop position. Here, he was one small part of a special landing force operation called Deckhouse IV that had been dovetailed into another operation called Desoto, now underway for several weeks.

Marines from 1st Battalion, 4th Marine Regiment, served as the main force in this operation, clearing the Duc Pho area of Viet Cong concentrations.

Hathcock had positioned the gun on a finger of the solitary hill so that he could cover much of the area between the coast and the mountains, but, sitting there on the hill also made him a target for daily fire from below. Those long shots sent lead splattering on the big rocks around the Marine sniper's nest, yet as long as he and Roberts kept low in their position, they were relatively safe.

From the hill, the snipers provided a blocking force and some security for the battalion during their sweeps through this broad, flat countryside. Hathcock's duty on this operation exercised very little of his ability as a sniper, requiring minimal stealth, just sharpshooting with the heavy machine gun. It was a sort of carnival shooting gallery where Viet Cong, rather than tin ducks and clay pipes, were the targets.

Hathcock had pioneered using the .50-caliber machine gun as a sniper weapon. The big gun's seven hundred-grain bullets offered a stable trajectory for nearly three thousand yards, extending the sniper's range of highly accurate fire well beyond two thousand yards, more than double the capability of his .30-06 rifle. The .50's cyclic rate was slow enough to allow for single shots with no difficulty. And, mounted on its T-and-E, a traversing and elevating tripod that accurately adjusted the machine-gun's fire with geared control knobs, the system served as a steady and finely tuned aiming platform for the eight-power telescopic sight, which was necessary to precisely train the gun on its distant targets.

The Marine sniper stretched. He was more tired than usual and glad the operation would soon end.

A star-filled sky greeted Carlos Hathcock the following morning. He sat in the dark, cross-legged behind his machine gun, waiting for the sun to share its new light with the enormous valley below. It would be a very busy day.

A Marine major stood behind Hathcock's right shoulder. He scanned the brightening horizon through powerful, green binoculars. Hathcock's wispy white feather quivered in his hatband as a steady westward breeze dried the dampness left by the ground fog and overnight dew. No one spoke.

Both Hathcock and the major listened for the sound of helicopters. That sound would signal the beginning of a final sweep through this area.

A dog barked in the darkness far below the group of Marines, and Hathcock glanced at the cooking fires that flickered near the huts where the dog lived. There, Vietnamese farmers prepared for another workday. He gazed farther out into the early morning grayness where other firelights twinkled. Viet Cong, he thought.

The major stuffed a load of chewing tobacco into his mouth and said, "Won't be long—sun's just about up. Sergeant, how does it look through your scope?"

Hathcock put his eye to the long and slender rifle scope mounted on the machine gun. He shook his head, "Still too dark. But when the frogs land, we should have plenty of light."

When he first came to this lonely hilltop, he had zeroed the gun sight to place his shots dead-on at twenty-five hundred yards, and now, from this sandbagged, promontory nest, he easily covered the entire valley with his deadly fire.

The sniper's victims never knew what hit them when his brand of whispering death struck—they only heard the heavy bullet's impact if he missed.

Today, Hathcock's gun would again serve as a blocking force for the battalion, turning the fleeing enemy back into the sweep, where they would either die or fall prisoner to the Marines. If they gambled to run, they must get by the sniper, who was already becoming famous among the Viet Cong as "Long Tra'ng"—The White Feather. To get by him, they must cross several hundred yards of open rice fields, flooded ankle deep in water.

The sniper waited and listened. He heard the distant mumbling of two Marines crouched up the hill among the rocks behind him. They had a radio beside them and were waiting to hear from the sweep leader that the operation had begun.

The distant sound of helicopters caught Hathcock's attention. Almost simultaneously, the radio crackled, "Red Man, Red Man. Evil Eyes three-six. Over." The Marine sitting next to the radio picked up the handset, answering the call, "Evil Eyes three-six. Red Man. Go ahead, over." The response came, "Roger, Red Man. Evil Eyes three-six at point Tango. Over."

The major searched the horizon and easily picked up three

helicopter silhouettes racing toward him just above the tree-tops. "I've got them," the major said. "Tell them we're ready here."

"Evil Eyes three-six, roger and tallyho. Red Man is ready," the radio operator responded.

The sweep began with three twin-rotor, CH-46 Sea Knight helicopters letting off their passengers in three "hot" landing zones. The chatter of small-arms fire filled the air as helicopters swept down the ridge lines, just above the treetops, and set down. In half a minute, this first wave of choppers was up and away, leaving the Marines to face the hostile fire that greeted them.

Farther to the west, other twin-rotor aircraft landed, unloading another company, blocking "Charlie's" hope for escape to the mountain ridges there. The two companies would push the entrenched Viet Cong out and into a cross-fire or into the blocking forces who now waited.

Hathcock watched the jungle that edged the expanse of flooded rice paddies beneath him. His eyes carefully searched each stretch of dense cover. Soon he realized that he could relax his grip on the machine-gun's handles. From the sounds of the fighting, the Viet Cong would not easily give up the security that their trenches and the tree cover offered. They held on as the Marines closed toward them. Hathcock knew that it would be awhile before he had any work.

The warm orange of the morning turned white as the sun climbed toward noon. The major stood staring through his binoculars, searching the trees and hedgerows for VC sneaking out of the sweep. Sweat trickled down Hathcock's neck as he scanned the tree line with his sniper scope.

The intense fighting had sent several Viet Cong retreating toward the southwest, only to meet the ambushing fire of blocking forces stationed there. The VC knew that the east's open fields would expose them, so they attempted to turn west, only to confront the widespread rifle squads of the flanking company. Hundreds died that day. Many others surrendered. By the end of February 1967, the landing force claimed more than a thousand Viet Cong confirmed dead, and they counted another thousand probable dead.

Two frightened Viet Cong guerrillas carefully crawled

through the brush at the edge of one water-covered rice field. They could hear the Marines closing swiftly behind them.

The two men searched the field's borders and saw nothing, and yet both men knew crossing it could mean certain death. Sweat soaked through their shirts. Their hair lay plastered flat and dripping. Their eyes burned from the perspiration that ran off their brows and down their faces. A decision could wait no longer.

When the men stood to run, Hathcock spotted them in his scope and said to the major, "Sir, two are breaking out on the left."

"Shoot to the side of them. Try to turn them back into the sweep."

Hathcock pressed the trigger and sent the first shot into the water ahead of the men. They had no place to hide, yet they kept running toward the far side of the rice field.

He sent two more shots down the hill, but the guerrillas continued to charge across the shining surface of the field. They seemed to be moving through the shin-deep mud and water in slow motion, their legs pumping like pistons and their feet splashing in the mire.

"Major, they're not turning," Hathcock said.

"Kill them," the major responded.

The sniper placed his scope's cross hairs on the first man and pressed the butterfly. The soldier splashed down dead in the muddy water.

"Good shot," the major said. He took the binoculars from his eyes and leaned slightly to his right, spitting a load of tobacco juice to one side of the sandbagged nest.

The second man wheeled, almost falling, and broke to his right, still headed away from the sweep. Carlos Hathcock laid his scope's cross hairs on the VC's back and again mashed the machine-gun's trigger. The second man tumbled into the water.

No one else broke out of the tree line during that day's sweep. When it was over, the major walked back to the command post, located on the other side of the hill, for an appraisal of the day's operation, and Hathcock waited and watched through the afternoon. He suspected that once the dogs had called off their hunt, "Homer the Hamburger" might show himself. For Hathcock, the Viet Cong had only two families—the Hamburgers and the Hot Dogs. They were all named Homer.

Sure enough, just as he had expected, he spotted a figure slipping from the trees to the edge of a distant rice field. He knelt and put his face in the water, and when Carlos put his scope on him, he could see a Chinese K-44 rifle slung across his back.

A lieutenant from a company that had participated in the sweep now sat next to the Marine sniper, staring through binoculars.

"You see him down there?" Hathcock asked the young officer.

The lieutenant shifted the binoculars toward the direction that the machine gun now pointed and found the Viet Cong soldier, still drinking. "I got him. How far you judge that to be?"

"Twenty-five hundred yards. He's right on the spot where I zeroed this gun when I first got here."

The lieutenant laughed, and Hathcock said, "Let's see if I can't rain all over his parade." He took a firm grip on the gun's two wooden handles, took a short breath, and began pressing the trigger, waiting for the recoil's surprise.

The lieutenant watched. He felt strange because even at this distance he could see the man's face and his eyes. He had never looked at a man's eyes just as a bullet killed him. The young officer jerked as the machine gun belched a single round down the hill. At that precise second, the enemy soldier started to rise and caught the bullet just below his chin.

The lieutenant saw the soldier kicking in the dirt and shouted, "You missed!"

In his Arkansas, low voice, Hathcock drawled, "He's dead, sir. They just flop around a lot when you shoot 'em in the head."

Hathcock never connected with a longer shot.

Later that day, he saw a Viet Cong soldier coming down a trail. On the same trail, an old woman was carrying water-filled buckets hung on the ends of a long pole, which she balanced across her shoulders like a yoke. She was teetering up the path when the Marine sniper's bullet struck the dirt between the soldier's legs and ricocheted over the woman's head. The frightened man charged right at her, and she attempted to set down her load. But, just as she began to squat, the soldier struck her head-on. The woman tumbled over backward into the dirt, spilling her buckets and losing her pole.

Hathcock had a chance at a second shot, but his laughter took charge of his aim. He continued chuckling as he dismantled the big machine gun. It was a satisfying end to his long watch atop the hill at Duc Pho.

The weapons platoon retook possession of their M-2 .50-caliber machine gun that had served as Carlos Hathcock's sniper weapon during his stay on the Duc Pho hilltop.

Hathcock fastened the long Unertl scope back on his sniper rifle—a match-conditioned, .30-06 Springfield caliber, Model-70 Winchester anchored at the receiver with precisely torqued screws that held it in a glass-bedded, Monte Carlo-style stock, above which the finely tuned barrel floated, less than the width of a dollar bill, allowing the barrel to flex freely when he fired the rifle. He again zeroed the weapon for seven hundred yards.

With his NVA pack* strapped snugly to his back and his rifle shouldered, Carlos Hathcock waited at the landing zone for the helicopter that would take him back to Hill 55, his base of operations. He liked Hill 55 because it overlooked miles of Viet Cong-controlled countryside—hot spots like Elephant Valley to the north and, to the south, Antenna Valley. East of Hill 55 were the friendly strongholds of Marble Mountain and Da Nang, but to the west lay the badlands known as Charlie Ridge and Happy Valley.

Hathcock felt glad to be getting back to his old hunting grounds. Charlie Roberts stood next to him and nudged him, "Looks like our frog." He pointed toward the twin-rotor helicopter that had just cleared the horizon along the northwest coastline and now raced toward them, skimming the treetops.

Hathcock said nothing to Roberts. It was typical of their

*North Vietnamese Army pack. It had a large cargo compartment and many pouches and pockets, ideal for snipers.

relationship. They had never gotten along, and Hathcock politely endured the staff sergeant while suppressing his often felt frustration with the senior Marine. As they waited, Hathcock recalled the first day on Duc Pho and how Roberts had stood atop the rocks surrounding the sniper position, admiring the breathtaking view, and drew a hail of enemy fire. A senior NCO in the battalion had yanked Roberts off the rocks just as the shooting began and then questioned the reliability of both the Marines. That insult had deeply wounded Hathcock's pride. From that day forward, the rift between the two men grew. Hathcock did his thing, and Roberts did his—mostly watching.

Hathcock smiled and took off his bush hat, holding his white feather secure in the hatband with his thumb.

More than seven years before, on a warm spring day in 1959, Carlos Hathcock had stood in the Marine recruiter's office in Little Rock, Arkansas, and watched his mother sign the papers giving him permission to join the Marine Corps. It was May 20—the day of his seventeenth birthday. He was fulfilling what for him was already an old dream.

That afternoon he got on a plane bound for San Diego, where he would have thirteen weeks at the Marine Corps Recruit Depot in which to prove himself man enough to join the United State's most elite society of warriors.

Carlos stood five feet ten inches tall and weighed one hundred forty pounds. Although slight in build, he could run all day and lift a load equal to his weight over his head. He had developed this strength after dropping out of high school at age fifteen and going to work for a Little Rock concrete contractor, shoveling cement ten hours a day, six days a week.

Boot camp wasn't going to be any picnic, but Carlos had the physical stamina to withstand the long, punishing days and nights. As for the mental pressures, he would handle them with the strong self-discipline that he had developed at an early age when he was forced to shoulder the responsibilities of his family.

Hathcock arrived at MCRD San Diego sitting on a brown, plastic-covered seat inside a dull gray bus with "U.S. Navy" stenciled on its side. He and approximately thirty other recruits had ridden it from Lindbergh Field to the recruit depot. Several of the young men talked loudly and smoked cigarettes, although the chubby, blond-haired Marine private who drove the bus had warned them that that wasn't the best way to start their military careers.

It was eleven o'clock of a warm, West Coast evening. The bus came to a halt, and a Marine sergeant wearing a tan uniform, with creases so sharp that they stood out a half inch from his chest, stepped briskly aboard.

The sergeant wore black, spit-shined shoes, which glistened like patent leather, and a brown, beaver-felt campaign hat with a wide, flat brim. Centered on the hat was a coal black Marine Corps emblem. The Marine walked directly to where one of the cockiest recruits was sitting.

During the ride from the airport, this loud-talking fellow boasted how tough his St. Louis gang had been. The young man wore his long and thick black hair heavily oiled and combed back in a ducktail. He sported a pack of Camels rolled in the sleeve of his black T-shirt. A smoking cigarette dangled from one corner of his mouth.

Without a word, the Marine drill instructor plucked the cigarette from the recruit's lips, dropped it on the black rubber mat that ran down the aisle of the bus, and crushed it out with a single twist of his toe. Half a dozen other lit cigarettes suddenly dropped to the floor in silence as the broad-shouldered sergeant gazed toward the rear of the bus with his stern, dark eyes, almost hidden under the brim of his hat.

Hathcock was in awe. "This is it!" he said loudly.

The Marine looked at him. Hathcock was just about to rise to his feet when he caught the drill instructor's cold stare.

"Ladies—you too, sweetheart," he said in a loud voice and looked directly at Hathcock. "You will not utter a word from this moment on, unless you are addressed by your drill instructor. When that occurs, the first word out of your mouth will be Sir," the DI growled emphatically, pausing for effect. "And the last word out of your mouth will be Sir. Is that clear?"

Only silence followed.

"When you are addressed by a drill instructor, and he asks you a question, you will respond with Sir, followed by the appropriate answer, and then finish with Sir. Is that clear?"

Again, only fearful silence met the DI's ears. He looked at Hathcock. "Private!"

Hathcock swallowed and answered him in a low, Arkansas drawl, "Yes Sir?"

"What did I just say?"

Hathcock felt the blood rushing through his face. He rose to his feet and mumbled, "Sir . . . ah . . . you ain't supposed to say nuthin . . ."

The Marine cut him off in mid-sentence. "You? You? Boy, do you know what a ewe is? That's a female sheep! You're a country boy, ain't ya. You ought to know what country boys does to them female sheeps. They fucks 'em, don't they— boooy. You want to fuck me?"

"Sir, no Sir," Hathcock quickly responded.

"Sit down, boy," the drill instructor barked.

"Sir, yes Sir," Hathcock said, gladly shrinking to his seat.

"I can't hear you, boy."

Hathcock responded loudly, "Sir, yes Sir!"

"Okay, ass eyes," the granite-faced sergeant said angrily. "When you answer me, you are on your feet, at the position of attention, and your asshole better pucker and your ears better pop. If they don't you ain't answering loud enough. You got that?"

Hathcock leaped to his feet, arching his back and jutting his chin straight up. He screamed with his eyes squeezed tightly shut and his veins bulging on his neck, "Sir, yesss Sirrr!"

The Marine sergeant walked down the aisle, "Ladies, any time a drill instructor addresses you as a group, you will answer as a group. You will answer properly and loudly. If you fail as a group, you will pay for your sins as a group. Is that clear?"

Thirty young men chimed together, assholes puckering and ears popping, "Sir, yes Sir."

"Very good."

"When you speak to a drill instructor, you will address him in the third person. That means if you have a request, such as one of you ladies might need to go tinkle, you would request it in this fashion, 'Sir, the private requests permission to make a head call, Sir.'

"Two words that will never be a part of your vocabulary are I or You. You will replace those words with The Private and The Drill Instructor, respectively. Is that clear?"

"Sir, yes Sir," thirty voices yelled.

"Now, when I step off of this bus, I don't want to hear the sound of anything but wind sucking in, filling the vacuum that you just left, and the thunder of your hooves hitting those yellow footprints painted out there on the concrete. You got that?"

"Sir, yes Sir."

"I will not hear one word out there. Marines are sleeping in the barracks just down the road and we don't want to disturb them, do we?"

"Sir, no Sir."

The Marine turned his back and stepped off the bus, followed by the stampede of thirty frightened recruits, including Hathcock.

That night they gave him a web belt, a pair of tennis shoes, a green utility cap, jacket and trousers, a large white T-shirt, a large pair of white boxer shorts, green wool socks, a blue, plastic soap dish, a bar of Dial soap, a blue, plastic toothbrush holder, a can of Barbasol shaving cream, a razor, a tube of Crest toothpaste, a toothbrush, a pair of rubber thongs that the marines called shower shoes, a pair of gray shorts, a yellow sweatshirt with a red Marine Corps emblem emblazoned on the front, a green canvas seabag with a wide strap that clipped through a ring on the top, a bucket, two sheets, a pillow, and a blanket. He got to bed at 4:00 A.M., and an hour and a half later a drill instructor rousted the exhausted recruits and sent them on the first day of their thirteen weeks of hell.

Hathcock chuckled as he recalled those unforgettable days. He gazed out the helicopter's door at the emerald-and-orange jungle, watching treetops blur past just a few feet beneath the chopper as it raced toward Hill 55. He thought how that first day in the Marine Corps had to be his most memorable birthday.

He thought that he could have married Jo on a May 20 also, but choosing the Marine Corps' birthday—November 10—seemed better, somehow. It balanced the year's celebrations, and it was a date that he remembered easily. November 10, 1967, would mark his fifth wedding anniversary. These five years of marriage had passed quickly for Hathcock. They had been happy for the couple, but not easy.

Jo did not like being a "shooting-team widow." However, when she married Carlos in 1962, she knew what lay ahead: He would be gone often, competing in regional, state, and national shooting matches throughout the United States. Carlos would leave Thursday and come home Sunday night. Monday, Tuesday, and Wednesday he worked from 5:00 A.M. until 6:00 P.M. at the rifle range. In the evenings, he lay on the floor in front of the television and practiced "getting into position"—the tightly contorted stances (standing, sitting, kneeling, and prone) from which he fired in the matches. From March through April he did nothing but shoot.

However, Jo had resigned herself to that life-style when she decided to become Mrs. Hathcock. Had someone asked her if she would ever make that decision when she first met him, she would have laughed in his face. Hathcock, on the other hand, had thought Jo was swell—nice looking and with a great personality. He formed that opinion the day that he walked into the bank in New Bern, North Carolina, where she worked as a teller. That was in January 1962.

Hathcock had just reported to the Marine Corps Air Station at Cherry Point from the 1st Marine Brigade in Hawaii, where he had spent the past two years cruising the exotic ports of the Far East and South Pacific.

It had been a dramatic change for Hathcock, departing that tropical paradise, with its brown-skinned girls and wonderful liberty nights, for coastal North Carolina, with its tobacco-lined country roads and gas-station entertainment.

After boot camp and basic infantry training, Hathcock had left Camp Pendleton for the base at Treasure Island in San Francisco Bay, where he sailed on a troop ship to Hawaii. There he became a machine gunner in the weapons platoon of Company E, 2nd Battalion, 4th Marines. And he did his best to maintain the image of the battalion's nickname—The Magnificent Bastards—during his liberty stops in Taipei, Tokyo, Papeete, and other exotic ports, as well as at home port in Honolulu.

When Hathcock reported to the air station in North Carolina, the first problem that the personnel chief had to solve was how does an air station employ an infantry Marine? The nearest infantry regiments were forty miles south at Camp Lejeune. The personnel chief asked Hathcock if he would like to work in special services, sweeping out the gym and passing out basketballs. Hathcock swallowed a lump in his throat and tried not to show the repulsion he felt at that idea.

He looked straight in the eyes of the ruddy-faced Marine and innocently asked, "Does Cherry Point have a rifle range?"

Hathcock knew that they did and that it was the home of an outstanding shooting team, too. He figured that if he asked to be assigned to the team right off, the personnel officer might not respond to the wishes of a private first class. But if he let them come up with the idea, it would be a sure thing.

"I have some experience shooting," Hathcock told the gunny. "I coached at Kaneohe Bay and shot on the Hawaii Marines team, too. You can call Gunner Terry or Lieutenant Land back in Hawaii. They put me through their scout/sniper school there. I might be of some use out at the range."

The gunnery sergeant listened and then said, "I'll call Gunny Paul Yeager down at the rifle range and see if he has a slot for you."

The phone call lasted but a moment. Yeager had heard that a hard-shooting PFC named Hathcock was headed his way and that this young Marine had won the Pacific division rifle championships the year before. He had already made plans to have Hathcock try out for the All-Marine Champion, Cherry Point Shooting Team.

In his three years of shooting at Cherry Point, Hathcock rose from a talented novice to become a Distinguished Marksman, winning Marine Corps, Interservice, and National shooting championships. He set the Marine Corps record on the "A" course by shooting 248 points out of a possible 250—a record never matched again—and retired with the course. That was during his first year there.

Hathcock spent his first Carolina Christmas alone in the barracks, where he read books and practiced squeezing his slim body into tight, rock-solid shooting positions. The South Pacific's liberty ports had been an unforgettable adventure, but competitive shooting was more fulfilling. For Hathcock, marksmanship represented the essence of a Marine: It was the skill of his trade. Hathcock did not mind the lonely Christmas. The thought of the rifle range opening for the new season and the opportunity to possibly make the Cherry Point shooting team kept his spirits high.

But some of the other Marines who lived with him during the holidays felt sorry for this quiet and unassuming shooter. He looked as though he could use a good time. One of the well-meaning Marines had a girl friend who worked in a bank in New Bern, North Carolina, a small community located a short drive west of the Cherry Point air station's main gate. She had a girl friend who might provide the perfect medicine for this lonely Marine.

It was a very cold January day when Carlos Hathcock walked inside the New Bern bank where Josephine Bryan Winstead worked. She was a woman who had just entered her thirties, yet looked hardly a day older than twenty-one. She wore the latest hairstyles and fashions and had adjusted to living independently again after an unhappy and unsuccessful marriage. Now she took care of her mother, who lived with her in a small apartment in New Bern. On weekends, she and her mother drove to Virginia Beach where they visited Jo's sister. She had dated little since her divorce.

On this brisk January morning, Hathcock wore a black, long-sleeved, polished-cotton shirt with white pearl buttons on his collar, cuffs, and shirtfront, and black sharkskin trousers. They were the only civilian clothes that he owned.

Hathcock usually wore his uniform. He was proud to be a Marine and loved to put on the tan outfit that had impressed him as an eight-year-old boy when he saw his first Marine. He had all of his uniforms tailored to fit perfectly. He even had his green herringbone utility shirts and trousers tailored and leather heels with horseshoe cleats put on his spit-shined boots. He was a poster-perfect Marine. He had never needed civilian clothes until his buddies at the air station's barracks convinced him that he would get much further with the ladies if he wore his civvies.

When Jo saw the slim, dark-eyed Marine with his jet black hair and clothes, she thought, "Oh my God! What on earth have I gotten myself into?" And when Hathcock swaggered across the bank's polished marble floor, the loud click of his heels added accent to Jo's first impression.

"Hi! I'm Carlos Hathcock," he said with cocky bravado. He locked his dark hazel eyes on hers without blinking and smiled, showing his sparkling, straight teeth.

Jo tried very hard to look beyond the bold clothing, and she noticed a very handsome young man who was slim and muscular, clean and clear-skinned. But his eyes seemed to dominate his entire presence—they pierced and flashed. It was a glance that overpowered Jo and left her blushing and turning her eyes toward the floor.

"I'm Jo," she said. She had not felt so uncomfortable since her teen years. She suddenly felt very shy.

As they walked down the street, she asked Hathcock, "Aren't you cold? I'm freezing! Where's your coat?"

Hathcock's face turned bright red and Jo suddenly knew that she had asked the wrong question. In a concerned tone she said, "I'm sorry."

"Oh, that's all right," he answered, holding his head high. "I just got here from Hawaii and haven't bought a coat yet. I'm freezing too."

Jo suddenly moved very close to Hathcock as they walked, putting her arm around him, trying to share her warmth. "Let's hurry. I don't want you to freeze."

A wide smile crossed his face.

Pay came twice monthly for Hathcock—less than $50 each fifteenth and thirtieth. He had bought U.S. savings bonds since his first week in boot camp. He had also taken out an allotment of $20 per month from his pay, which went into his savings account. After slightly more than two years, he had amassed more than $500 cash, not counting his bonds. He had planned to buy a car when he made corporal. Meeting Jo caused him to alter those plans. He barely had enough to cover the monthly payments, but the $500 that he paid down on the Chevrolet Bel Aire kept the total cost within his range.

Gunnery Sergeant Yeager lost his temper when he saw what the underpaid private first class had done. "Hathcock! Are you out of your mind, or do you come by that special brand of stupidity naturally? What are you going to do for spending money? After you pay for your haircuts and cleaning and then make your car payment and buy gas, you won't have a dime left to your name."

"I eat in the chow hall. I sleep in the barracks. That's all free. And haircuts cost a quarter, and I spend five dollars a month on cleaning. I won't have any problem making the payment," Hathcock retorted.

Hathcock spent the summer dating Jo and not spending more than $5 a week doing it. But for Jo, that didn't matter. She had come to know and love this gentle young man. He had a boyish nature, full of ideals and dreams. He made her feel very comfortable. By August she had fallen deeply in love with Carlos, and he in love with her. Their relationship had gone for nearly nine months, and Hathcock made no overtures beyond their frequent dating. Jo felt it was up to her to make the next move—he certainly was not doing it.

"You and I have to stop seeing each other," she told Hathcock as they drove away from the bank on a warm August evening. "We have no future like this. I don't want to go on just seeing a movie on Friday nights and riding in the country on Saturdays and Sundays. I want more. I'm a woman, not a little girl."

"I can't get married," Hathcock said in a low, almost inaudible voice. "You gotta be a sergeant. I got busted to private already twice now, and I just sewed on my PFC stripe for the third time. Do you think that they will give me permission to get married?"

"I won't wait," she said. "And they can't tell you no, either."

Hathcock saw there was no use in arguing with her on this subject. He had never asked any of his superiors about marriage; he only knew the scuttlebutt that fellow snuffies* told concerning the Marine Corps' feelings about it. He did know

*A slang word describing lower ranked enlisted Marines. Derived from "Snuffie Smiths," meaning little guys.

that a PFC's or even a corporal's pay was not nearly enough with which to even dream of supporting a wife. But Hathcock loved Jo, and he did not want to lose her. He felt that he could suffer through anything, as long as she was willing, too.

When the alarm buzzed next to Hathcock's head at four thirty Monday morning, the sleepy Marine put his feet on the floor and struggled to stand. He felt as though he would throw up. "Oh God!" he moaned as he walked down the aisle between the rows of racks and wall lockers in the squad bay, heading toward the showers. An hour later he stood at the brink of the confrontation that he had dreaded all night.

"Gunny Yeager, Jo and I are getting married," Hathcock told his NCO-in-charge.

"No you're not." Yeager told Hathcock in a matter-of-fact voice.

"Yes I am. I've already made all the plans. She's got a good job and I love her."

The gunny looked at Hathcock and shook his head. "You will get married anyway, won't you. It's just like that car. I gotta know this. Is she in trouble."

Hathcock looked angrily at the gunny. "No. And why would you think such a thing? She's a nice girl."

"Back off! I have to see the captain, and he will ask."

The gunny looked at him appraisingly. "How you going to live? On her pay? You gonna sell your car? Where you going to live? And what if she does get pregnant? What then? You better think of all this too. You know that bank won't let her work pregnant! If she loses that job, you're shit out of luck."

Hathcock looked at the gunny and said in a calm, low voice, "I'm getting married. You're invited to the wedding. It's November 10."

The next year, Jo became pregnant and had to quit her job, and Hathcock managed to make meritorious corporal.

Once safely on the ground, Hathcock headed for his bunker. He was thinking about the past and the future. He knew his wife would be happier if he left the Marines and put down roots somewhere—got a job and a house. But he loved the Marines, and he had already given a lot of his life to it.

"Eight years already," he said aloud as he walked down a

path that led to a waist-high ring of sandbags that surrounded the plywood-and-screen-sided, tin-roofed building, the Marines called a hooch, which housed 1st Marine Division's scout/sniper instructors.

Lance Corporal John Roland Burke lay on a cot. Carlos Hathcock regarded him as the best spotter with whom he had ever worked. The young Alabama Marine looked up and said, "Sergeant Hathcock, you say something?"

Hathcock leaned his shoulder against one side of the long, narrow building's doorway. "No. Just talking to myself. You gonna be ready to move out tomorrow? Gonna work north, I think. Up around Elephant Valley."

Burke nodded, "I'm set. Sure don't look forward to another week of peanut butter, cheese, and John Wayne crackers. Think I'll pack a few cans of jelly, too. Need something different."

Since the snipers had to travel light they were used to carrying nothing but the small, flat cans of peanut butter and cheese. The bulkier C-ration cans were not for them.

Hathcock laughed. "You want to eat good? Learn how to type. They'll have you over on Hill 327, sittin' around camp and gettin' fat in a heartbeat."

"No thanks," Burke said. "I'm no pogey."*

Hathcock headed for the chow line near Hill 55's mess tent. One last good meal for another week, he thought. Tomorrow's chow would be the standard peanut butter-and-cheese entrée.

Resting a tablet on his thigh, Hathcock sat on the edge of his cot and wrote another letter home to Jo. She had no idea that he did anything beyond instructing Marines in marksmanship —the only job that she had known him to do in the Marine Corps outside of competing on the rifle team and being an MP for a while. She had no way of knowing that her husband—a soft-spoken, country boy—was now the Marine Corps' deadliest sniper.

---

*A pogey is slang for a Marine, such as an administrative clerk or typist, who works in an office. Marines would convince pogeys to do special administrative chores by offering them candy and soda pop, which is appropriately called, "pogey bait."

He told her little of his job. He had written about being an MP at Chu Lai and how he hadn't liked it.

She'd been relieved when he wrote in October telling her that he had been taken out of the MPs and was now with his old shooting teammate Capt. E. J. "Jim" Land, forming a new school to instruct Marines in marksmanship. His letters told her how he missed her, but they never mentioned going into "Indian Country" to hunt and stalk "Charlie."

In New Bern, North Carolina, Jo Hathcock picked up her daily copy of the *Raleigh News and Observer* from where the delivery boy had tossed it in the front yard of her 1303 Bray Avenue home. She slid the green rubber band off the large, tightly rolled newspaper and opened it to the front page. As she had done each day since her husband's departure for that far side of the world, she looked for news of the war, turning to the column marked SERVICE NEWS. There she hoped to read about people whom she and Hathcock might know. She sometimes clipped items and sent them to Carlos. Her eyes found a paragraph headed A SCOUT-SNIPER. It told of the Marine Corps' deadliest gun in Vietnam—Carlos Hathcock.

Jo's hands trembled as she read of how her husband regularly crept into enemy territory alone, or with only one other Marine, and stalked the Viet Cong. The story began:

> A SCOUT-SNIPER with the 1st Marine Division in Vietnam earned praise from his commanding officer for "making life miserable for the Viet Cong." Sgt. Carlos N. Hathcock of New Bern is one of several "expert marksmen" credited with killing more than 65 enemy. Firing at ranges up to 1,125 yards, Hathcock and the "crew" have been picking off better than two enemy a day—without a friendly casualty.

Jo quickly folded the newspaper, walked in her house, and slammed the front door shut. She never had liked Carlos's being in the Marine Corps. She hated Vietnam. She only tolerated the Marine Corps because Carlos loved it so dearly. She had often felt jealous of the Marines, especially when he spent nights away from home with the rifle team, competing. Now she felt both fearful and angry.

Jo Hathcock sat at her kitchen table, her young son playing on the floor near her chair. She sipped a cup of coffee as she wrote her husband a long letter.

In a darkened hut half a world away from New Bern, North Carolina, Carlos Hathcock licked the envelope's flap and pressed it shut. He addressed the letter and jotted the word FREE on the upper-right-hand corner. "No tax, no stamps," he reminded himself. Hathcock laid the letter on his footlocker and flipped open his Zippo to light a cigarette—his last for a week.

While in the bush, Hathcock wanted to smell like the jungle—not tobacco smoke. The Viet Cong could smell the stuff a mile away. As the Marine Corps' best sniper, Hathcock had a healthy respect for the abilities of his foe. A pinch of chewing tobacco generally kept his nicotine craving controlled.

With lights out, only the glow of his cigarette illuminated the inside of his hard-backed hooch. He lay and listened to the sounds of the night and the war.

Carlos Hathcock lay back on his air mattress and thought about home and his twenty-fifth birthday. He sighed, "Twenty-five—my car insurance will go down, and I get a pay raise. Eight years in the Corps. It don't seem like it.

"Seems like yesterday when Daddy came home from Europe and brought me that old Mauser rifle. Boy, those were the days. I could barely lift the thing. I must have been ten or twelve years old before I finally got to where I could take aim with it."

Hathcock closed his eyes. A gentle rain began falling. He listened to its patter on the sandbags that ringed his hooch. He quickly fell asleep.

2

The Nature of Things

MAY 7, 1954 — it was only thirteen days before Carlos Hathcock's twelfth birthday.

The boy was going out to play in the woods with an old German Mauser rifle. Its barrel was plugged shut but, even though he couldn't shoot with it, he loved the gun. His father, Carlos Norman Hathcock, Sr., had brought the rifle home as a war relic nine years before and given it to three-year-old Carlos II. Carlos's family background was WASP with a touch of Cherokee Indian, and no one knew quite why the first name of Carlos had become traditional for the men in the family.

As young Carlos walked toward the woods that stood behind his grandmother's rural home, a white frame house next to a gravel road in a tiny farming community near Little Rock, the hourly news that crackled from the radio could have been reporting that the French Union Army's 167-day defense of a place called Dien Bien Phu had ended. That was the day the French fell to Gen. Vo Nguyan Giap's Viet Minh forces. General Giap had managed to starve them out and now the Geneva Conference, called that spring, seemed heavily tilted toward the Communists.

But, if that was the news on the air, Carlos cared nothing for it. That conflict did not involve America or the U.S. Marines. He had John Wayne, Japanese, and a real war on his mind today. Sergeant Stryker in the *Sands of Iwo Jima* was one of the few movies in which the "bad guys" had killed

25

"The Duke." Carlos mourned Stryker's death, and he cheered as Marines from Echo Company, 28th Regimental Combat Team, raised the Stars and Stripes atop Mount Suribachi.

He, after all, was a Marine, too. He had decided four years earlier, when he was eight, that he would join the United States Marine Corps someday. Carlos felt certain that no greater calling could exist in this life.

He hummed the Marines' Hymn as he marched toward the woods, his Shetland collie dog, Sassy, trotting at his heels and Carlos squarely holding the rifle at "right shoulder arms."

Carlos saw his first Marine at age eight, in the Memphis apartment building where he and his parents lived. His father had quit his Arkansas railroad job to work in the Mississippi River port city as a welder for the Tennessee Fabricating Company.

A young Marine and his wife lived downstairs from the Hathcock family then, and from the first time that Carlos had set eyes on the trim and straight man who had a square jaw and rock-hard arms, he could imagine no greater thing than to become a Marine.

Bill Monroe sang nasally about his "Brown Eyed Darlin'" following the radio news. Carlos's grandmother hummed along with the bluegrass melody as she opened her kitchen's screen door, causing its rusty spring to sing out when the old door swung wide.

"Carlos!" she shouted in a voice that cracked slightly from age—a sing-song grandmotherly voice that young boys, now grown old, associate with barefoot memories of warm summers and goodness. "Supper's gonna be ready soon. Don't you go runnin' off and gettin' yourself dirty. You hear me?"

"Yes ma'am," Carlos called back. "I'll be right out here—me an' Sassy."

Now, once behind the dense, green cover of the weeds and bushes and trees that grew on the edge of his grandmother's backyard, Carlos dropped to his knees. He knelt next to the thick trunk of an old pine that overlooked the yard and magically projected his imagination through space and time to the jungles of Guadalcanal, where he joined the 1st Marine Raider Battalion in action.

The skinny, black-haired boy no longer wore jeans and T-shirt but Marine Corps herringbone and boondocker boots. He faced the Japanese enemy alone. They hid behind every tree, stump, and rock.

Quietly, Carlos shoved the muzzle of his rifle through the prickly vines of a blackberry bush. Pushing with his toes, he slid across pine needles and damp earth without making a sound. There he lay hidden beneath an umbrella of tangled vines.

Today, he hunted the Japanese, much the way he stalked squirrels and rabbits with his J. C. Higgins .22-caliber, single-shot rifle, which he had gotten for his tenth birthday. He rarely missed a shot.

Carlos hunted small game to put meat on the family table. His mother and father had separated, and now he and his two-year-old brother, Billy Jack, had accompanied their mother here to live with their grandmother. They were poor.

But peering down the old Mauser's sights on this warm spring day, Carlos did not think of food as he drew bead on a tortoise. A tortoise, which now became a well-camouflaged Japanese sniper—the deadliest sworn enemy of Edson's Raiders, heroes of the Pacific.

However, the young warrior's dog failed to appreciate the intense situation, and she trotted over to the tortoise, nudged it with her nose, and began barking. The tortoise clamped shut.

Carlos rolled from under the vines and thorns and stood erect, holding the long rifle by its muzzle and resting its butt on his toe. "Sassy!" he shouted, frowning at the dog. Then he glanced down at his clothes. No longer in the South Pacific, but back in the woods of Geyer Springs, Arkansas, he realized that he had trouble. Muddy circles outlined the knees on his once-clean jeans. His T-shirt had fared no better. He frantically dusted off the loose soil, but the muddy stains on his knees and T-shirt remained. That meant a problem at home.

Carlos's grandmother never understood that Marines cannot fight in combat and keep their knees clean—especially twelve-year-old Marines.

"Carrr-looos," her voice sang through the woods.

"Commm-inggg," he answered apprehensively.

* * *

May 20, Carlos celebrated his twelfth birthday and opened his gifts. He found one special present that dwarfed the importance of all the others—a Remington 12-gauge, single-shot shotgun. His mother and grandmother both thought that he should have something for his twelfth birthday that required more responsibility, something that would give him a better edge than his .22 rifle.

Carlos Hathcock had an exceptional ability to shoot a rifle well, even at age twelve. When he saw the long and narrow box, he knew that its contents could only be one thing—a new rifle or a shotgun.

There was a certain fineness about firearms for the young shooter. He never saw them as toys but as tools crafted for a purpose that he greatly respected and enjoyed—hunting.

Now, with a shotgun, Carlos's grandmother thought, he could hunt dove and pheasant and quail when they came in season. Carlos saw the shotgun as a more efficient firepower to snap-shoot the squirrels and rabbits that often flashed through the brush before he could draw down on them with his rifle.

Carlos opened the box containing his new shotgun and shells at nine o'clock that morning. By nine thirty he walked in the woods with the gun resting over his forearm, its breach broken open and a shell chambered.

A sudden gray flash caught his attention. In a single motion, Carlos snapped the breach shut and raised the gun to his shoulder. He heard the rabbit skitter through the weeds ahead, so he waited for another flash of fur. This time he would be ready.

The flash again caught his eye, but this time it was several yards away. He fired the gun and watched the rabbit run up and over a hill. He had missed.

By eleven o'clock Carlos had killed nothing, and he had missed several shots—easy shots. He put the shotgun away and returned to the woods with his single-shot rifle. The .22 may not have had the spread, but with it Carlos never failed to bring home meat. Just past noon, he returned home with two squirrels and a cottontail rabbit dangling from a tether.

Carlos never mastered the knack of hunting with the shotgun, although he tried shooting dove and pheasant and quail. He hunted with the shotgun often, but always wound up getting his old single-shot rifle to bring home the game.

Warm damp air hung heavily in the morning stillness when pleasant childhood memories blurred into conscious thought and Hathcock awoke. He felt sticky and uncomfortable. The rain, which had lulled him into a restful sleep, now heralded the beginning of another humid day in Vietnam.

Outside Hathcock's hooch, Lance Corporal Burke sat quietly whittling on a stick. Hathcock saw the back of Burke's bush hat resting against the wire screen and called out drowsily, "You been there long?"

"No, not really. Figured you weren't in any special hurry since we're going for the week. Thought I'd let you sleep some."

"Let me grab my pack and rifle, and I'll be with you. What's the time?"

"Almost six thirty."

Hathcock and Burke walked to the Combat Operations Center, where radios crackled around the clock and a tired-eyed gunnery sergeant sat at a field desk jotting notes on a yellow pad, assembling bits and pieces of an intelligence report from messages scrawled in pencil on flimsy, yellow slips of paper.

"Morning, Gunny," Hathcock said in a low voice to the intelligence chief.

"Hi there, Sergeant Hathcock. Want some coffee? That jug's fresh."

Each man poured himself a cup and then Hathcock looked over at the sergeant. "Anything going on north—up around Elephant Valley?"

"Happenings everywhere, Sergeant Hathcock. Take your pick. Recon's sighted lots of movement. Already had reports of contact this morning from two patrols—one up toward Elephant Valley. You planning to work up there?"

"Had that in mind, unless someone has something else to offer. Lance Corporal Burke and I coordinated a long-range mission up that direction."

"Good. I could use some intel-reps from up there. Let me

know your call sign when you check out with operations. And be careful—Charlie's up to something."

Hathcock finished checking out in the operations center and joined Burke outside in the drizzle.

"What's the plan on getting up there?" Burke asked.

We chop north to a fire base where we join a patrol. They'll take us to a good drop-off point. After that, we'll be by our lonesome. A long-range patrol will pick us up on its way in Sunday, at the edge of Elephant Valley. That's six days alone with no rear guard.

"We're Bravo-Hotel on the radio net. We will only make contact on the move or when departing our position."

"Or in case shit hits the fan?" Burke added with a sarcastic smile.

Hathcock unfolded a map that he had made waterproof with a clear-plastic laminating film. "We've got a battery of 105s here," he told Burke, pointing to a hill located southeast of Elephant Valley. "They'll fire on our call, if we need help. If we need air or some other kind of help, we call the S-3."

"Sounds good, Sergeant." The rain was ending, and Burke looked up at the brightening sky. "Weatherman says possible light showers off and on in the evening, and sunny days."

"Good. We ought to be able to move pretty fast. Shouldn't make any noise with the world soft and soggy."

In less than an hour, the two snipers were climbing out of a helicopter at the fire base* where a rifle squad stood in a U-shaped formation. A tall, black corporal moved from man to man, checking each rifle and inspecting each Marine. Two Marine sentries sat behind sandbags, near a gap in the barbed wire that encircled the compound. The corporal turned toward the approaching snipers. A Marine standing in the squad crowed, "Looky here. It's Murder Incorporated!"

"Shut the fuck up, asshole," the black corporal snapped. "You the snipers we're taking up toward Dong Den and Nam Yen?"

---

*A fire support base is a bivouac established to support operations in extended or remote locations, usually away from the main body of the regiment.

"That's us. I'm Sergeant Hathcock and he's Lance Corporal Burke."

"I'm Corporal Perry."

The men shook hands, and, in less than ten minutes, the patrol set out, moving quickly through the wire, one man at a time. Once they reached the far side of the tangled maze of barbed wire surrounding the fire base, stretched in crisscrossing patterns, each Marine took a covered position, widely spaced and on line along a hedgerow near a well-traveled road.

Perry took a quick head count and motioned to the point man to move out. One at a time, each Marine stood and followed the lead, the men taking positions staggered from right to left and spaced thirty feet apart. They maintained this discipline of wide dispersion to lessen the effects of ambush or booby traps.

Hathcock and Burke joined the column near the patrol's rear guard—a heavyset and already sweating Marine whose boots had worn nearly white from lack of polish. Hathcock had seen many Marines like this one—Marines who neared the end of their tours, their clothes showing the wear of a year at war. He could see beginnings of the telltale one thousand-yard stare, the stoic expression on a face that had seen its fill of combat.

Hathcock looked at his own faded uniform—Marines called it "salt." That lance corporal walking rear guard looked salty, but, except for his boots, no more salty than he or Burke did. The snipers used plenty of black paste wax on their boots, but they left it unbuffed so as not to reflect sunlight and draw fire.

Hathcock thought about the wisecrack the Marine had made when he and Burke turned up. It was the sort of thing he had had to get used to. He remembered Capt. Jim Land, the man largely responsible for selling the sniper program to the Marines, saying, "When you react to their brand of bullshit, you just buy more. Keep this in mind, they don't understand snipers because snipers are new. They may be a little scared of you, too. Show them you're a pro by not letting their crap get in your way."

It was Land who had recruited Hathcock and Burke and

fifteen other men as snipers, and he had known perfectly well what he was doing. Land looked for a special breed of Marine to join his unit—the 1st Marine Division's Scout/Sniper Instructors. Good marksmanship was important, but that was a skill one could acquire. He picked men like Hathcock because they possessed the more important skills—great knowledge of nature and the outdoors, a sense of belonging to the wilds, extensive field-craft skills, and, most important, strong mental stability and extreme patience. So far Land's judgment had paid off.

The patrol walked for two hours through the bush, and engaged in one fire fight that could have been costly but wasn't because they had approached an area that seemed ideal for a Viet Cong ambush with caution. The ambush had come, but the Marines hadn't been where the enemy expected them to be. Result: six dead Viet Cong and a massive string of mines the Cong had laid along a trail set off by one of their own men.

The Marines departed from the scene of the action and moved through more acres of hills and thorns and tall grass. The sun baked the ground dry from the morning rain. The weeds crunched under their steps as the patrol approached a stream that led northwest, toward Elephant Valley.

"Sergeant Hathcock, I guess this is it for now," the black corporal said to the snipers. "I hope I see you again. You two Marines take care of yourselves."

Hathcock and Burke dropped away as the patrol moved westward. This was the start point from which the sniper team moved into Elephant Valley for the week.

They had a long trek ahead that would be at a much slower pace. Beneath the thick undergrowth they went forward cautiously, on constant alert for the slightest hint of Charlie's presence. Hathcock faced the inner struggle of speed versus stealth. He wanted to be hidden by nightfall—in position and ready to start hunting Charlie at first light. But he was going to see to it that even their presence in this area would be unknown to the enemy.

3

Elephant Valley

BAIE DE TOURANE, as the French called it, serves as the city of Tourane's gateway to the South China Sea. When the French left Tourane, the Vietnamese, and later the Americans, called the city Da Nang. The muddy water of the Ca De Song— known to U.S. Marines as the Cade River—finds its end at this city, emptying into the bay that is guarded by a prominent peak the Americans named Monkey Mountain.

Ca De Song flows wide from the west's high mountains, into the thousands of rice fields that border the northern edge of Da Nang. During this region's monsoon season—November through February—more than one hundred inches of rain swells the river, flooding the rice fields along its banks. Those farmlands, vulnerable to the river's monsoon ravages, stretch from Da Nang's northern limits to where the river's valley begins gashing between the Annamite Cordillera's eight thousand-feet-high peaks.

Along the southern bank of the river, a dirt road winds just above the highest points that the monsoon floodwaters reach. This road serves the farmers, who grow rice along this river, as a pathway to Da Nang's market. During the monsoon floods, it also serves as their escape route from the deep, rushing water as it courses eastward between densely forested granite mountains. No one knows who first built the road. For the Vietnamese farmers, it has always been there—the only trafficable route out of this mountainous jungle. Because it is the only road, the Viet Cong and the North Vietnamese Army depended on it for supplies and reinforcements from Laos.

More than twenty kilometers northwest of Da Nang, heading up river to where the Ca De Song bends north and then west again, rises a velvety green mountain, thirty-three hundred feet high, called Dong Den. Below Dong Den stretches the narrow, elbow-shaped run that infantrymen from the 3rd Marine Regiment named Elephant Valley.

It got its name one June night in 1965 when the Marines atop Dong Den's jungle-covered ridges heard the trumpeting of elephants. An illumination round was fired to light the valley, and it revealed a train of eight elephants, loaded with heavy cannons. The Marines called for naval gunfire, and after two spotter rounds, the eastern horizon came ablaze with the flash of the ship's broadside fire. In the valley, the barrage struck, obliterating the Viet Cong and their elephants.

The elephants died near the hamlet of Nam Yen, the heart of Elephant Valley. There the river runs eastward. Two kilometers downriver, where the elbow crooks southward, is the hamlet of Pho Nan Thuong Ha. And two kilometers below this crook, the river again bends eastward at a hamlet called Truong Dinh—the end of Elephant Valley.

It is here at Elephant Valley's eastern limit that the mountains become hills and the river spreads flat across the rice land, scattering sandbars between its wide channels and dumping silt into Baie de Tourane.

Darkness had swallowed this country as Carlos Hathcock and Johnny Burke slowly made their way over the hills east of Dong Den and descended into Elephant Valley where the Ca De Song bends from its southward to its eastward flow at Truong Dinh. Hathcock planned to move into the big elbow's crook at Pho Nan Thuong Ha where the valley broadened between the dense mountain jungles.

"We have two, maybe three kilometers left before we're at the big bend," Hathcock whispered to Burke as they paused to examine their map and survey this end of the long and crooked valley. "I think we'd be too close for comfort here. Only six hundred meters to work in. Up at the big bend where the valley widens we'll have a thousand to shoot across, and, by moving into a couple of different positions, we have open fields of fire that extend two or three thousand meters up or down the valley." The slim Marine stood up and said to Burke with a smile, "It'll be gooooood huntin'."

These were the first words they had spoken since they separated from Corporal Perry's patrol. On the move, they communicated with hand signs and facial expressions.

While Hathcock and Burke slipped along the valley's edge at Truong Dinh, heading toward the big bend, as many as one hundred fifty newly trained North Vietnamese soldiers and their leaders tromped into the western reaches of the valley that follows the Ca De Song.

The NVA company consisted mostly of sixteen- and seventeen-year-old boys. They were the children of the new society of Uncle Ho—its first generation. They began school under the Communist state, established in 1954, and passed from childhood into adolescence following the valiant struggle of the Viet Minh rebels against Ngo Dinh Diem. Diem was overthrown on November 1, 1963, by Gen. Duong Van Minh, and unrest lasted through 1964. It seemed as if the National Liberation Front and its National Liberation Army, the Viet Cong, would finally claim victory and bring about the unification of Vietnam. But the United States stepped in following the ouster of Minh, propping up the south's new chief of state, Gen. Nguyen Van Thieu, and premier Gen. Nguyen Cao Ky, and flooding South Vietnam with American forces.

Now the young Communist soldiers realized that the war might rage for years. They were valiant enough, these young men, but they were new to combat. Their uniforms looked fresh, their turtle-shell-shaped helmets showed no dents or scars, and each man's Kalashnikov rifle looked as if it had just been unpacked.

They were a far cry from the typical National Liberation Army soldiers who had no uniforms other than khaki shirts and shorts, or black pajamas, and whose rifles were old and well worn. Men like these had often been in the jungle for years, and they waged war with whatever they could steal or capture, and with what little they could carry over the mountains from Laos.

These youngsters followed an officer who had only a little more experience than they did and who was assisted by a few subordinate officers and NCOs, who had seen some combat. Each officer and NCO carried a pistol—a symbol of authority—on his hip.

As the company route-stepped* along the rice fields, the commander kept his position at the lead. Behind him his senior NCO followed closely. The young officer who led the company planned to join his battalion in the jungles on the northern side of Elephant Valley, and rather than climb through the rough mountains at a crawl, he marched his men through the flat valleys at a rapid pace. This cut days off his trek, getting badly needed soldiers to his commander, whose battalion's numbers had been cut drastically by the search-and-destroy attacks that the growing American forces had launched against them.

Concealed in the thick jungle growth at the valley's edge, the two Marine snipers peered from behind a tree fall covered with broad-leafed vines, scanning the open fields through which the Ca De Song snaked. They rubbed light and dark green greasepaint on their faces, necks, ears, and hands. The whiteness of their eyes contrasted sharply with the mixture of green hues that surrounded them, like pearls laid in a mossy pool.

The white feather festooning the senior sniper's bush hat lay motionless in the still morning air. Soon dawn's first gray light began to reveal more and more of the wide and flat river valley to Carlos Hathcock's and John Burke's shifting and searching eyes. Both snipers felt knots tighten in the pit of their stomachs. As the early morning brightened, they could hear the muffled sounds of men on the march.

A thick fog hung just above the valley, hiding the upper reaches of the mountains that surrounded this place, offering the two snipers a field of fire that faded into grayness eight hundred yards from where they hid.

The distant sound of many voices became audible to the Marine duo. Hathcock searched for scouts who might be moving ahead of what he now concluded was a large unit that he knew could not be friendly. The brashness of their march

---

*A march that is followed without cadence—usually out of step. Used for movement on long treks through rough terrain.

puzzled him. Was it a ploy by an even larger organization to draw fire and expose an ambush to devastation by a hidden NVA battalion?

The snipers saw no scouts.

Hathcock tasted a mixture of salt and camouflage paint that dripped from above his upper lip into the crease of his mouth. He wrestled with a decision to shoot or wait, as dark silhouettes appeared through the fog directly before him in a lengthening column of march. The men were marching straight across the dried-out paddy fields that lay between the river and the hills and jungle beyond.

Hathcock glanced left at Burke who rested prone behind his M-14, aiming at the line of targets that grew in number with each passing second. In a whisper soft as the still air, he said, "Be ready to call for arty and move out quickly. I'm gonna shoot the one on the far right. Back me up on the left."

Burke confirmed receipt of the order with a slow, subtle nod and then trained his aim to the column's rear, waiting to follow the Winchester's report. His heart pounded against the mulch of decayed leaves beneath his chest. The Marine's coursing blood caused his front sight blade to rise and fall with the rhythm of his pulse.

Hathcock's heart pounded too, sending the rifle scope's cross hairs rising and falling over his target—the man who walked at the head of the column and wore a pistol. The sniper waited for his pulse to again settle. He had faced the same dilemma at Camp Perry, Ohio, when he won the Wimbledon Cup in 1965. This shot was not nearly as difficult as firing at a 20-inch V-ring from one thousand yards away.

As his concentration narrowed more and more on the accuracy of this first shot, the pitch of his sight's cross hairs grew less and less erratic until the steadiness of a national champion marksman held the scope's center point steadily on the NVA commander.

The surprise of the sniper rifle's discharge caused Burke to blink, and as he heard the sound of Hathcock's bolt ejecting the shell and sending a second into the Winchester's chamber, Burke fired at the suddenly frozen figure on the far left of the advancing column.

The NVA leader lay dead at the feet of his company. A

seventeen-year-old recruit lay dead at the company's rear. A third shot cracked from the distant jungle, and another NVA soldier wearing a pistol reared back with a .30-caliber hole in his chest.

A short dike, approximately one hundred yards long, ran parallel with the column of soldiers. Other than the nearest tree line, nearly one thousand yards away on the base of the mountain slopes, nothing else offered cover to the company. They scrambled to the dike, and as they ran, Hathcock's and Burke's shots followed them, claiming soldiers with each report.

"We better move before they figure out what's going on," Hathcock whispered to Burke, expecting this company to react as a seasoned one might.

"Right," Burke said—his first words in nearly a day.

"We're going over to the other side of this little finger we're sitting on," Hathcock told Burke. "They might buy the bluff that we are spread out along this ridge. We'll pick at 'em right and left. Keep your eyes and ears open. They could have friendlies closing on our flanks."

Hathcock moved first and took up a position fifty feet to the left of his previous firing point. Burke followed.

Behind the dike, an NCO raised his head above the mud wall. He tried to locate his enemy's position in the silence that now met his ears. Wondering if the attackers had gone, he slowly stood. Lifting his leg to step onto the dike, he suddenly bounded backward and crashed into the thick grass—his throat torn away from his collar bones. The fatal crack of another rifle shot echoed through Elephant Valley.

On the right and left ends of the dike, eight frightened soldiers leaped to their feet, set their rifles into action, and charged toward the mountain's tree-covered base and their enemy.

"Here they come," Burke spoke.

Hathcock answered with a shot that dropped one young soldier, and Burke replied with a crack that dropped another. Hathcock worked his rifle's bolt so rapidly that his fire kept pace with Burke's, whose bolt operated automatically.

After they had downed six men, the charge evaporated; the last two retreated toward the dike but were shot before they reached it. All the enemy fire was wild.

At that moment, one of the North Vietnamese officers scrambled to his feet and ran toward the river, which was five hundred yards behind the company. After he had gone fifty yards, he leaped into a flooded rice field. His cries echoed across the valley as he splashed and churned his way through the knee-deep bog. Just as he was about to disappear in the fog, a rifle shot cracked from the tree line, and he fell on his face with a .30-caliber boat-tailed bullet lodged in his spine.

The officer frantically struggled to raise his head above the rice paddy's slime, but the paralysis caused by his shattered spine made it impossible, and he sank beneath the muddy water.

Now none of the frightened soldiers moved, for they saw that cowardice and valor purchased equal plots in the snipers' killing field.

The two snipers crept cautiously and silently around the broadly curving base of Dong Den mountain, hoping to expose the NVA's left flank. The three hundred-yard move took the pair more than two hours to complete. It offered only a slightly new angle of attack.

The sun climbed in the March sky, lifting and clearing away the morning's foggy shroud. It revealed a blue heaven scattered with white puffy clouds that towered above the mountains and grew ever higher on thermal currents, reflected from the earth's surface. By mid-afternoon, the towering cumuli changed to cumulonimbi with great anvil-shaped heads and broad, black bottoms that flashed lightning and rumbled thunder down the Ca De Song and through Elephant Valley.

Hathcock listened to the rumble of the approaching storm. He caught the refreshing scent of rain, carried into the deep valley by a breeze that drifted down Dong Den's slopes. The first few drops of rain pattered on the broad leaves that hid the two snipers. They continued to watch the short mud dike where the North Vietnamese soldiers awaited the night and the possibility of escape.

The afternoon wore on, and Burke lay back to rest while Hathcock continued to observe the dike. The enemy had remained still and quiet for more than seven hours. It was clear the snipers held the upper hand.

With each passing hour, the Communist soldiers' situation became more desperate. They lay unshaded and baking in the midday heat. The sound of the river's refreshing coolness teased them with its inaccessible nearness. Their water supply was being quickly consumed. They impatiently watched the thunder shower's black cloak sweep down Dong Den and wished that it would hurry toward them.

In the lush shade where Hathcock and Burke lay hidden, alternating shifts of observing and resting, the heat also rose, raising sweat on both men. Hathcock took a slow sip from his canteen, "Those guys have got to be miserable out there, cooking under that sun. It's way over ninety degrees right here. It's gotta to be close to a hundred out there."

"Think they'll make a move with this storm blowing in on us?"

"Not unless it gives them enough of a screen. They might make a run for it then. It would have to get pretty bad, though." Hathcock capped the canteen and looked down at the long line of the dike. "My guess is after dark. We'll let them try to slip out and then catch them with illumes—light up those hamburgers and rain all over them."

"Rain would feel good," Burke said, wiping sweat off his head. "These few little drops just make you wish it would hurry up and turn loose."

"Think of what it's doing to them," Hathcock said.

On Hill 55, an assistant operations officer dropped a stack of yellow message slips on the intelligence chief's field desk. The gunnery sergeant took the stack and peeled through the first few until he saw Hathcock's sniper report.

"What's going on with Hathcock and Burke?" he asked the young lieutenant.

"They reported contact this morning and asked for illumination rounds on call through the night. They say they have a sizable NVA unit pinned behind a paddy dike in Elephant Valley. Division wants to wait and see what develops."

"What's Division going to do if the NVA decide to overrun Hathcock?"

"They have units ready to move by chopper. They can be

in there in less than an hour. I think Division wants to see if the enemy goes in to pull their pork out of the fire, and then they'll hit 'em.

"You think those two can hold for an hour if they're stormed?"

"No. But I don't think they'll storm Hathcock. He probably has those gooners scared shitless."

Rain partially obscured the valley, but it did not provide the cover for which the pinned NVA soldiers had hoped. The two snipers lay in their leafy blind and watched heads pop above the dike and quickly drop back down.

"Those hamburgers are getting ready to move," Hathcock whispered to Burke. "Sun's going fast and I'd stake my stripes on them making a run for the trees or them hooches down the valley soon as it is dark. Just hope those cannon cockers give us the illumes when we need 'em."

Burke nodded and put his binoculars back up to his eyes. Hathcock lay behind his rifle and slowly moved his scope along the paddy dike, watching and waiting.

The afternoon showers faded and left the sky orange above the western mountains as the sun set behind them. Long shadows from the high peaks crossed Elephant Valley, and as darkness descended, the two snipers watched for movement emerging from behind the dike.

"I can't see a thing," Burke said, dropping the binoculars from his eyes.

"Call in an illum," Hathcock said.

Humid air hung through the dark valley, and only water dripping from the jungle's leaves offered any sound for the two snipers to hear.

High overhead a muffled bang echoed, and like a miniature sun dangling beneath a small parachute the illumination round exposed the NVA soldiers nearly one hundred yards from the dike, moving eastward down the valley toward a group of huts that lay another one thousand yards away.

Without a word, both snipers' rifles fired on the line of men who ran toward the huts.

"Turn 'em back," Hathcock told Burke. "Concentrate the fire at the head of their column."

As quickly as he could squeeze the trigger, Burke fired on the fleeing men. Hathcock followed as rapidly as he could work his rifle's bolt.

One after another the soldiers at the front of the column fell. The rest of the company hurtled back to the dike, leaving their fallen comrades behind them.

"Well, I guess they won't try that again for a while," Burke said.

"Don't count on it. If I were them, I'd make a run for it right now."

A second illumination round burst overhead, lighting the valley with its eerie glow, showing no movement.

"Sergeant Hathcock, those guys are just plain scared to move. I don't think they're going anywhere."

"Let's give 'em some dark for a while and see what they try. Tell them to hold the illumes for a few minutes. Maybe they'll make another run for it."

The two snipers lay quiet, listening to the sounds of the dark jungle. Croaking gecko lizards and small tree frogs chirped. Echoing through the jungle came the shrill cry of a foul-sounding bird, "Fauk-U, fauk-U, faaauk-uuuu."

"My sentiments exactly," Hathcock mumbled.

Down below, in the rice paddies of the valley, they could hear only a deep silence, but, as soon as they called for another flare, it exposed a squad-sized group dashing for the huts that were just beyond the trees, east of the dike.

"Don't let 'em get to those huts. We'll lose them in the trees and they'll be on our backside in no time."

Both Marines fired as rapidly as their rifles could chamber rounds. The running NVA soldiers dropped to the ground and began returning fire.

"Tell that battery to keep the illumes rolling in here. We can't let it get dark or we're dead," Hathcock commanded Burke.

The soldiers who remained behind the wall now joined in the fire, shooting toward the muzzle flashes that gave away the Marines' position.

"Concentrate on those hamburgers out in the open. Well-aimed shots—don't waste your fire," Hathcock told Burke, as he rejoined the battle.

Hathcock laid his cross hairs on one prone NVA soldier after another and squeezed the trigger, killing a man each time.

Burke shifted his fire to the NVA company's main body, which now appeared to be charging over the dike. "They're coming at us!" he shouted at Hathcock.

"Well-aimed shots, Burke, well-aimed shots." Hathcock turned his rifle on the charging company and began dropping a soldier with each shot.

"If they don't give up, we're going over the ridge and up the draw, and let them have this place," he told Burke, pumping his bolt back and forth as rapidly as he could shoot.

"I'm ready any time you are."

But, just at that moment, the steam went out of the attack, and the soldiers who were left dashed toward the dike.

"Keep shootin', Burke—don't cut 'em any slack."

Hathcock turned his scope to the right of the dike where the escaping squad had thrown themselves down. "I don't see any life out there. If anyone made it, he got to that hooch down yonder. We better watch our backsides real close from here on out."

The night passed. The Marines lay listening for any sound that might mean attack. Under the dim light of the illumes, they potshot at any enemy soldiers whose heads popped up.

"You reckon we ought to call in the cavalry? We've been hammering those guys nearly twenty-four hours. Sun'll be up in an hour," Burke said.

"I'll wait till we run out of lead or Division sends in troops. We can hold here awhile. We've knocked out a good third of them already."

The sun rose, and the two men began rest cycles—one watched while the other napped. Throughout the second day, the North Vietnamese stayed behind their mud wall. During the twelve hours of daylight, the snipers fired three shots, merely letting the enemy know that nothing had changed.

The first illumination rounds came at sunset and lit the valley at intervals throughout the night. This small battle had reached a stand-off. For the two Marines, time meant little. They took turns shooting and resting, eating their rations of cheese, peanut butter, jelly and John Wayne crackers (large round crackers packed in C-ration cans). They felt confident and completely in control.

They lay in the shade with water and food, while the enemy starved in the sun and exhausted what little water remained to them. Yet the NVA continued to wait.

The third day began as the second had and followed through to the fourth without change. Hathcock knew that unless something happened, he and Burke would move out on the afternoon of the fifth day and leave the NVA company to a sweep team from the 26th Marine Regiment.

Hathcock rested against a tree trunk and spread cheese on a cracker. Burke lay behind the sniper rifle, staring through the scope, slowly moving it along the length of the dike. "Sergeant Hathcock, you reckon that we set some sort of record pinning these guys for as long as we have?"

"I don't know, Burke. Reckon we'll find out when we get outa here. Anyway, it don't mean anything to me. It wasn't like we were holding them off. These guys just want out of here. But I imagine that if we were to let them go, they'd come after us once they reached the jungle. When we leave, we'll slip off before they know we're gone and let the sweep team have 'em.

"When you compare it to some of the times we had when we started up the sniper school last October, this is pretty tame."

Without lifting his eye from the rifle scope, Burke said, "Wonder how Captain Land is getting along back home?"

"I imagine he's enjoying life one hell of a lot more than we are. He'll be getting ready for the Division Matches down at Camp Lejeune. I may see him when I get home. Those matches go about a week after I get back to New Bern—about six weeks from now."

"Intramurals ought to be in full swing right now," Burke followed. "When did you first shoot in intramurals, Sergeant Hathcock."

"Back in Hawaii. I won the individuals. That's where I met Captain Land—he and Gunner Arthur Terry ran the shooting team and the sniper school. I won the individuals and went to the All-Marine shooting matches. You get outa here, look into the shooting team wherever you end up. That's one thing in the Marine Corps that I really love. I got my greatest sense of accomplishment from shooting and teaching other Marines how to shoot. I guess that the biggest moment in my life came when I won the 1,000-yard championship at Camp Perry.

"Did I ever tell you about winning the Wimbledon Cup?"

"No," Burke replied, still staring down the sniper scope. "I've heard other guys tell about it, but I never heard you. I'd sure like to hear your side of it. We got lots of time. Those guys out there aren't going anywhere."

"Yeah, I know. I won the Wimbledon at Camp Perry, Ohio, on August 26, 1965—the day after I went distinguished."

Burke asked with a tone of hesitancy in his voice, "Don't think I'm stupid or anything, but I've heard you and Captain Land and Gunny Wilson all talk about distinguished for six months, and to be honest with you, I never really understood exactly what it is. I figure that it is a high honor for a shooter, but nobody ever told me how you become distinguished."

"Well, you become distinguished by placing in so many shooting matches. Every time you win a gold, silver, or bronze medal in matches, you get points toward becoming distinguished. A Distinguished Marksman in the Marine Corps is the top dog among shooters. He wears a gold shooting badge and is a member of an elite few marksmen. There are some great Marines among them, for example, Major General Merit A. Edson is distinguished. He died a while back, but he won the Medal of Honor on Guadalcanal leading the 1st Marine Raider Battalion. He went on to become the executive director of the National Rifle Association.

"I went distinguished in 1965. When we got to Camp Perry that year, I was hard as woodpecker lips. I just missed the National Match Championship by a couple of marks, but the silver medal I won gave me the last few points that I needed to make thirty and go distinguished. The day that I won the Wimbledon Cup was special. It was the biggest day of my life, as far as shooting goes."

Burke turned from the scope and smiled. "Captain Land talked about Camp Perry and you winning the Wimbledon Cup. I think he was as proud about it as you were. He said that when the smoke cleared, there was one Marine Corps meatball down on the line, and that was you.

"He said that everybody who was anybody, including the Commandant of the Marine Corps was there. The whole National Rifle Association was there, and you beat them all."

Burke turned back to the scope and again began scanning the dike. Hathcock stretched out and rested his shoulders and head against the base of the tree. He watched the jungle behind their position, and in a soft-spoken voice he began his story, pausing with caution after every few words to listen for any sounds that might signal an unwelcome visitor.

4

The Best Shot in America

COMPETITIVE SHOOTING IN the United States comes to a climax at one place every year—Camp Perry, Ohio. It is a small red square on many road maps, along Ohio's Route 2. There State Highway 358 begins and then dead-ends less than a mile north at a gigantic complex of rifle and pistol ranges located on Lake Erie's southern shore. There, military and civilian marksmen fire side-by-side in the single elimination tournaments that end with one shooter alone on the firing line, declared a national champion.

There are various team and individual championships, such as the National Match Championship, but the single title that marksmen from all walks of life desire most is the 1,000-Yard National High-Power Rifle Championship—the Wimbledon Cup.

On August 25, 1965, Carlos Hathcock was one of 130 marksmen lying prone on the firing line at Camp Perry, focusing through their rifles' scopes at a target that at 1,000 yards resembled a pin's head. The bull's-eye at which they aimed measured 36 inches across, and inside that black field was a 20-inch circle painted in white with 5-V marked in its center. That small circle within a circle, the V-ring, was the very center of the target, and championships usually rested on the number of times the marksman's bullets struck that circle—that number was the V-count.

It was opening day for the first elimination round for the

Wimbledon Cup. The high shooter from this 130-man relay would join the single high shooters from 19 other relays, also competing for the 1,000-yard championship, and shoot the sudden-death relay for the title—firing a single round at a time in three minutes.

These 2,600 marksmen began the elimination with 10 rounds and 10 minutes in which to fire them. One shot out of the black, 5-point center and they could forget that dream of capturing the Wimbledon for another year. In order to advance from this first day of shooting, the marksman had to outpoint the other 129 shooters in his relay. Since most of the competitors shot a possible 50 out of 50 points, the selection of high shooter usually ended with a count of V-ring shots.

Captain Jim Land, now shooting as a teammate of Corporal Hathcock on the Marine Corps Rifle Team, watched the skinny kid from Arkansas survive the cuts and make the semifinals, where he had competed against nearly 3,000 other crack shots for one of the 20 targets set aside for the final's sudden-death showdown.

And when the first day ended, Hathcock and a sergeant named Danny Sanchez remained the only Marines firing bolt-action rifles—still in contention for the coveted Wimbledon Cup.

August 26, 1965, blew in with such a wind that a bullet fired at the 1,000-yard target carried more than 190 inches to the right before it struck home.

Twenty men lay on the line, ten behind bolt-action rifles and ten behind semiautomatic weapons, classified as "service rifles." Beside going for the Wimbledon Cup, those shooting the service rifle also contended for a special award for their class alone, the Farr Trophy.

Land looked at the backs of the men lying prone on the line, many wearing heavy, leather, shooting jackets, which were belted and strapped on them so tightly that each man had to force his breathing. He searched the line until he saw the round, yellow patch, with a red Marine Corps emblem in its center, sewn on the back of Hathcock's green canvas shooting jacket.

"There's Hathcock," Land told two of the team members

who sat with him, high in grandstands filled with hundreds of people, including NRA officials, other marksmen who had been eliminated earlier, and family and friends of shooters who were on the line. And among those seated on the front row, center, with the NRA's top brass, was Gen. Wallace M. Greene, Jr., Commandant of the Marine Corps.

Before the marksmen had taken their positions on the line, Greene had met with the Marine Corps team and shook Hathcock's and Sanchez's hands. "Go out there and win," he told the young corporal and sergeant. "You have 196,000 Marines counting on you."

Land sat on the high wooden bleachers and watched Hathcock making notes in his data book, sighting down his rifle, and then writing again. Brass bands filled the air with patriotic march music. Booths and exhibits capped off the atmosphere, which resembled a county fair. Press photographers, reporters, and television crews swarmed along the front line as each shooter prepared to crawl down into his shooting position. Land spoke aloud to the Marines seated around him, "I wonder if he's feeling the lump?"

The lump, as competitive marksmen call it, is the tightness that builds in a shooter's throat when the pressure of the competition becomes too much for him.

As Hathcock began putting his shooting gear together on the firing line, he felt the lump building. His tension caused that cramped feeling in the pit of his stomach—a feeling that he dealt with the day prior when he lost the National Match by three points. He had won a silver medal in that competition, facing thousands of other marksmen, shooting his service rifle—an M-1 Garand—in slow and rapid fire matches at 200 and 300 yards, firing at 12-inch bulls'-eyes, and in slow fire matches at 600 yards, firing at 12-inch bulls'-eyes. And in it, one point could separate 20 shooters in the final standings. He looked at his data book and began concentrating on today's marksmanship tasks, busying himself to the point that thoughts of General Greene and 196,000 other Marines left him.

Hathcock looked down the firing lane. Twenty red, pennant-shaped flags, each one twenty feet long, lined the range's sides at one hundred-yard increments. They ruffled in the wind that blew directly across Hathcock's line of fire. He let out a deep breath and looked again at his data book containing his notations from the days of practice and the semifinal round. Leaning over his left elbow, he put his shooting eye up to the rear of a spotting scope, mounted low on a stand next to him, and watched the mirage, its layers of heat waves concentrated by his telescope, dancing and rolling from the left side of his view to the right, affected by the wind in the same way that the wind would effect his bullet. "I'm gonna go fourteen minutes left," he told himself, calculating the effect the wind would have during a lull. "I'll watch the flag and when it drops, I'll shoot."

He laid his rifle on its side and began counting clicks as he turned the windage knob on the side of his rifle's telescopic sight. After noting the change in his data book, he checked his leather sling, making sure that it was adjusted to the proper length and wrapped around his upper arm at the exact spot where he had looped it each time he fired. With the sling making a half-twist around his forearm, he slid his left hand, shielded by a thick leather shooting glove, up the hand guard of his rifle's stock and jammed it tightly against the D-ring and swivel that held the sling to the rifle.

Slowly, Hathcock leaned his weight on his left elbow and began working the rifle's butt tightly into his right shoulder. "Got to be tight. No room for it to slip—not here." As the sling tightened and stretched to accommodate the tight fit of the rifle into his shoulder, he felt the strap bite painfully into his upper arm and trap the blood in his left hand and fingers. He looked at their tips protruding from the shooting glove and watched them turn red and deepen to purple.

"Gentlemen, your prep time has begun," a voice from the tower at the center of the line echoed over the public address system. Hathcock laid his cheek on his rifle and rested his right elbow on his shooting pad. Reaching his right hand around the grip of his stock, he laid his finger on the rifle's trigger and sighted in on the small black dot of a target that appeared above the center of his scope's reticle.

Pulling his body backward with his toes, the rifle's cross

hairs rose slowly into the small target. Hathcock closed his eyes for a moment and then opened them to see where his sights might have drifted. They remained exactly where he had held them before, center of the target.

Looking out the corner of his eye, Hathcock shifted his legs left, moving the cross hairs until the small round target sat on the right corner of the sight. "If the flag drops, I'll turn the first one loose at center-mast bull's-eye. If I miss, that's it, but I'm gonna gamble that I'm in there. If the flag don't fall, all I have to do is pull to this spot—a hair left."

With the rifle still in his shoulder and being careful not to move his elbow, which supported his weapon, Hathcock leaned to his left and glanced through the spotting scope to see the mirage once more.

"Gentlemen, your prep time has ended," the voice from the center of the line announced. And with that announcement, the bands stopped, the crowd silenced, and the targets dropped from sight into the pits. All Hathcock could now hear was the wind. All he could now see was the white top-edge of his target resting at half mast in the pits and, in the corner of his eye, a red range flag, billowing in the wind.

Hathcock let out a short breath and looked at the single .300 Winchester Magnum shell that lay shaded beneath a towel on his mat, next to his right arm. The voice from the center of the line came on the public address system, "Gentlemen, you may load one round."

Hathcock took the long brass shell, dropped it into the breach of his rifle, and shoved the bolt forward, locking it into the chamber. He snuggled his cheek back against the rifle stock and waited, sighting across Lake Erie, which was behind the targets, and watched his scope's center rise and fall as his heart coursed blood through his tightly strapped body.

Hathcock thought of nothing except that one round sealed in his rifle's chamber, the firing pin drawn back by the spring in his bolt, awaiting the trigger's release that would send the 176-grain Sierra bullet one thousand yards downrange, into the V-ring.

"Gentlemen, when the targets come out of the pits, you will have three minutes to fire one round," the voice announced. And as the last word echoed downrange, twenty targets rose from the Camp Perry pits, shuddering in the crosswind.

Hathcock waited for the red range flag in the right-hand corner of his eye to drop.

In the stands, the Marine Corps' rifle team and the Marine Corps' commandant felt the lump as they watched marksman after marksman fire off their rounds. Hathcock lay silent behind his rifle, sighted in and waiting.

He watched the red range flag and waited for a lull in the wind when his bullet would travel the one thousand yards to the mark with as little distortion in its trajectory as possible. Hathcock watched the second hand on his wristwatch, which he laid next to his data book, tick away the time. He hoped that within the three minutes allowed, the wind would drop.

After nearly two minutes, the flags fell and Hathcock squeezed his trigger, sending his first shot into the target. He looked at his target for the remaining minute, wondering where his shot had gone.

"Cease fire, cease fire," the voice called through the PA system. At the sound of the line boss's voice, the twenty targets dropped into the pits.

In the target pits, match officials checked and verified the bullet strikes in each target. With this task completed in a matter of minutes, the pit crews stood ready to score the shots by means of a twenty-inch metal disk, painted red on one side and white on the other, and mounted on a five-foot-long pole.

They signaled a miss—a shot outside the fifty-inch-diameter three-ring—by passing the red disk across the face of the target from left to right. A shot in the three-ring was scored with the red disk held at center-mast on the left side of the target. A shot within the forty-inch-diameter four-ring was scored with the red disk held at center-mast on the right side of the target. A shot within the thirty-six-inch, black bull's-eye, but outside the twenty-inch V-ring was scored with the red disk being held directly over the bull's-eye. And a shot within the V-ring was scored with the white disk being held over the bull's-eye.

As Hathcock waited for the disking procedure to begin, he confidently drew out his second round and laid it on the shooting mat next to his data book, where he prepared to record the strike of his bullet. He leaned to his left and peered through the spotting scope, watching the mirage dance across his firing lane, and waited for his target to appear.

Like a coordinated drill movement, the targets rose to half-mast, hiding their black centers below the berm, and a voice came on the public address system. "Ladies and gentlemen, we will now disk all misses." There was a momentary pause. "There are no misses."

Behind Hathcock several thousand hands came together in applause at the announcement. The anticipation gathered again in the pit of Hathcock's stomach as he began to wonder if his call had been on-target.

"Ladies and gentlemen, we will now disk all threes."

A target frightenly close to Hathcock's rose from the pit, sending a chill through him. He saw the black spotter two inches right of the four-ring's line at the three o'clock position on the target. "Wind got him," Hathcock silently concluded. And as the disk rose to the left side of the target, the shooter to the right of Hathcock rolled up his mat, lay his rifle across his folding stool, stuffed his gear into his shooting bag, and carried his equipment off the firing line.

A murmur rose from the stands, followed by consolatory applause as the eliminated marksman walked to a group of people, who huddled around him. A dark-haired woman hugged the man, and in a matter of seconds the group turned to watch the next targets to rise from the pits.

"Ladies and gentlemen, we will now disk all fours."

Two targets rose from the pits and the two shooters walked away from the line, as the audience applauded their efforts.

"Ladies and gentlemen, we will now disk all fives."

Four targets rose from the pits, one to the left of Hathcock. Those shooters joined the other eliminated marksmen and became spectators.

"Ladies and gentlemen, we will now disk all Vees."

Hathcock's target rose from the pit with a white spotter in the center of the target. He leaned away from the spotting scope and again worked himself into the position that gave him the first center shot.

Again sighting in on the target, he found his natural point

of aim and awaited the call from the center of the line to load his second round.

The remaining thirteen targets dropped into the pits and, in a moment, rose to half-mast.

"Gentlemen," the voice from center line announced, "you may load one round."

Thirteen bolts shoved thirteen shells into thirteen chambers with a ripple and clatter.

Hathcock settled behind his rifle for the second shot. He found the bull's-eye and closed his eyes for a moment, then opened them to find his sights still in position. "Good," he reassured himself as the announcement from the center line again broke the morguelike hush.

As the preparatory time ended, the targets dropped together into the pits and the voice announced, "Gentlemen, when your targets come out of the pits, you will have three minutes to fire one round."

Next to his data book, Hathcock's watch ticked the seconds away. He glanced at the row of red flags, peered at the mirage through the spotting scope, and then glanced at his watch.

"You got all the time in the world, Carlos," he reassured himself. "Don't rush the shot. Wait for the lull."

With one and a half minutes gone, the flag dropped and Hathcock fired. It felt good. His trigger squeeze was steady. He knew that it would have to be a major problem with the round, or his rifle, in order for that shot to not find the center of the target. Hathcock picked up the pencil that lay on his data book and drew a small black dot in the center of the small target on the page that represented the call of his second shot. He again jotted 14-L in the square above the small target, reminding himself of the 14 minutes of left windage he had turned on his scope.

With the second entry made in his data book, Hathcock relaxed over his rifle and awaited the call from the center of the line to cease-fire. He now felt more relaxed. He had forgotten the crowd, the bands, the cameras, and the Commandant of the Marine Corps, who intensely watched for the second round of eliminations' verdict—who would walk and who would stay.

"Cease-fire, cease-fire," the voice called to all the participants.

The targets again disappeared into the pits, and quickly, one after the other, their top edges appeared above the berm as the pit crew raised the targets to half-mast.

"Ladies and gentlemen, we will now disk all misses." Again there was the hushed pause followed by the announcement, "There are no misses."

The crowd cheered, and Hathcock, oblivious to the sound of the spectators, looked downrange through his spotting scope, awaiting his target.

Two shooters hit the three-ring and left the line. They were followed by four men who shot into the four-ring. There were no fives. Hathcock and the other six remaining marksmen, one of whom was Sanchez, had again found the center of the target.

In the stands, Land and the others on the rifle team now felt excitement as they looked down at the last seven shooters and realized that both Sergeant Sanchez and young Corporal Hathcock had a real chance at taking the national one thousand-yard championship—the Wimbledon Cup.

Hathcock felt his stomach tighten as he drew out his third round and lay it under the towel next to his data book. He glanced downrange at the red flags fluttering and pushed himself back into position, again locking into his natural point of aim at the black center of the target.

"Gentlemen, you may load one round," the voice from center-line announced. And again the rippling sound of seven bolts locking home broke the windy quietness on the Camp Perry one thousand-yard range.

For the third time, Hathcock double-checked his position and natural point of aim and again checked the movement of the mirage while he awaited the targets rise from the pits.

"Gentlemen, when your target appears, you will have three minutes to fire one round."

As Hathcock's target rose from the pits and steadied on its carriage, the range flags fell with the wind and he fired. Again he felt certain that he had found the center of the target. He felt that he could now win the title that just one hour earlier had seemed a dream. The three minutes slowly passed.

"Cease-fire, cease-fire," the command from center line came for the third time as the targets descended into the pits for scoring and marking.

On this round, there were no misses, threes or fours. Four marksmen shot into the black but penetrated the paper to the right of the white circle that marked the V-ring.

Hathcock watched them leave and felt the tension, irrepressibly tight in his stomach, now closing on his throat. "You've got to settle down," he commanded himself sternly. "You have to concentrate on your next shot. It could be the difference between another handshake and victory."

He looked at the mirage rolling and then again at the range flags fluttering in the strong wind. "Looks like it's picking up some," he told himself. "Hathcock, watch the flags and don't forget the time." He looked at the second hand sweeping around his watch face and thought, "Three trips around the dial, that's all. Three sweeps of that hand. Watch it. Watch the wind."

"Gentlemen," the voice again announced, "you may load one round."

Hathcock took the round that he had laid beneath his towel and dropped it into the breach of his rifle. In one smooth stroke, he shoved his rifle's bolt forward and locked the handle down. Taking a deep breath, he sighted in on the horizon above Lake Erie behind where his target would stand.

The targets came up, and the three minutes began.

"Get aligned, sight on the target, and then concentrate. Watch the cross hairs. Watch the clock. Watch the wind."

The lump left him. He thought of nothing but what he had to do to make his shot find black paper within the center ring, one thousand yards in front of him.

Two other shooters, one of them Sergeant Sanchez, lay contemplating the same puzzle—when to shoot and where to hold.

The wind continued blowing, and Hathcock watched the second hand on his watch finish its first sweep around the dial. Crack, came the sound far to his left where Sanchez lay. Hathcock glanced through his spotting scope at the rolling heat waves and then looked at the range flag. He wondered if

Sanchez had allowed for that much wind. Hathcock continued to wait while the second hand on his watch ticked on and the wind blew the range flag straight.

Boom. The sound of the other marksman with a bolt-action rifle sending his round downrange caused Hathcock to again glance at his watch and follow the second hand as it completed its second trip around the dial.

"Less than a minute left," Hathcock told himself. He leaned to his side, taking a quick glance at the mirage, and then lay back into his position. He focused on his rifle's cross hairs and watched the range flag continue to ripple in the periphery of his vision. The second hand ticked, forty-five seconds left. Now thirty . . . now twenty seconds.

Hathcock looked at the watch as the second hand swept past the fifteen-second mark, pulled slightly with his right toe, shifting his reticle to the seven-o'clock position of the bull's-eye, and began squeezing the trigger.

Focused on the cross that the fine wires inside his sight formed, Hathcock noticed the range flag dip somewhat as the wind's speed dropped. A sudden feeling of relief filled him.

Jim Land sat on the bleachers with Hathcock's other teammates, nervously counting the ticks of the sweep hand of his watch. "Shoot, damn it, Carlos," Land said aloud as the second hand drew itself across the final few seconds of the three-minute time limit.

It was almost as though Hathcock had heard Land's tension-filled plea, the report of the rifle following on his last syllable. The target dropped as the bullet ripped through the target and disappeared into Lake Erie. "Cease-fire, cease-fire," the voice from the public address system again commanded.

Two minutes later, the tops of three targets emerged together from the pits and stopped at their half-mast position.

"Ladies and gentlemen, at this time we will disk all misses. There are no misses.

"At this time we will disk all threes. There are no threes.

"At this time we will disk all fours."

Two targets emerged from the pits. Both had black spotters three inches to the right of bull's-eye.

Hathcock kept his eye fixed in the rear lens of his spotting scope, waiting to see his target. He did not hear the grandstands filled with cheering people, applauding his victory.

"Ladies and gentlemen, we will now disk the score of the 1965 National Champion, Marine Corporal Carlos N. Hathcock II of New Bern, North Carolina," the voice from the tower at the center of the line announced. And as Hathcock's target emerged from the pits, a red disk rose to the center of the target, covering the bull's-eye. Hathcock looked through the scope, and when the disk lowered, he saw a white spotter in the outer edge of the black. He thought to himself, the wait for the slight break in the wind had been worth the gamble. He had won by a matter of four inches.

5

Elephant Valley Roundup

BURKE LOOKED OVER his shoulder at Hathcock, "What did you do when you found out you won?"

"I had completely shut out everything. You could have walked up and stood on my back and yelled at me. I wouldn't have heard you. I was so intent on looking at where I had hit the target and so disturbed that I had landed outside the V-ring that I hadn't even stopped to realize that the other two guys were out and I had won.

"I was still staring through the spotting scope when one of the other shooters grabbed my shoulder and wanted to shake my hand. Then everything was like a whirlwind. I don't think that it soaked in until they handed me that big trophy and took my picture. The rest of that day is still a blur."

Burke smiled and put his eye back to the scope, "Boy, that's something—really something. No wonder you busted so many of these hamburgers over here."

"You ready to switch over?" Hathcock asked.

"Sure. Not a thing moving out there."

Hathcock eased himself through the tangle of vines and jungle growth to where the rifle lay benched on a fallen log; he tucked it into his shoulder while Burke rolled to one side.

"If they don't try something tonight, what are we going to do tomorrow?" Burke asked.

"We need to be moving out of here by ten o'clock, no matter what. We'll signal the sweep team at about nine thirty.

One way or another, those hamburgers are gonna get some relief tomorrow."

Burke chuckled. "Too bad we won't be around to watch the round-up. This has wound up pretty slow."

"Don't count those guys out. They may just be a waitin' for us to lull off. When that sun goes down, you better be on your toes."

Burke closed his eyes and caught up on his sleep.

Hathcock lay behind the sniper rifle and glassed the short dike with the weapon's telescopic sight. He searched for a target to shoot that would remind the NVA that he remained their adversary—ready for whatever the night might bring.

As the afternoon wore toward evening, the sky turned hazy. By the time the sun set forty-five degrees above the horizon, the hazy sky had turned gray with thick clouds that threatened rain.

"Burke," Hathcock whispered. "Sun's going fast, and it looks like rain."

"Yeah, we'll probably get wet about midnight or so," Burke answered, opening his eyes and raising on his elbows. "Those clouds will make watchin' Charlie a lot tougher. Light from the illumes won't break through the clouds until they're right down on top of us."

"Some just might slip through the crack tonight," Hathcock said. "We have to stay on our toes tonight. At this stage of the game, the tables could turn real easy. Just about the time we start thinking we got 'em whipped, they could wipe us out.

"Just keep this in the back of your head, those bastards are gettin' more and more desperate the longer we sit on 'em. I think that if somebody was going to rescue them, they would have been here by now, and I think they realize that, too. Plus, they're probably runnin' a mite short on vittles and real short on water. Those hot dogs are at the point where they either have to do something or get off the pot.

"We ain't got a whole lot left either. Our food is running short, and the way we been pot shootin' the past four days, our ammo won't stretch a whole lot further."

The two snipers waited for the sun to disappear behind the mountains and usher in their final and their darkest night in Elephant Valley.

Behind the low dike, fewer than one hundred bewildered and desperate soldiers of the NVA company remained. They continued to huddle and wait behind the protective wall like frightened puppies in a storm, cowering beneath a house's eaves to stay dry.

The youthful soldiers who sang songs of triumph as they marched through Laos along the Ho Chi Minh Trail now finalized their plans for one last desperate act. They, too, watched the overcast sky grow dark and knew that the heavy cloud cover gave them a greater chance for escape.

"It's startin' to smell like shit out there," Burke told Hathcock, wrinkling his nose after catching a whiff of the breeze that drifted across the wide valley. "They're gonna have a hell of a time sneakin' through the dark like that."

"I know. It's gotten worse today. I think a bunch of them may have a bad case of the squirts, being hunkered down back there for so long. And they can't have much water left, if they got any at all. With diarrhea, on top of the effects of cooking out there in the sun, dehydration is gonna start taking its toll on 'em."

The sun was setting over the western mountain tops as a platoon of weary boys crouched at the eastern end of the dike, hoping to make a run in the gray evening twilight—ahead of the nightly barrage of illumination rounds.

Hathcock and Burke watched as the dike faded from view.

"There's something moving," Hathcock whispered as he shifted his rifle scope's reticle onto a dark lump that appeared to the right of the wall. He had already called the artillery battery to request flares.

Burke put his binoculars to his eyes and saw the motion.

"It's too dark to be sure of my shot," Hathcock said, "I can barely pick up my cross hairs. Where's those illumes?"

High overhead, three muffled pops echoed through the valley, and three bright spots appeared in the clouds.

"They're running," Burke cautioned, and just as he spoke, Hathcock's Winchester broke the silence with a shot that sent the cluster of dark shadows rushing across the open terrain.

"Shoot, Burke, shoot! They're getting away!" Hathcock said as he rapidly drew his rifle's bolt back, ejecting a smoking brass casing. As he shoved the bolt forward, chambering a second round, Burke's M-14 began to pop and flash in the darkness.

"I can barely see 'em, Sergeant Hathcock, we need more light."

"Just shoot into the crowd. Those illumes will brighten up pretty quick once they drift to the bottom of these clouds."

Three muffled pops ignited more illumination rounds. As the glowing flares, swinging beneath small parachutes, flooded light across Elephant Valley, the soldiers who remained behind the mud wall sprayed a broadside hail of bullets at the tree line, hoping to suppress the snipers' fire and allow their comrades to reach the huts. Once there, they would set up a second base of suppression fire, allowing the men behind the dike to follow them.

Beneath the forest's umbrella, and behind the thick knot of brush and fallen timber that had filled with silt and dirt, Hathcock and Burke continued their assault on the fleeing platoon. They had already shot the first few leaders of the escaping band, and now, midway between the mud dike and the huts, the remaining troops fell into prone positions in the dried out rice paddies and began shooting back.

"Damn," Hathcock said.

"Those guys gonna lay there?" Burke asked. Both snipers dropped their heads behind the upper edge of the log that they had used as a bench-rest for their rifles. Above them hundreds of bullets sang and popped as they struck the broad leaves and branches along the tree line.

"I reckon," Hathcock answered. "I suppose we're gonna have to pick at 'em down there until they decide to go back to the dike."

"Reckon we ought to radio operations and tell them what's happening?" Burke asked.

"Let's give the gooners a chance to regroup behind the dike. I'd a whole lot rather wait until daylight before we drop our people in on them. We would stand a better chance of sweeping them out with fewer casualties."

Placing his rifle on the log, Hathcock put his eye to the scope and fired another carefully placed round. Then he said to Burke, "If you think that the calvary can ride to the rescue for us if we start losing ground down here, you better think again. I ain't about to wait around if things start to fold up too fast. That happens, I plan for us to be up on the ridge, looking down and moving out.

"If the sweep team catches the bastards after that, then good for them. I'm not about to let anybody come in here and die trying to save you and me. Besides, those hamburgers ain't worth a thing, except maybe to those shaved-headed bozos at ITT" (Interrogator Translator Team).

Burke laughed.

"What's so damn funny?"

"I'll bet that ugly gunny at ITT would love to hear you call him a shaved-headed bozo. As big and mean looking as he is—what with his head shaved slicker than a peeled onion and that long black handlebar mustache curling out past his jaws—he'd probably melt you into the ground with just a look."

"Burke . . . shoot."

"And you better not say anything to him either, or I'll tell him what you said about his face and you shaving your dog's butt."

Above the firefight, more flares burned their way through the clouds. Hathcock and Burke continued picking at the platoon of soldiers who hugged the earth. The Marines were connecting with one shot in four, and now once again the North Vietnamese rushed back to cover.

Huddled behind the dike, a second platoon of young Communist soldiers crouched ready to run. They counted on their comrades to provide a more effective suppression fire this time.

At exactly 8:20 P.M., just as more illumination rounds exploded in the clouds, the NVA opened a hail of fire that struck much lower in the trees and sent dirt flying from the deadwood behind which Hathcock and Burke lay hidden.

"We're gonna move out of here and take up positions higher up the hillside and on down toward those huts so that we got those hot dogs running right down our barrels," Hathcock told Burke. "Let's turn them back behind that wall and then scoot."

Both Marines began firing at the east end of the dike, daring anyone to venture past its corner.

The hail of fire began to concentrate into the downed dead

tree and tangle of brush, yet the two Marines continued to pop the end of the dike with single shots that kept the waiting platoon sitting in place.

"Let's go, Burke," Hathcock said, and began to low-crawl from behind the log barrier and through the vines and thickets that lined the hillside.

Burke continued shooting until Hathcock reached a sheltered point, where he opened fire and allowed his partner to move away from the cover that now attracted the majority of enemy bullets.

As the two Marines leapfrogged their way to a small ridge that jutted out ahead of the group of mud-and-straw huts, the desperate platoon emerged from behind the dike and began running toward them.

Hathcock sat cross-legged behind a tree fifty feet away from Burke and opened fire. Burke hurried past him and crawled into a sinkhole surrounded by roots and brush that were piled with dirt and covered with vines. He laid his rifle across the mound and fired.

Hathcock swiftly crawled to a small rise and lay behind it, resting his rifle across its top and aiming at the soldiers who now ran through his field of fire at a forty-five-degree angle toward him.

His first shot sent the lead soldier tumbling head over heels. It reminded Hathcock of when he shot jackrabbits on the run in Arkansas—how they seemed to roll like a ball when his .22-caliber, hollow-point bullets struck them. This time it was a teenage boy who lay kicking and screaming as he died from a bullet that had ripped through his middle, disemboweling him.

A second soldier fell to his knees at the screaming youth's side and Hathcock sent a round straight through the young man's chest, reeling him backward with his knees folded beneath him.

Realizing that they now ran directly into a new field of fire, the remaining NVA soldiers turned and retreated to the dike.

"Burke," Hathcock whispered into the darkness.

"Yo," Burke responded.

"You OK?"

"Yeah."

"Let's move on over to that ridge."

Quietly the two snipers crept through the jungle to a hump on the ridge and settled behind it. They looked at the dike surrounded by open terrain and at the small mud-and-grass huts at their right.

"Let me see your map," Hathcock told Burke, who lay five feet away, at his right. "If I'm not mistaken, these are the same huts that we have marked as on-call targets for the artillery battery."

"You're right, Sergeant Hathcock. We gave them these huts here and the set of huts around the bend to the west as primary targets. They should have these spots bore-sighted."

"If what I have in mind works, we'll send most of the rest of these hot dogs back to Hanoi in pieces. We're gonna let them eventually reach these huts . . . just about daylight.

"We'll defend these huts for now. Later on, we'll move up this ridge and go back over to where we first caught these hamburgers on the march, but just a little higher up the slope. We'll start hammerin' on 'em and let them see that we moved to the opposite end from the huts. Once they start out, we'll have the arty hit our on-call targets, while we do a Hank Snow and go a movin' on, over the hill."

"What about the sweep team?" Burke asked.

"We have to call operations and ask them to move up their timetable a couple of hours. We'll leave the sweep team a real easy operation, once we're done."

By midnight, the NVA had made a fourth push toward the group of huts and each time lost men. Each time they turned back, the two Marines ceased fire—encouraging the retreat.

For three hours after midnight, neither side fired a shot. And, for three hours after midnight, a drizzle soaked Elephant Valley and the men who lay imprisoned behind the mud wall, as well as their captors. Other than the drip and patter of the light rain, only the sound of the Ca De Song's rushing water and the intermittent popping of the illumination rounds overhead broke Elephant Valley's silence.

Both snipers lay quiet, their rifles trained at the end of the dike now nearest to them. Nothing but stillness met their eyes as they monotonously watched the low mud wall through the night.

"Burke," Hathcock whispered.

"Yeah," came his quiet reply.

"Let's get ready for the big adios. It's just past four o'clock and I'll bet those shovel heads are sleeping. When we get to the other end, we'll wake 'em up."

Slowly and silently, the two Marines crept up the ridge and edged across the lower face of Dong Den.

Two hours later, they reached the ridge that overlooked the western end of the paddy dike. Hathcock slipped through the thick vines and brush like a snake, hardly making a sound as he pushed himself up to a place where the ground leveled off. Carefully he pulled a thick branch from one side and bench-rested his rifle across it, focusing his scope on the west end of the mud wall.

Above and to the right of Hathcock, Burke bellied himself behind a fallen tree where he sat cross-legged with his body following the contour formed by upward-turning roots that jutted at a right angle from the fallen trunk. He took out his binoculars and began searching for movement along the low dike below him.

Hathcock looked at his watch and offered a thumbs-up sign to Burke. Burke smiled back, and taking the handset, he called the artillery battery, warning them to ready their guns for the fire mission.

Hathcock looked at the thick black clouds that hid the sunrise and allowed only dim gray light to usher a new day into Elephant Valley. He hoped that the clouds were high enough to allow helicopters to land the sweep team into the eastern end of the valley, near the tree line.

He pointed at the sky and shrugged at Burke.

Burke took the signal and radioed the sweep team, which now sat mustered in the landing zone south of Dong Den with their three CH-46 Sea Knight helicopters prepared for takeoff. He glanced back at Hathcock and put his thumb straight up.

Hathcock sighted down his scope, picking the corner of the west end of the low dike, and sent a round whining toward the river after it ricocheted at a right angle off the wall. Moving his scope along the dike, he found a tuft of black protruding from behind. One of the soldiers attempted to peek over the top and locate the snipers' position. Hathcock took a short breath and held it, bringing his scope's reticle on the black tuft. Slowly he tightened his grip around the small of the rifle stock and began squeezing the trigger.

Burke winced as Hathcock's bullet struck the soldier's skull, showering the young NVA troops who huddled beside him with blood, bone, and brains. The sudden bloody shower sent a dozen soldiers scurrying down the wall toward the eastern end, and Burke followed them with three shots from his M-14.

Hathcock shot once more and sent two soldiers dashing from the dike's east end toward the distant huts. Both snipers concentrated their fire toward the middle section of the wall as more of the soldiers saw the escape unfolding and followed their brothers' lead.

"Call the artillery, Burke."

Burke called the fire mission, instructing the battery to fire for effect.

"Let's go," Hathcock said.

Both men moved quickly up the ridge and began their trek around Dong Den to their rendezvous with the patrol that would take them back to the fire base and their helicopter ride home.

The two Marines walked up Hill 55 toward the operations tent.

"You two look like shit!" the stocky intelligence chief called out to the pair. Between laughs he said, "The word's out on you two—all the way up to General Walt. Pinning down those NVA like that. What were they, a Boy Scout troop?"

"Durn near, I suppose," Hathcock responded. "Their big mistake was walking smack down the middle of that valley. I was going to watch the other side of the river where that opening runs between the hills at the big turn. I had that all staked out to catch a patrol crossing there.

"When these hamburgers come marching down the middle of the valley—on my side—just like a Saint Patrick's Day parade, I knew I had them. But one thing that I can't figure out is why didn't they move out at night. All they had to do was run out to the river and jump in. I couldn't have gotten more than a dozen of them like that. They kept going for those huts that sit on the east end of the bend, you know, just out of the trees where that ridge runs down into the valley.

"I let that work in my favor when we had to pull out. We called in the fire mission and dropped over the ridge. We never saw what happened, but I know plenty of artillery dusted them at those huts, if the rounds were on target."

The gunny put his arm over Hathcock's shoulder and said, "Come on in my house. We'll debrief and I'll tell you about that artillery mission."

The three Marines sat down inside the tent. Hathcock took a cigarette from the gunny's pack, which lay open on the field desk, and lit up.

"What about that artillery."

The gunny chuckled and said, "You boys were real smart getting out before the H-Es* hit—all over that valley. You probably would have taken a few. When Lance Corporal Burke radioed for the fire mission and said 'fire for effect,' they did. Those cannon cockers opened every gun they had and hit every one of your on-call targets at both ends of the valley . . . and everything in between, too.

"By the time the shooting stopped and the sweep team got in there, that NVA company scattered over every mountain around that valley, and they may still be running. The sweep team picked up one prisoner. And nobody can make heads or tails of any kind of body count out there."

"What did the prisoner have to say?" Hathcock asked.

"Well, that company was close to being a troop of Boy Scouts. They had just finished training in the north when their captain—whom you killed right out of the gate—marched them south to join up with an NVA battalion that was supposed to be waiting for them on the north side of Elephant Valley.

"We had pretty well ground that particular battalion down to nothing in the past two weeks—they needed these guys bad. But not bad enough to come down and face whatever it was that had them pinned. They figured you controlled the high ground on the south side, and they didn't want to screw around with you guys. That NVA prisoner said that they had

*High-velocity explosive

no idea what in hell they faced up on that hillside, but whatever it was, it was deadly."

Hathcock took a final draw off the cigarette and crushed it into the brass ash tray that sat on the corner of the gunny's desk. Exhaling a cloud of smoke, he smiled and then tucked his bush hat back on his head, stroking the white feather in its band.

The two Marines walked away from the buzzing command tent toward their hooches, where they would clean their gear, then themselves, and get some rest. Hathcock looked at Burke and rubbed his finger down the Marine's cheek where sweat had washed white streaks through the light and dark green camouflage greasepaint that both snipers had caked on their skin. Hathcock shook his head and then lazily drawled, "Come on, Burke, let's get cleaned up, your mascara has done run all over your face."

6

In the Beginning...

A STACK OF mail lay on Carlos Hathcock's field desk when he walked inside the 1st Marine Division Scout/Sniper School's hard-backed tent. Two letters were from Jo—one thick and one thin.

Hathcock looked at the postmarks and opened the letter that bore the oldest date first—the thick letter. As he unfolded the letter, a small clipping from the *Raleigh News and Observer* fell onto a copy of *Leatherneck Magazine* that lay on his desk.

Hathcock grunted as he read the bold print that led the story. A sharp knot tightened in his stomach as he laid the clipping aside and began to read the letter.

"Dear Carlos," the letter began, "they wrote about you in the newspaper. I don't quite understand, but I hope you can explain...

"Now every day I wonder what you are doing. I keep waiting for them to come up the sidewalk and tell me you're dead...

"I thought you were safe at the headquarters, teaching. Now I read that you go out alone, or with one other Marine, sniping in enemy territory. I want to know how you are. I want to know the truth."

Hathcock folded the fat letter and looked at the thin one that was postmarked the following day. It was two pages long and began, "I'm sorry that I was angry with you. I know that you don't need to be getting negative letters. I understand that you just didn't want me to worry..."

The letter also told about their son and what Jo hoped to do once her husband was home. It asked, "Have you decided about staying in the Marines?"

Hathcock took a tablet of paper from the field desk's right-hand drawer and scrawled, "Dear Jo, I'm sorry. I didn't think telling you would make the waiting better for you. I didn't want you to worry.

"I know that I'm not invincible, but none of these hamburgers are smart enough to get me. I promise you that. Don't you worry about me...

"I have decided to quit the Marine Corps and settle down there in New Bern.

"I'll see you in a couple of weeks... Love, Carlos."

Gunnery Sgt. James D. Wilson, the noncommissioned officer in charge of the 1st Marine Division sniper school, walked in the hooch just as Hathcock licked the envelope's flap and pressed it closed.

"Letter home?"

"Yeah. I gotta bone to pick with that reporter who was up here a couple of months ago. You know, the one who interviewed me and Captain Land after Charlie put out the bounty on us?"

"Sure. What happened?" the gunny asked.

"You remember Captain Land tellin' that guy that the story he wrote was just for the *Sea Tiger?* That it was for in-country, only?"

"Yeah?"

"His story—almost word for word—appeared in the Raleigh newspaper. My wife just mailed me the clipping."

"No shit. That's a hell of a way for a woman to find out about her husband, by reading it in the newspaper."

"That's what she thought, too."

"You know, you lead the list of confirmed kills, and that makes you the Marine Corps' number one sniper. And there is no way you can keep that secret from her. How's she going to handle that news?"

Hathcock lit a cigarette and inhaled deeply. Blowing a cloud of smoke toward the mud- and oil-stained plywood floor, he said, "I never looked at it like this was some sort of shooting match where the man with the most kills wins the gold medal. Hell, Gunny, anybody would be crazy to like to go out and kill folks.

"As far as I'm concerned, you can take those numbers and give 'em to someone who gives a damn about 'em. I like shooting, and I love hunting. But I never did enjoy killing anybody. It's my job. If I don't get those bastards, then they're gonna kill a lot of these kids dressed up like Marines. That's the way I look at it.

"Besides, Gunny, I got a lot more kills unconfirmed than confirmed, and so does every sniper over here, including you. So what the hell does it mean? Who really has the most? And who gives a shit—this ain't Camp Perry."

"The fact that you got as many kills as you do isn't the issue," the gunny said. "It's the way you got that many that's impressive. The Army has this fella that they say has got a hundred confirmed kills. They take him by helicopter and drop him on a hilltop. He'll sit there awhile and sharpshoot folks, and then they'll lift him off and drop him somewhere else. I don't think he knows stalking from Shineola. He sure as hell ain't a real sniper—not like you or anybody else who learned in this school.

"You'll go home next month with more than eighty kills, and the Marine Corps might just want to do something about that. That's my point. Like it or not, you are Super Sniper."

"I never set out to be no Super Sniper," Hathcock said sharply. "I just did my job."

"Hathcock, you did your job . . . and kept doing it over and over when any other sniper would have reported back after completing the original assignment he was sent on. Hell, Hathcock, you started a regular campaign selling yourself to every battalion and company commander in I Corps. Remember Captain Land sending me down to Chu Lai to bring you back to Hill 55—under restriction? Tell me about just doing your job and nothing more.

"Also, stop and think about the fact that you and Captain

Land were the first snipers to have the big bounties put out on your heads by the North Vietnamese. They didn't do that because they thought your white feather looks cute in your hat —you're hard on their health. In fact, the sight of a white feather in anybody's hat scares hell out of half the country.

"I've heard you tell how there ain't no VC or NVA smart enough to get you, and that's why you wear that white feather, to dare 'em to try. You wear that feather in your hat like some of these assholes wear a bull's-eye painted on their flack jackets. Now, you can't tell me that you don't enjoy your work. And you may not like killing, but I remember about six weeks after we moved up here when you killed that woman sniper platoon leader. Hell, you were dancing around like you had won the National Match Championship."

Hathcock nodded, "I was happy about getting her. But you know why—She was bad. Real bad! I still say I do my job and nothing more, but I don't wait until somebody orders me out to the field. If I did, I'd be laying in here and have no kills. I know my job, and maybe I am the best there is at it. So if that makes me Super Sniper, so be it. But I never went on any mission with anything in mind other than winning this war and keeping those shovel-headed bastards from killing more Americans. I never got pleasure out of killing anybody, not even that woman that they code-named the Apache. No. Not even her, and you know she tortured and killed a hell of a lot of people before we got her."

Five months earlier, on September 30, 1966, a stretch DC-8C airliner landed at Da Nang and unloaded another 200 soldiers bound for I Corps' battlefields. When it took off again, it was carrying 219 cheering soldiers, sailors, airmen, and Marines whose tours in Vietnam were over.

Sitting on his tightly stuffed military suitcase, Capt. Jim Land watched the big jet, which had now become what American servicemen called a "Freedom Bird," lumber down the runway and lift into the hazy sky, headed for Kadena Air Force Base, Okinawa. Land awaited transportation to Chu Lai, where he would check in at 1st Marine Division's headquarters and begin the task of establishing a sniper program—

per his commanding general's orders, issued to him a few weeks earlier in Okinawa.

It was Land who had put sniper teams back into Marine Corps thinking for this war. He had written papers on the merits of training and using scout/snipers well before the United States became involved militarily in Vietnam. He told how commanders could use snipers to penetrate the enemy, deny him leadership by killing his officers and NCOs, demoralize him by random hit-and-run attacks, and cut off his support from crew-served weapons by sniping those who operated them.

In 1960, Lieutenant Land, who was then officer in charge of the Hawaii Marines shooting team, organized a scout/sniper school. He had spent the previous year as an infantry platoon commander with the 4th Marine Regiment—the same organization to which Private Carlos Hathcock belonged.

A chief warrant officer named Arthur Terry assisted Land with the shooting team. Gunner Terry had survived Wake Island in World War II and had competed on rifle and pistol teams throughout all his years as a Marine. Terry had been the one who turned Land's attention to sniper warfare—not from his Wake Island experience, but from another angle. "If we don't provide a *service* as a rifle and pistol team, we're going to wind up losing our happy home. They're not going to pay for us to run around the country and shoot—we have to deliver something worth the money.

"There are no sniper units in the Marine Corps, although we do have sniper rifles in every Marine infantry battalion's inventory. I think that because sniping requires fine-tuned marksmanship, we might give the team new meaning by pushing the sniper angle."

Land listened, and what the old Marine veteran said made sense. Both men dearly loved the shooting team, and Land liked the idea of an insurance policy to keep their competition-in-arms program going.

"Gunner, how will we sell it to the Marine Corps, though? You know that if they have the sniper rifles in the inventory, and they don't have any sniper units, there has to be a reason."

"I've thought of that, E.J. I've got the selling point to put it over. We send men back stateside every few weeks to attend scout school at Camp Pendleton. If we combine sniping and scouting into one school and call our graduates Scout/Snipers, I think that they'll buy it for the scouting aspect alone. The sniper training will be just sweetening."

Land did some homework and wrote a proposal that began:

THE NEGLECTED ART OF SNIPING

There is an extremely accurate, helicopter-transportable, self-supporting weapon available to the Marine Infantry Commander. This weapon, which is easily adapted to either the attack or defense, is the M-1C sniper rifle with the M-82 telescopic sight in the hands of a properly trained sniper.

Every infantry battalion has twenty of these rifles. Too often it will be found that through lack of knowledge and lack of qualified instructors these weapons are packed away and virtually forgotten. Very little or no time is devoted to training personnel in the operation, maintenance, and employment of this valuable equipment.

There are several problems that will be encountered in organizing a training program for snipers. The first, and probably the most handicapping, is the lack of reference material. Most of the information found in the field manuals presently in use is very limited, and only through research can much of the needed information be found. Two excellent books on sniping and related subjects are *A Rifleman Went to War* by Captain Herbert W. McBride and *Field Craft, Sniping and Intelligence* by the late Major Neville A. D. Armstrong, O.B.E., F.R.G.S., Chief Reconnaissance Officer, Canadian Army. Although these books are written of World War I, it is evident that sniping is not outmoded with trench warfare, but is really just coming into its own with the present emphasis on dispersed units and on guerrilla warfare . . .

There are several prerequisites that need to be considered before selecting a Marine for training as a sniper. Due to the nature of his duties, a Marine selected for sniper training must have physical and mental capabilities not normally found in the average Marine. Excellent physical condition is a must. The sniper must be able to move rapidly over great distances. Good physical condition also builds the courage, confidence, and self-discipline necessary for the Marine sniper who will be required to work in pairs and, at times, alone. He must have better than average ability with the rifle; while marksmanship can be taught, it is very time consuming. To achieve a highly skilled state of training in marksmanship, it is imperative that the shooter have excellent noncorrected vision, both day and night. It is very desirable to use men with an out-of-doors background, such as experienced hunters, trappers, game wardens, or hunting guides. The late Major Armstrong expressed it in this manner:

> The art of a hunger coupled with the wiles of a poacher and the skill of a target expert, armed with the best aids that science can produce, equal success.

A sniper's mission requires that he be able to score a hit on small, and sometimes moving, targets at great distances with the first or second shot. To accomplish this feat, he should be armed with the best aids that science can produce. I would recommend an accurized, bolt-action rifle such as the Winchester Model 70, caliber .30-06, equipped with a variable-power telescopic sight. Although, I feel it is highly desirable that this equipment be made standard issue for Marine snipers, it is realized that such a change in Table of Equipment would create some problem. Nevertheless, the Winchester Model 70 is already available in sufficient number to outfit the Marine sniper in event of an emergency. Since they are presently in the supply system, it should not be difficult to acquire more as needed . . .

Our potential enemies have large numbers of well-trained snipers. With a Marine sniper's knowledge of the art of sniping he would be the best man available to cope with the enemy sniper. Here, if I may use an old adage to illustrate, it takes a thief to catch a thief . . .

It was 1960, and in that year the first scout/sniper school commenced under Land's and Terry's direction. The course lasted two weeks—one week of marksmanship skills and a second week of field crafts and land navigation training. Hathcock graduated in 1961, from the second class that Land taught.

In 1965, the United States forces operating in Vietnam suffered under an unchecked sniper war leveled at them by an enemy who stalked and killed Americans at will. Land served then at Quantico, Virginia's Marksmanship Training Unit, as a member of the Marine Corps Rifle and Pistol Team, and, by this time, he had written papers that advocated a sniper and countersniper doctrine.

That year, the Marine Corps, frustrated by the casualties inflicted by an unchecked enemy who moved with ease, set the wheels in motion. They took Land's and other sniper advocates' arguments to the drawing board and initiated sniper warfare against the enemy in Vietnam.

While in Miami, competing in a rifle match at Trail Glades Range, Land spoke with a reporter from the *Miami News*— Jim Hardie, their outdoor editor.

His December 6, 1965, story quoted Land:

I've helped in the initial planning of a new Marine Corps program to place snipers in Vietnam. A group of us interested in marksmanship had been trying to sell the Corps on the idea of training snipers for the past four years.

Six months ago the Corps decided to set up a special sniper program. Starting in January, a training program will begin at Camp Pendleton, California...

We have been sending out patrols in sizable numbers which the VC could avoid. But they can't avoid a sniper slipping up on them. This will be an entirely new threat to them. Now they won't be safe anywhere they go.

Major General Lewis W. Walt, 3rd Marine Division's commanding general, organized the first sniper unit in Vietnam. Land and his counterparts at Quantico developed the weapons and a doctrine to support the sniper effort.

After several months of testing, the choice came down between two rifles—the Winchester Model 70 and the Remington 700. Remington won out. They mounted a Redfield 3-to-9-power scope atop the rifle.

During that time, Land had been transferred to an ordnance job on Okinawa.

In August of 1966, Maj. Gen. Herman Nickerson was on his way to Chu Lai, Vietnam, to assume command of the 1st Marine Division, and he stopped for staging at Camp Butler, Okinawa, where Land commanded the ordnance company.

It was a twist of fate that brought Capt. Jim Land and General Nickerson together, and it was that chance meeting that caused a major turn in the life and future of Carlos Hathcock.

Nickerson encountered Land by coincidence at a command briefing. "Captain!" the general said, "What are you doing here?"

"I'm Ordnance Company's commander."

"Ordnance! You're no ordnance officer—you're a shooter. You did all that work selling and developing the sniper program. Why aren't you over in Vietnam, killing the Viet Cong?"

"Sir, I'm afraid I don't have an answer for you," Land said bravely.

"I have a proposal for you, Captain Land. You get your gear together and report to me in Chu Lai. You have thirty days to be effecting sniper casualties on the enemy in Vietnam."

Now Land was here in Vietnam, standing in the bright sunlight of Da Nang. The stocky Marine captain with the short-cut hair and the bulldog expression pulled a list of names from his pocket and began reading through them. He recognized many teammates from the Marine Corps Rifle and Pistol Team. He searched the unit designations for Marines who belonged to 1st Marine Division, since they would be easiest to have placed under his command.

Many of the Marines belonged to 3rd Marine Division, which had a sniper program started some months earlier. Major Robert A. Russell headed the snipers there and already employed several of the men whose names appeared on Land's list.

Land took a pen from his pocket and circled several names, one of which was Sgt. Carlos Hathcock, who had been serving as a military policeman at Chu Lai since April.

By October 3, Hathcock had joined Land at the 1st Marine Division headquarters in Chu Lai. There they, together with M. Sgt. Donald L. Reinke, Gunnery Sergeant Wilson, and Staff Sgt. Charles A. Roberts made preparations to move north into the Da Nang Tactical Area of Responsibility, where 1st Marine Division would relieve 3rd Marine Division.

The move was well timed as far as the new sniper school staff was concerned. The small nucleus of snipers had spent every waking hour searching for rifles and scopes with which they could begin their own training operations. After Land obtained rifles, he had them all rebuilt and put into match condition by former shooting team armorers. By the time the sniper school staff had fully equipped themselves, the move north was ready to begin. They could start shooting the enemy as soon as they reached Hill 55, their base of operations, thirty miles southwest of Da Nang.

When the school formed at Hill 55, Captain Land managed to interview several other prospective sniper instructors, among them Lance Corporal Burke.

Careful searching had produced the sort of men he was after: good marksmen, but, above all, men who had both good outdoor skills and strong mental and moral stability. He needed no hotshots; Land knew that type well, and he had seen that the loudmouths and braggarts tended to fold when the going got really tough, and their precious lives were on the line.

Land outfitted each team of two men with an M-14 for the spotter and one of the odd bolt-action rifles for the sniper. They ranged from Remingtons to Winchesters to M-1D (Korean War vintage) sniper rifles. He married the M-84 scope to the M-1 rifles and used a variety of eight- and ten-power scopes, developed by a World War I German sniper named John Unertl, which he mounted on the Remingtons and Winchesters.

Land managed to add to his men's confidence and chances for success by obtaining a large lot of match ammunition, direct from the Lake City Arsenal—the same ammo used in national and international shooting competition. It had 173-grain, boat-tailed bullets that traveled at 2,550 feet per second and would strike the target at the same spot with every shot.

A dozen strong, the classes began.

When word spread of the sniper school's creation, reactions ranged from the snide to the complimentary. But one request came through very clearly to the entire sniper school staff—get the Viet Cong woman who led a guerrilla platoon that terrorized the Marines at Hill 55.

7

The Apache

THE STEAMINESS OF the hot October morning left a foggy pall across Hill 55 as Marine helicopters approached from the south. The rippling, thumping sound of their rotor blades beating the heavy air echoed across the rice paddies beneath the dusty hill, and a dirty-faced young woman turned and searched the hazy southern skies.

She was attractive, about thirty years old, and stood just five feet tall. She wore her shiny black hair pulled into a tight bun on the back of her head. Her nose was small and pointed, and her eyes were wide and light brown, hinting at a partially French ancestry.

In her left hand she held a three-inch by five-inch notebook whose narrow-lined pages were bound together with paper tape that she had carefully removed from the cardboard containers in which the Americans' artillery shells had been wrapped for shipment to Vietnam. She had bought the small notebook in Hanoi, nearly a year ago, while she was training to become a sniper platoon commander and intelligence expert. The notebook was mildewed now, and its water-stained pages were filled with the records of her numerous encounters with the enemy.

She looked at the large face of the man's wristwatch that she wore on her left arm, opened the book to a clean page, and began writing of the activity that she observed.

Squatting in the tall, saw-blade elephant grass, she swore

in Vietnamese and spit out the betel nut she had been chewing. She realized that the Marines she had tormented so successfully were leaving, and an entirely new unit was replacing
them. The progress she had made with the old residents of
Hill 55 was nullified. She would have to begin anew.

She crawled through the thick grass to the edge of a rice
field where other women, dressed as she was—in black silk
blouses and pants and wearing broad-brimmed, rice-straw
hats—worked. The women knew better than to take any notice of her. When a few of them walked back toward the
village, she followed behind them. Once they reached the
cluster of huts, she made her way to a hut at the far side of the
village, next to the edge of the jungle and, reaching in its
doorway, took hold of a canvas rucksack and her most prized
possession, a Russian M1891/30 Mosin-Nagant 7.62 x 54mm
sniper rifle with a 3.5-power PU scope mounted atop its receiver.

Glancing over her shoulder at the women huddled at the
other end of the village, their eyes turned away, she stepped
quickly behind the hut and disappeared into the jungle.

On Hill 55, four Marines who had gotten off one of the helicopters that had flown them there from Chu Lai, walked to an
empty, hard-backed tent on the edge of the compound and laid
down their packs. A lieutenant from the intelligence section
met them outside the dark green canvas-covered, plywood-
and-pine-board structure, with its large, screen-covered windows and doors, and introduced himself to Captain Land.

"What's the good word, Lieutenant?" Land asked cheer-
fully, as he pulled a handkerchief from his hip pocket and
wiped the sweat from his face.

"How soon are you and your men going to be in operation?"

"Give us a little time to get our racks made and office in
order, and I'll tell you."

"Come see me when you're ready to go after Charlie," the
lieutenant said casually. "I can put you onto some leads, and I
can certainly use the input from your sightings."

"I plan to do that. What can you tell me about this place?"

"It's one of the most active areas in the country," the young officer said. He unfolded a plastic-covered map that he carried in the cargo pocket on the leg of his trousers. "Our west are Charlie Ridge and Happy Valley. Just south is An Hoa, and right there is Dodge City. Up north we have Elephant Valley, and over here, across this river, is Oklahoma Territory—all Indian country, just crawling with gooks.

"You could set up on finger four of this very hill, just out back of this hooch," he said, pointing toward a panorama of rice fields, hedgerows, and jungle overlooked by a small bunker a few feet away from the tent's rear screen door, "shoot off into that general area and probably kill or wound more VC than you ever saw down at Chu Lai. If you're into huntin' Charlie, you've come to the right place—he lives down there.

"The boys that vacated this fine country estate tell me that Charlie puts on his own special brand of entertainment for the troops at night. The local VC hatchet lady, who we code-named Apache, likes to get her hands on a young boy and make him sing real loud to the troops on the hill. I haven't heard it yet, but I figure it's only a matter of time before we get our first serenade. I could tell you stories though."

Land glanced down at his three Marine snipers, who had sat down on the wooden cots that lined one side of their new home, "You want to hear about this?"

The three Marines nodded and Land and the lieutenant sat on the racks by them, and the intelligence officer began to tell what he knew.

"I think this woman has some sort of sexual problem concerning men—she hates them. She's been known to carve on a man all night long, just to hear him yell, and she's always coming up with new innovations in torture, which serves to demoralize the hell out of anybody going on patrol. For example, it seems there was this civilian contractor over here a few weeks ago who farted around and got himself kidnapped by the VC. I guess she figured that he was some sort of CIA spook, and he might have been, for all I know. But she wanted to make him talk about all the secret shit that the spooks got going on over here.

"She cut on him awhile, and that didn't do anything but make him scream. Finally, she gets this great brain stroke and has a couple of her boys go out in the trash pile and catch a bunch of rats—you know the kind, those great big mother-fuckers that eat cats and shit and attack you if you get close to them.

"Well, she has this poor asshole stripped naked and tied to a bamboo rack where he can't move. She gets a big straw basket and sticks it on the guy's head and sews the bottom up around this bastard's neck.

"Her henchmen come back with a half-dozen big rats and they drop them in the basket and sew the lid shut.

"I don't know how long it took for that son-of-a-bitch to die, but when the patrol found him, there was nothing left of his head except for hair and bone and a two-inch hole in the basket where the rats gnawed their way out."

Land looked at the lieutenant and shook his head. Hathcock shrugged his shoulders and shivered, "Sir, I reckon we ought to put this Apache right at the top of our list."

"Hathcock, she will be our top priority," Land said tersely. "How many Marines did she torture like that?"

The lieutenant frowned, "I don't have a firm number for you, Skipper, but I know it's more than a dozen in the past three months. She's done it to ARVN troops too. Tied them to trees and skinned them alive. She keeps the fear factor high."

"Well," Land said, "maybe we can increase her fear factor in the next few weeks. I'd love to snag her up and feed her to the fish."

"You and every Marine who has cut down a buddy from a tree after she finished with him," the lieutenant said.

Hathcock gazed through the screen windows of the hooch, staring down the hill at the rooftops of the huts that surrounded the rice fields, and the emerald jungle and bush country that surrounded them.

A faint wisp of white smoke drifted from a small hole in the ground hidden by thorn bushes northwest of Hill 55. The smoke came from cooking fires in a kitchen chamber. It was part of a tunnel network that comprised the company headquarters of the Viet Cong sniper platoon that hunted the Marines of Hill 55. The underground compound consisted of an ammunition bunker, three sleeping chambers, a conference room, and, finally, an observation chamber that was some distance from the main body of tunnels and chambers, connected to them by a narrow spider hole.

Beyond the kitchen a network of tunnels lay booby-trapped, to welcome any Marine or ARVN patrol that happened upon them. Just beneath the ground's surface, in the opposite direction from where the faint white smoke drifted and disappeared into the hazy morning air, the woman sat beneath the light of a kerosene lantern. She was marking notes on a map spread across the top of a crude table made of rough pine boards taken from ammunition crates. Two men sat across from her. They watched as she moved her index finger down a page in her small notebook and then wrote on the map.

Across the many rice fields and hedgerows that stood between the Viet Cong headquarters and the Marine compound atop Hill 55, six Marines dressed in camouflage uniforms and wearing bush hats boarded a green, twin-rotor helicopter that would take them and two companies from the 26th Marine Regiment to a hill position. From there, the men would sweep for three days the broad flood plain that flanked a wide and muddy river. The snipers, led by Captain Land, would guard their flanks at a sandy point, checkered with rice fields and tall grass, that jutted into a wide bend in the river. From that position, they could cover an expansive area of tall grass and low-growing bushes and trees.

A tall, thin Marine major met the snipers as they bounded from the roaring helicopter.

"Captain Land?" the major said.

"Yes, Sir."

"Follow me. You can brief me on your plan while we walk."

Sergeant Carlos Hathcock, Gunnery Sgt. James Wilson, Lance Cpl. John Burke, Staff Sgt. Charles Roberts, and M. Sgt. Donald Reinke followed Land and the major to the far side of the hill where a general purpose tent, sprouting antennae and draped with camouflage netting, billowed in the easterly breeze. Inside the tent was a large acetate-covered map mounted on a four-foot by eight-foot sheet of plywood.

Land stood before the map and pointed to the bend in the river, "We'll set up three two-man positions along that point and cover the flats on the far side of the river. I'll use the knoll located behind these rice paddies as my rally point."

The major nodded in agreement as the five snipers under Land's command looked closely at known enemy positions plotted on the map in red grease pencil. The markings showed heavy VC concentrations across the river on low hills overlooking the flats—the snipers' principal fields of fire.

As the six Marines walked from the bustling tent, Hathcock looked at his captain, "Sir, it looks like pretty good huntin' over there."

"Could be, Hathcock. It just could be."

"Reckon the gooners will try to come across there? The water's pretty shallow."

"No. But I think we may catch a few breaking across those flats, trying to sneak around by the back door. One thing we have to keep on guard for is that concentration of gooners on those low hills. If they pick out our positions and set up on us, it could get a little hairy. The only high ground we have is that five-foot-high knoll behind the rice paddies, and that ain't much. You guys look for my signal. Something breaks— we're gone."

The six Marines slipped down the hill, edged around the rice paddies, and made their way toward the sandy point. Burke and Reinke assumed the forward-most position in the center. Roberts and Wilson took the left flank, while Land and Hathcock set up on the right.

Hidden in the tall grass, the six snipers watched the hillsides and the flat country across the river.

Hathcock's heart pounded against the matted grass as he lay prone behind his rifle. He saw something—a flicker of white. Just a flash. But it was enough to tell him that someone was moving through the thicket at the base of the hills, six hundred yards across the river.

Hathcock nudged Land, who nodded slightly. As they strained all their senses to detect any sign of the enemy, they suddenly heard the report of a rifle, three hundred yards to their left.

Land turned his binocular toward the brush-covered river-bank opposite Burke and Reinke. Draped across an upturned tangle of roots a body hung with a crimson stain running down its back. Leaning into the roots, just beyond the dead man's fingertips, rested a K-44 rifle.

The single shot also informed the Viet Cong in the hills above the river that their lone scout had met with trouble. The next patrol would be larger.

Several hours passed before Land sighted the VC patrol's point man moving along the same route that the scout had taken. He knew Hathcock had seen him too, by the way he stiffened behind his rifle. Soon more men followed. Land found his sight picture and waited to fire following the report of Hathcock's rifle.

Sweat seeped into the corners of Hathcock's eyes as he put his scope's reticle on the guerrilla in the center of the group, who appeared to be the officer in charge. He felt a tightness grow in his throat and stomach as he drew the slack from the rifle's trigger—shooting men rather than targets was still something new and uncomfortable for him.

A matter of seconds seemed an eternity to him, as the rifle finally discharged the 172-grain bullet and sent it ripping into the soldier's chest. Before the rifle returned to its rest from the recoil, Hathcock had drawn the bolt to the rear and had chambered a second round.

Land fired and caught the patrol's point man in the hip. The other guerrillas had scurried for cover, and the wounded soldier disappeared into the brush before either Marine could finish him. "One KIA and one WIA," Land said softly to Hathcock.

A few seconds passed and then the sound of gunfire broke the stillness. "Sounds like they slipped past us and got caught by the Top and Burke," Hathcock said.

"I think that once the shooting stops, we'll move out," Land whispered. "We could wind up sitting ducks down here if we hang around too long. They have all their cousins up in those hills, and next time, they won't send another patrol—they'll blast us out of here."

"Just give the word, Sir. I'm ready when you are."

Land patted Hathcock on the shoulder and said, "Let's go. I'll pop a green star to signal the others."

Thirty minutes later after the green pyrotechnic burned high in the air over the sandy point, the six Marines huddled at their rally point behind the five-foot knoll that offered them protection from direct fire. There they waited until the daylight faded.

After dark, the men reached the safety of the fire base. Inside the now sandbag-reinforced tent that housed the large operations map and the crackling radios, Captain Land and the major stood before the map talking. Land's five snipers sat quietly outside in the darkness, waiting for their captain and straining to hear the conversation he was having with the major.

"Sir," Land said, "I understand how rich a hunting ground that flood plain looks, and we did make contact. But that's what worries me. I think the VC will be ready for us tomorrow. I wouldn't be surprised if they move in rockets or heavy mortars on us.

"I'd rather move on the hillside off to the right. We can still cover that area. We will just have to shoot at a thousand yards instead of six hundred. And all my snipers are excellent thousand-yard shooters. Hathcock, as a matter of fact, is the United States champion at a thousand yards."

"Captain, I appreciate the skill of your Marines, but I don't believe that you can compare fast-moving targets with the bull's-eyes that you shoot out at the rifle range. If you're more than half a mile away from your major area of responsibility, you'll miss more than you hit."

"If they kill us, Sir, we won't be any good to anybody."

"I don't think that they will kill you. You didn't do that much damage today. Take my word for it, Skipper, they won't be looking for you."

"Well, Sir, you may be right, but I feel uneasy about going back into the same position two days running. It goes against all sniper doctrine that I have read or encountered."

Land saw it was no use discussing it further and agreed to go out the next day, only asking that some covering fire be prepared for them.

"We'll plot some targets on the hills above that flat," said the major. "If you take fire, it will come from there. A pair of red stars will turn on the fireworks. Good luck, Captain."

Land shook the major's hand and walked out of the tent, tripping over Burke, who had crawled next to the doorway where he could hear the conversation more clearly.

"Do I need to explain anything to you men, or did you get it all?" Land said sourly.

"We got it all, sir," Reinke said.

"What time we humpin' out there, Skipper?" Hathcock said quickly, hoping to smooth over the mood of his captain.

"Plan on a zero four wake up. We'll start down the hill at four thirty. We should be back in position well before daylight."

The I Corps' darkness that morning was blacker than any night Hathcock could remember. The dark shapes of the bushes and grass blended with the sky, offering his eyes no firm definition of form. He searched the horizon for a line of reference—straining his eyes, he finally saw the hilltops standing mute against the starless heavens.

As the troop of snipers descended into the black valley, Hathcock looked down at the river and its broad, flat bend. There he would spend his second day on this operation—and possibly, it occurred to him, his last day on earth.

Hathcock thought of the conversation he overheard the night before. He knew that Land had been right—it was foolish to move back into that flat two days in a row.

Hathcock sniffed the air, searching for the familiar scent of river mud and mildew. It was a sign that they were nearing their trek's end. But at this point, all he could smell was the sour odor of sweat from his fellow snipers as they made their way across the flats toward the small knoll that would be their rally point.

There, the three teams checked their bearings and departed in three directions.

For Hathcock, the sound of his breathing and heart beating seemed amplified in the predawn's stillness—as loud to him as the roar of the broad, muddy river fifty yards ahead. The two men had reached their firing point, and they crouched in the brush.

Soon Burke and Reinke, Roberts and Wilson also lay in position, awaiting the first gray light of day.

Hathcock focused on the input of his senses to keep his sharpness. He tasted the hint of salt in the air and smelled the faint fragrance of fish coming from a shallow cove where the river water eddied in a foamy swirl. In the distance he saw and heard a flock of white birds suddenly rise up screeching from the shallows. He also heard something else down river—it was the faint clank of metal.

Slowly, yet deliberately, he shifted his scope to his right, trying to find the source of the sound. He thought he saw a flicker through the dense brush. He listened and heard the clanking again, but he saw nothing more as the sound now moved across his front and slowly made its way to his left.

"Burke and the Top will get these guys, too," he whispered to Land.

"Shushhh," came the captain's response, as Land leaned on his elbows and continued scanning the opposite side of the river with his twenty-power spotting scope.

Hathcock glanced at his wristwatch. It was exactly eight o'clock.

Burke and Reinke had taken their positions on the sandy point of the river bend and had a broad view of a gap in the brush where a shallow ditch emerged from the low grass and brush and joined the river. There they saw the enemy patrol slowly emerge from the pale green undergrowth that had hidden their movement between here and the hill.

Carefully, Burke set his scope's reticle on the point man's head and began squeezing the trigger on his rifle.

Land flinched when he heard the sudden crack of the Winchester a short distance to his left. He looked at Hathcock and then lay behind his spotting scope, searching the far bank for the target at which Burke had shot. A second shot echoed through the wide valley—and then a third.

Suddenly the air was alive with heavy bullets cracking through the tops of the bushes and the tall grass in which the six snipers lay.

"What in the hell?" Land said aloud. "God damn

quad-.51s. They're going to cut this riverbank into pieces with their heavy machine guns."

"Where they at?" Hathcock asked anxiously.

"Up on the hill. Right where I thought they would be. Only I thought they'd be shooting rockets or mortars, not .51s. They must have a hell of a lot of shit up there. We've got to get the hell out of Dodge, now!"

In the midst of the crackling shower of .51-caliber machine-gun fire, streaked with red tracers, Land sent two, red-star, cluster pyrotechnics skyward. The six snipers scrambled for their lives, running toward the low knoll that offered protection from the half-dozen four-barrel machine guns the Viet Cong had trained on them. The ground was checkered with rice fields, and knee deep in mud. Roberts and Wilson sprinted first through one of the paddies, followed by Burke —then Hathcock, Land, and Reinke.

Hathcock pumped his legs like pistons as he drove them through the mire of mud and water. He looked to his right and saw Land, his square face flushed, his eyes opened wide and his mouth agape, inhaling every drop of air that he could force into his burning lungs.

The first three Marines disappeared into the brush and found their safety behind the knoll, while Hathcock, Land, and Reinke crossed the midpoint of the boggy rice field. Hathcock pulled his legs up and down as hard as he could and saw that bullets were exploding into the water around him.

"Go for it, Hathcock!" Land yelled, "they've got us bore-sighted."

Hathcock suddenly looked back. "Top!" he hollered. "Are ya hit?"

The master sergeant's head and shoulders were just above the muddy water. He appeared to be struggling to get back on his feet.

"You hit bad, Top?" Land yelled.

Reinke motioned to the Marines to go on and leave him.

"God damn it, Hathcock. Top's hit. I can't leave him there to die. You go ahead."

"You can't get him alone," Hathcock yelled back to Land, and the two Marines ran toward their downed comrade who was splashing the water with his hands and trying to pull his body forward through the heavy mud.

"We ain't gonna leave you out here for that Apache woman, Top," Land called.

The two Marines reached Reinke. All around them bullets were pelting the water.

"Where you hit?" Land gasped.

"I'm not hit," the master sergeant said. "I stepped in a fuckin' hole. Grab hold and get me out of here."

Hathcock and Land grasped the master sergeant near his armpits and pulled as hard as they could. Slowly, the sucking mud gave way and the Marine slid free, splashing in the water on his belly. The captain and Hathcock each lost their balance and fell to their hands and knees, soaking themselves in the mire.

"Gooooooo!" Land cried. The three Marines charged through the knee-deep mud and water. Hundreds of bullets sent tall, liquid shafts splashing up from the paddy's surface.

Hathcock felt the blood surging through his veins at such pressure that his ears pounded and his vision blurred. He knew he was running for his life. He took a long, stride through the deep muck and plunged headfirst into the black water, gulping what seemed gallons of filth before he breathed air again.

Land and Reinke were doing no better. Now that they had gotten near the low dike that retained the water in the rice paddy, the three exhausted Marines frantically swam on their bellies through the mire the last few yards. They emerged on dry land, caked from head to toe in stinking mud and, straining their last resources of strength, crossed the final few yards of open grassland. As Land, Reinke, and Hathcock fell behind the cover of the low knoll, they heard the first rounds of Marine mortar fire striking the enemy's positions in the hills. All six men lay on the ground shaking, amazed that they had survived.

"I must have sucked in a gallon of that shit," Land said, spitting kernels of mud and sod from his mouth.

"Better a bellyful of that than your ass full of lead," Reinke said between heavy breaths.

Hathcock pulled a package of Salem cigarettes encased in a yellow plastic box from his soaked shirt pocket. "Well, I managed to keep something dry," he said and put a white filter tip in his mouth.

"Anyone else for a dry cigarette?"

Land looked at the five Marines and then took the package from Hathcock's hands, "I don't smoke, but I think this time I deserve a cigarette. That was just too damn close."

Hathcock threw him the lighter and, holding it in his right hand, Land flipped the top back and struck the flame. As he drew the lighter toward the cigarette between his lips, his right hand, which was holding it, shook violently. Land's entire body began to tremble so badly he couldn't light the cigarette.

Hathcock took the captain's hands and guided the flame toward the cigarette, which also shook in the Marine's lips. The four men who lay watching them roared with laughter.

Land looked at them, drew the smoke in, and said, "Fuck every one of you! You're shaking just as much as I am."

Reinke and Hathcock lay on the ground laughing, and with a gasp Carlos said, "I don't think I'd ever believed you could get so shook."

Land finally laughed too, after he saw one of the other men trying to put some purification tablets in a canteen spill half the water. Each one of them was astonished to find himself still alive.

The six snipers lay behind the knoll more than an hour, waiting for the exchange of fire to cease and then they spent the remainder of the day cleaning their equipment, preparing to return to Hill 55 that night.

8

A Nightmare's Witness

NONE OF THE six Marines discussed that near-disaster at the riverbend for several days after they returned to Hill 55. They felt embarrassed about it. But even if the mission was a failure in every other sense, it had reinforced Land's and his men's confidence in the tactical principles of sniping, which they were adapting by trial and error from those of World War I Europe and tailoring to the jungle environment of Vietnam.

The rule that one should never hunt the same ground twice —and never set a pattern or establish predictable habits—became profoundly important for Hathcock after that day on the river. He saw it as a major key to survival and success.

Hathcock began dissecting and analyzing every activity in which he, or the Marines under his supervision, involved themselves. He concluded that even the call of nature could have deadly results if the trip to the privy took place at approximately the same time each day. He was determined that the only consistent thing about him or the snipers he instructed would be their complete unpredictability.

Hathcock was beginning to regard sniper warfare in a new perspective. He saw it as a complex craft that required scientific skill, total self-discipline, and absolute awareness of every aspect of the sniper and his environment. This, he told his students, was not a goal for them to strive for but a necessity that they would master if they intended to survive. Mistakes meant death. "In this shooting match," he told them, "second place is a body bag."

The first class of the 1st Marine Division Scout/Sniper School commenced during November 1966. It was a learning experience for both student and instructor alike.

November arrived at Hill 55 with torrents of rain. Inside the sniper school's damp, hard-back tent, twenty wet and muddy Marines sat on long wooden benches listening to Captain Land welcoming them as the school's first students. He told them that they would be divided into two-man teams and that each team would have the benefit of a sniper instructor who would not only take them through their paces at Hill 55 but accompany them on every assignment in the bush.

Like a football coach welcoming a new squad to summer practice, the captain stepped atop a wooden footlocker and began to preach to the men, telling them why they were so special and why they should work hard to succeed in the school.

"Gentlemen," Land told the men, "you have been selected to become scout/snipers not because you are the meanest sons-of-a-bitches in the valley, nor was it for showin' off what a tough guy you are to the gang back on the block. You were chosen not because you have muscles in your do-do, and not because you have potential to become some sort of cold-blooded killer who would just as soon blow the eyes out of a baby as step on a bug.

"Your units selected each of you to become snipers because you are good Marines—men who are well disciplined . . . courageous . . . duty-bound . . . and loyal to your country and your Corps. You have been screened and found to be in top physical condition, mentally sound, and very patient. Each man here has demonstrated to his commander that he has good moral character and a strong sense of values, among which he holds life sacred.

"These attributes are important to be a successful sniper. When you go on a mission, there is no crowd to applaud you—no one for whom you can flex your muscles or show

how tough you are. When you go on a mission, you're alone.

"You have to be strong enough to physically endure lying in the weeds day after day, letting the bugs crawl over you and bite you, letting the sun cook you and the rain boil you. shitting and pissing in your pants, but lying there. Lying there because you know that Charlie's coming, and you're gonna kill him.

"You don't shoot the first gooner that walks into your field of fire, either. You select your target carefully, making sure that the gooner you kill is Charlie, so that you can waste the bastard with no doubts or remorse.

"When you kill ole Nguyen Schwartz, other than you added another digit to your company's body count for that month, nobody will give a shit.

"But you give a shit! You acted as a professional. You identified and put an end to a man, a woman, or even a child who would have killed your best friend, most of your friend's friends, and you. And that's what is important to you.

"I know that as grunts, it was easy for you to feel justified in killing the enemy when he attacked you—he was trying to kill you. If you attacked him, he also had a choice to fight or surrender—you did not murder him, because he died trying to kill you. That's self-defense.

"As a sniper, you do not have that luxury. You will be killing the enemy when he is unaware of your presence. You will be assassinating him without giving him the option to run or fight, surrender or die. You will be, in a sense, committing murder on him—premeditated.

"To deal with this successfully, you must be mentally strong. You must believe in what you are doing—that these efforts are defeating our enemy and that your selected kills of their leaders and key personnel are preventing death and carnage that this enemy would otherwise bring upon your brothers."

The captain stood silent, looking at his new students' solemn faces, allowing this sermon to digest. He cleared his throat. "Gentlemen, the screening is not done. It has only begun. We want strong, good men—the best. We will weed out the ear, finger, and tooth collectors and send them pack-

ing. We will eliminate the hot dogs and cowards and send
them packing with the dummies, liars, and thieves. I will tolerate none of these among my snipers.

"I will tolerate only hard work and dedication. You give us
that, and we will make you the deadliest creature on earth—a
sniper."

The muggy tent erupted with cheers and whistles from the
Marines. Hathcock stood near the back door, clapping.

The rain continued falling that warm November day. It soaked
the many rice fields, hedgerows, and jungles that surrounded
Hill 55. At the edge of the barbed-wire perimeter that surrounded the Marine encampment atop the hill, a rifle squad
passed through a checkpoint as they left the compound's security. The Marines making up this patrol were mostly cooks,
administrative clerks, and supply personnel. It was a chance
for them to see action and earn medals.

The patrol was a routine one. They would walk down the
hill to a crossroads, where they would check the local citi-
zenry's identification cards and possibly return with some Viet
Cong suspects for interrogation.

Hathcock stood at the back door of the snipers' hooch,
looking at the gray afternoon and watching the distant figures
walking at the sides of the water-covered road. Stepping back
inside the hooch, he sat next to his cot and began cleaning his
rifle. The sound of the rain spattering against the canvas left
him relaxed, feeling warmly secure as he scrubbed the rifle's
bolt with a solvent-soaked rag. The solvent's pleasant, aro-
matic smell spread throughout the tent, wafted on the cool
afternoon breeze that came through the hooch's large,
screened windows.

The quiet afternoon was suddenly shattered by the sound of
rifle fire below the hill. The sound of a command-detonated
mine exploding brought Hathcock to his feet. Even before he
reached the door, he knew that the patrol that had just left Hill
55 had walked into an ambush.

He saw several Marines running for cover, trying to regroup and fight. But the enemy's fire was heavy, and the best
that the patrol could do was try to survive. The Viet Cong had

set up their ambush in a tree line and planted claymore mines* along the edges of a rice paddy dike that served as a trail cutting across a series of rice fields. The Marine patrol frequently used it as a shortcut to the crossroads. When the patrol turned up the well-traveled pathway, the Viet Cong opened fire. They then detonated the claymores as the Marines leaped into the rice paddy—the VC's killing zone.

Realizing their tragic error, the dazed Marines mounted the dike and turned their rifle fire toward the tree line as they ran for their lives. Four bodies, partially in the water, lay sprawled against the dike, including that of one Marine who lay unconscious from a round that penetrated his steel helmet, cut his scalp, and knocked him out.

"Damned VC," Hathcock said, pounding the door with the heel of his hand. "It's like trying to kill ants: You can burn 'em, poison 'em, and stomp on 'em, but they just keep crawling up out of the ground."

The sergeant who led the patrol reported to the intelligence chief that four of his Marines had died on the rice paddy dike and that the remainder of the patrol, including two seriously wounded men, had made it back to the hill. His report had been accurate, except that the fourth Marine did not die on the dike.

A reinforced platoon descended on the ambush site, but the woman who had led the attack had already told her guerrillas to carry the living Marine away.

The platoon searched the tree line and hedgerows for the fourth Marine until well after dark. When they quit looking for their fallen comrade it appeared certain that the Viet Cong had him.

The rain stopped just after nightfall and ushered in a light shroud of fog, which covered the low rice land surrounding Hill 55 like sheer, white chiffon. Inside a sandbagged bunker, where Marines drank beer and listened to rock 'n roll music,

---

*An antipersonnel mine shaped in a curved rectangle filled with heavy explosive and ball bearings (grape shot). Each ball is approximately ¼-inch in diameter. It can be set off by trip wire or by a remote control on command. The curved shape enables the user to direct the blast (and thousands of shot) in a specific direction or killing zone. It is ideal for ambush or perimeter defense.

Hathcock listened to the stories that the survivors of the ambush told. He felt both grief and anger about the wounded Marine being left behind, but he said nothing to these men who now spoke in slurred phrases, trying to purge the sorrow from their minds with beer. He knew that their grief was much greater than his—the man had been their friend.

The din of the music shut out the war but soon, one after another, Marines began disappearing from the dimly lit room. A corporal tapped Hathcock on the shoulder, "Some poor bastard is screaming bloody murder outside the wire."

Carlos left his beer and walked over to where Captain Land and Gunnery Sergeant Wilson knelt behind sandbags, searching the tree line with a starlight scope.

"I can't see a damn thing, Gunny," Land told Wilson, as he passed the scope to him. Resting the scope across the sandbag, Wilson slowly panned across the tree line from where shrill cries echoed over the rice paddies.

Hathcock knelt beside Wilson. "That bitch! That filthy-assed Communist whore!" Wilson growled.

Across the quarter-mile of rice fields that separated the tree line from the hill, the tormented Marine who had been taken prisoner that afternoon hung naked on a rack made of bamboo. He wore only his boots and the green wool socks that had his name stamped in black ink across the tops. Blood streamed down his cheeks, mixed with tears.

The boy, just out of his teens, tried to blink, but the effort only obscured his vision with blood that flooded from where his eyelids had been cut away. He cried and prayed aloud, reacting to the pain each time he strained to blink.

The Viet Cong woman had pried off each of his fingernails and was now in the process of bending his fingers backward, snapping them at their middle joints. She had finished with the left and right little fingers and was working her way toward the index fingers, one at a time. Breaking a finger every twenty minutes, she followed a well-planned timetable of torture that covered her prisoner's entire body and would carry the session through the night. At a few minutes before midnight, she had eight fingers to go.

The woman and four men from her platoon sat at the Marine's feet, speaking softly in Vietnamese and laughing. The remainder of her platoon lay quietly surrounding her in a maze of sniper hides, ready to ambush anyone who might try to come to rescue the prisoner.

The woman chewed betel nut, spitting the juice between her feet as she squatted with her arms resting across the tops of her knees. She looked at the youthful Marine. "You cherry boy? I think maybe no. You get plenty pussy back stateside, yeah. You get Vietnamese pussy too? I think you do. You go China Beach swimming, fuck plenty.

"You like get cherry pussy? Plenty American GI like cherry pussy. Rape many young girl—take cherry pussy. True! I know true."

She shouted in Vietnamese at the men squatted by her, and they glared at the Marine. The woman walked to where the boy hung limp on the bamboo rack and spit a mouthful of betel nut into his eyes. "You goddamn-fucking GI!" she said.

Hathcock sat on an empty ammunition crate, his arms folded across the top layer of sandbags and his chin resting on them. He stared into the darkness, feeling more and more frustrated as the hours passed. A major sat next to Captain Land, who was still searching the tree line, and talked of sending a company out to find the Marine.

"You'll end up killing more men and that poor guy, too," Land told him. "During World War I, the Germans used a tactic of catching a man in the open, shooting him in the legs, and letting him lie there and beg for help. Pretty soon, there would be some hero who couldn't bear to hear any more, who would organize a rescue. It was always a big mistake.

"We've done it here, ourselves. We'll wound some gooner in a rice paddy and wait for his buddies to drag him away. We'll sometimes get two or three that way.

"I'll bet you money they have more mines, booby traps, and snipers between us and that man than you or any other Marine here would care to face in a month."

"Well, Captain," the major said, "what do you propose?"

"Sir, just what we're doing now. We locate them and maybe my snipers can get the bitch. It takes a thief to catch a thief."

The major stood, cleared his throat with a grunt, and walked away. Hathcock sat motionless, his eyes closed, trying to picture in his mind the rocks, trees, trails, and streams that lay beyond the tree line.

"Hathcock," Wilson said, "hit the rack. You're not doing any good here. The skipper and I won't be worth a shit in the morning, and somebody's got to be functional tomorrow."

Hathcock spent most of the night awake on his cot, listening to the screams.

As the fog thickened just before dawn, the Viet Cong woman torturer completed her work on her prisoner. "Goddamn-fucking GI. You no fuck no more," she said, as she approached him with a long, curved knife in her hand. Taking his genitals in her left hand, she jammed the blade's point beneath the base of his penis, grazing his pubic bone. She pulled the knife with a sweeping, circular cut that released both testicles and his penis in one large handful of flesh that gushed with blood.

Blood surged from the gaping cavity left between his legs. She knew that this man could not last long, and, quickly cutting away the cords that bound him to the bamboo rack, she said, shaking with laughter, "Run, GI. Maybe you live—you find doctor in time! Run to wire. We watch Marines shoot you fucking ass."

The Marine ran, shouting unintelligibly, as blood gushed so rapidly from his body that it left jellylike pools on the compost of decaying leaves that covered the forest floor. And when he emerged from the trees on the far side of a rice field that lay below the observation post where Land and Wilson watched, he began waving his arms, screaming incoherently and sobbing.

"The poor bastard's trying to tell us not to shoot," Land said. "Look at him, Gunny. That bitch has emasculated him."

Several Marines ran toward the wire, only to see him fall headlong into the curled strands of concertina wire, dead.

The final nightmarish cries had awakened Hathcock, and he had just reached the observation point when the Marine ran the final yards of his life. The sniper hung his head and shook, his anger rising to a nearly uncontrollable peak.

"I want her!" Hathcock said in a strained voice, his teeth and fists clinched.

Land didn't speak, but wrapped his arm around Hathcock's shoulders. He, too, felt the need for revenge.

9

Sign of the Sniper

"SERGEANT HATHCOCK," A voice whispered in the darkness, "the time on deck is zero three hundred." Hathcock opened his eyes to see a black figure at the foot of his cot. The Marine standing the duty watch, who now was making his wake-up rounds, pushed the button on his flashlight and pointed the beam at him. "You awake?"

"Turn that off," Hathcock ordered, holding one hand in front of his face to block the light. "I'm awake."

The Marine woke two other men, then he walked out of the hooch and let the screen door slam.

Hathcock gave instructions to the two Marines, then laced his boots and headed toward the mess tent. He would spend the day leading a student sniper team in the farmlands and forests west of Hill 55. He felt that area offered the best hunting and an ideal classroom for teaching his new snipers the craft of operating from a hide.

As he sat sipping coffee and reading notes scrawled in his sniper log, the two sergeants joined him. The three Marines huddled in the dim glow of a small lantern set on their table, sipping coffee and discussing the best combinations of men to team for this day's missions.

Two hours later, Hathcock and his sniper students were hidden at the edge of a forest that climbed the hills up to Charlie Ridge. Their hide overlooked a patchwork of rice paddies and trails, bordered by a community of thatched huts.

To their right, Hathcock could see Hill 55's dark blue peak jutting through a thin, white veil of fog.

The edge of the sun boiled above Hill 55. A flock of white sea birds silently flew across the sunrise, and Hathcock wondered at the contrast between the morning's beauty and the war's ugliness.

He knew that in this land few people noticed the beauty of a sunrise. Mornings were a time for making war. Hathcock gazed across the wide patchwork of fields and scattered huts, his thoughts of peace and beauty dissipating from his consciousness. He thought of the woman who butchered the young Marine a fortnight ago and wondered where she was hiding now. He was certain that this new day represented nothing for her except a time for war. And with that thought, it became that for him as well.

He watched three silhouette figures walking along the dikes that divided the rice fields and lotus ponds and, as they emerged into a streak of sunlight that stretched down the length of the valley between Hill 55 and Charlie Ridge, he put his eye to the M-49 spotting scope on the tripod in front of him. Examining them closely through the twenty-power telescope, he saw that the men carried hoes, not rifles. They were farmers on their way to the fields.

In the corner of his eye, Hathcock caught the student who took the first watch behind the sniper rifle—a burly private first class—tightening his grip around the small of the gun's stock, preparing to shoot one of the men. Saying nothing, Hathcock placed his hand over the rear optic of the rifle's scope. The PFC turned and smiled guiltily.

Hathcock motioned for the other student to take the sniper rifle. The first Marine would spend the remainder of the day with his instructor, but once they returned to the hill, he would be gone.

The three Marines continued their vigil, quietly hidden among the soft, green ferns and grass, beneath a low umbrella of broad-leafed trees and palms. To the right of the rice field where the farmers busily chopped weeds along a dike, Hathcock watched a lone man wearing a khaki shirt and black shorts walk to and from a hut that hugged the edge of the forest.

Slowly, Hathcock moved his rifle to his right and lay behind it, watching the hut through his telescopic sight. The way that the man kept walking back to the hut and nervously stepping in and out the door made him suspicious.

In the distance came the rumble of heavy explosions, the sounds of an arc-light raid—Air Force B-52s dropping their tons of bombs on targets high in the steep mountains that stood well beyond Charlie Ridge and Happy Valley. That was where the enemy leaders hid and controlled the guerrilla war. Hathcock had seen that country only on maps and in aerial recon photographs. Even from such a sanitary perspective, he did not like the looks of it. He knew that for an American to go into those mountains that faced the Laotian border took great courage. The terrain alone could kill a man.

The bombs fell on those distant Viet cong and NVA strongholds that morning, but did not strike the headquarters of the North Vietnamese Army division general, who commanded thousands of soldiers from there. Hathcock knew nothing of this man, yet the man already knew of Hathcock and his fellow snipers. The commander carefully read a report sent to his headquarters by the cruel woman who led the Viet Cong near Hill 55. She told of the new school at the hill and the sniper tactics that she had observed being taught. She felt certain that American sniper operations were potentially very harmful.

In little more than a month, this general would read much more about the snipers who operated from Hill 55. He would also know many of them by name including Sergeant Carlos N. Hathcock, the sniper they would call "Long Tra'ng," White Feather. Even as he read the report on this morning that the bombs fell dangerously close to his office, hidden beneath a camouflaged umbrella of netting and foliage, he contemplated means of stopping this new threat of sniper warfare. He knew that if it were left unchecked, it would badly cripple his operations near Da Nang.

The old man scratched a message on a narrow pad with his black, mother-of-pearl-finished fountain pen. He pressed the ink dry with a small ivory rocking horse blotter, a gift from his daughter, folded the paper double and sealed it shut with a drop of red wax, on which he pressed the impression of a crimson, enamel-inlaid, five-point star, a gift presented to him in China.

A soldier wearing a tan uniform and pith helmet marched smartly from the headquarters, with the note secured inside a small leather pouch that hung from a strap across his shoulder. The neatly dressed soldier stopped at the end of the walkway and looked up at the sun, which stood at its noonday peak. He lifted the tan helmet from his head, wiped sweat from his brow, and turned his eyes toward the towering clouds that loomed in the east and promised rain that evening.

Sheets of rain fell on the three Marines as they hid silently observing all activity around the rice fields and huts. The men who had worked chopping weeds from the edge of the rice paddy now huddled inside the doorway of a hut that faced the three Marines. Hathcock was not concerned with them, but the man who squatted just inside the door of the hut at the edge of the forest continued to hold the sniper's interest.

The monsoon rained through the afternoon, and Hathcock and his two students lay soaked at the edge of the jungle, watching intently for the man who squatted in the hut to confirm himself as Charlie.

"Let's go," the burley PFC whispered to Hathcock. "It's almost time for us to get back. There ain't no VC to shoot out here anyway. And besides, I'm hungry."

Hathcock looked at the young Marine's round face with a glance that easily told the man that he should keep his thoughts to himself. Crooking his finger in a motion for the man to come closer, Hathcock whispered tersely, "Sit still and don't make any more noise. You got enough explaining to do, with you trying to kill them farmers."

The Marine lay flat on his stomach and rested his chin on his hands, which he clasped together. He said nothing more until he spoke to the captain that night.

The rain lightened to a drizzle and a soft breeze began to blow from the east, clearing the hazy pall that had gathered over the fields. In the doorway of the hut that hugged the edge of the forest, the man who wore the khaki shirt and black shorts stood. He stepped outside and looked to his right, and then to his left, before disappearing behind the hut.

"He's up to something," Hathcock thought to himself, as he watched through his rifle's scope.

Ten minutes later the man returned with a white canvas bag strapped over his shoulder. He looked again to his right, and then to his left. And when he felt certain that no one watched him, he reached inside the hut's doorway and took an SKS rifle from its hiding place there.

"Got you, Charlie," Hathcock thought, as he gently squeezed his rifle's trigger and dropped the man dead in his tracks.

"Let's go home," Hathcock told the burly PFC.

The three Marines silently slipped into the tree line and, following the edge of the forest, came abreast of the hut where Hathcock had killed the Viet Cong soldier. They stopped and looked at the man lying dead only a few feet from the forest's edge. Next to him lay the SKS rifle.

"I'm gonna capture that weapon," Hathcock told the two students.

As they cautiously walked to the forest's edge and peered from behind its dense cover, Hathcock scrambled to where the body lay and snatched the rifle. He turned to retreat quickly when he noticed a broad, white feather, three inches long, lying at his feet. The sight of it reminded him of the white sea birds that he watched fly over this valley at sunrise.

He knelt and took the delicate plume in his left hand, and without another pause, stepped rapidly behind the jungle's green curtain.

As the trio of men made their way to the rally point, Hathcock twirled the feather between his fingers and thought again of the peaceful dawn and the white birds. It might well have been a feather dropped by a chicken that had strayed to that far end of the community, but for Hathcock, the white birds of the morning seemed a more meaningful source. And in the same respect that hundreds of Marines and soldiers would occasionally wear a small flower on their helmets, representing a simple beauty that still survived in the midst of war's thorns and fires, he took his bush hat from his head and inserted the feather into its band.

Shoving the hat back on his head, Hathcock turned his interest to the rifle he had captured. He would tag it and turn it in at the command post. Hopefully, he would be able to take it home as a souvenir, just as his father had done with the old Mauser.

The march home took much longer than the trek out that morning. The squad took a return route that brought them to the opposite side of Hill 55 from where they had departed. They knew that often the Viet Cong would rig explosives in trails left by outbound patrols, in hopes of blowing away the soldiers as they backtracked home.

By the time Hathcock reached his hooch, he felt extraordinarily tired—physically drained from the long day, the rain, and the extra miles home. Cleaning his rifle and combat gear seemed a dismal chore, one he had to force himself to complete.

That night, Hathcock sat shaking on the edge of his cot. His legs trembled and his vision blurred. His head buzzed as though he had taken a marathon roller coaster ride. He thought that it may have resulted from the soaking he took during the day. But deep in his consciousness he knew that it had to be something else. Something that he did not like. A thing that had been subtly attacking him—coming and going—for three years.

It began when Jo gave birth to Carlos Norman Hathcock III. She herself had had to call the Naval Hospital ambulance at Cherry Point to get to the delivery room. Hathcock had suffered fainting and dizzy spells two weeks before that, and the doctors had hospitalized him, as a precaution.

He had been in the hospital when his son was born. It had upset him at the time—he would have liked to have been with his wife—but he sometimes felt it had hardened his resolution to get out of the hospital and take up his responsibilities, even though his physical unsteadiness hadn't entirely disappeared.

This evening in the sniper hooch on Hill 55, he felt much worse than in many months. He sat there visibly shaking when a meaty hand took him by the shoulder.

"You okay, Carlos?"

Hathcock turned to see his captain standing at the foot of his cot. "Get over to the sick bay," Land said in his gruff voice. "You look pretty well wrung out."

"Skipper," Hathcock said in a high-pitched, singsong voice, "I'm really all right. I just got a little chill from the rain today. I'm gonna get me something hot to drink, and I'll crawl in the rack. I'll be okay."

Land looked at him quizzically, but decided to accept his sergeant's opinion of when he was sick enough to need a doctor. "I guess that will do, but I'm gonna be keeping an eye on you. I don't like the way you look. Just remember—life is hard. But it's one hell of a lot harder if you're stupid."

Hathcock smiled as he recalled the John Wayne movie where he had first heard that line. "Yes, Sir. Don't you worry about me. I may be ignorant, but I ain't stupid."

In his heart, however, he knew that life was getting one hell of a lot harder, and he could remain stupid only so long. Some day his secret would be out. The doctors would have to know. But now was not the time.

Less than twenty minutes later, the captain returned to Hathcock, carrying a canteen cup filled with hot chicken soup. "Here, drink this."

"What is it? Chicken soup? Where you find that?"

The captain smiled, "That staff sergeant at the mess tent. I just asked him for some hot soup and he came up with this. I didn't ask where or how . . . I just thanked him and left."

Land picked up an ammunition crate that the Marines who lived in the hooch with Hathcock had used as a stool and set it down next to the cot and took a seat on it. "You sure you don't need to talk to a doctor about this? You're shaking pretty bad."

"I'm okay, really. I just got a little flu or something today and got the shakes from it."

Gently cupping his palm over Hathcock's forehead, the captain did not feel any sign of fever. "You don't seem to have a temperature. I guess you'll be okay. Probably is just a little chill. You stay in that rack tomorrow."

"I will, Sir, unless I feel real fit. I'll come see you first."

"You be sure you do."

At one o'clock that morning, Hathcock walked to the privy. He stumbled and staggered as though he had been drinking heavily. He was frightened that the problem would not leave before dawn.

Inside the plywood hut, he took short breaths and held them for several seconds each, trying to avoid smelling the stench of the excrement that filled a cut-down fifty-five-gallon drum positioned below the wooden throne on which he sat. He recalled watching a private lift the heavy cans onto the bed of a mule* and how the foul liquid sloshed on the man's hands and clothes—how his utility uniform bore greasy black stains across the chest and down both legs from this chore.

Hathcock thought how lucky he was to be a sergeant. He did not have to pull shit detail, hauling the shit-filled cans down to the west side of the hill, topping them off with kerosene, and setting them on fire.

When Hathcock awoke the following morning, he felt better. The dizziness had almost gone. The trembling had settled to a slight twitching in his legs. He smiled as he put his feet on the oil-stained plywood floor and stood, feeling steady. "Maybe it was the soaking I took," he thought.

Although he felt better, he did not go to the field for several days. He spent his time writing lesson plans and debriefing students. And planning patrols—patrols that he longed to lead.

On a sweltering monsoon afternoon, with the temperature and humidity both hovering near 95, Hathcock was writing the day's report at the green, clapboard field desk. He took off his shirt and wore only his camouflage utility trousers and boots. The snipers had returned from the field early and empty-handed again. Their debrief was short.

Carlos sipped a cold beer. The gunny had bought six when the service club opened at five o'clock, and now two cans sat on the corner of the field desk, water beading down their sides, awaiting the captain.

A large, black mosquito landed on Hathcock's arm and began drawing blood from skin marked by a tattoo of the confederate flag and the word "Rebel" written beneath it. "Go

---

*A small, flatbed motor-driven, four-wheel-drive vehicle with a driver-seat and steering control suspended over the forward edge of the cart. It is a light-duty utility vehicle, but also served as a mobile platform for the 106mm recoilless rifle, which was mounted on the rear of the vehicle when used in that capacity.

ahead and suck," Hathcock said, watching the insect fill its stomach, stretching it round. Just as the mosquito was about to withdraw its proboscis, Hathcock pressed the tip of his finger on the insect and burst it, leaving a bloody smear on the red-and-blue tattoo.

"Damn mosquitos," Wilson said, slapping one that bit his neck as he sat on an ammo crate and reclined on his shoulders against the wall of the hooch. "One way or another, I'm gonna wind up leaving most of my blood over here—if Charlie don't get us, then the bugs will."

"Gunny," the captain said, as he walked through the doorway, "if it wasn't the bugs, you'd be bitchin' about the heat or the dirt."

"Now that you mention it, Skipper, this is about the hottest, filthiest sandpile I've ever spent time at anyway. I'd just as soon be livin' inside a shit-can on the Sahara," Wilson fired back.

"Don't be joking about that, we'll probably wind up there next," Land said.

Hathcock smiled and said, "I don't know what is so bad about living in this nice little house we got here."

"You would like this dump, Hathcock. I forgot about you coming from Arkansas. It was probably a step up for you to come here and wear shoes," Wilson said, evoking a chuckle from Land and a finger from Hathcock.

"We're going out tomorrow," the captain said, taking a healthy swallow from one of the dripping beer cans."

"Sir, does that 'we' include me?" Hathcock asked hopefully.

"Yes it does, Sergeant Hathcock."

When the sun rose, Hathcock and Captain Land already rested beneath the leaves of a short palm in a grassy hide that overlooked a clearing fifty yards wide that the Marines often used as a landing zone. Beyond the clearing grew short bushes and plants with broad, flat leaves. Farther on, a tree line followed the edge of a narrow stream. The water ran along the base of a hill that a barrage of napalm and heavy explosives had left bare except for splintered trees bristling up like the pins in a pincushion. A faint trail led across the front of the two snipers' hiding place, made a left turn in the clearing, and etched its way between the bushes and plants, through the shattered timber and onto the top of the hill, where it connected with a road.

This junction was the focal point of the two Marines' interests. Here they watched for the enemy to emerge, crossing one of the openings below this denuded hill, on the way to ambush American forces. And here they hoped they might also get a glimpse of the woman torturer who led the Viet Cong snipers thereabouts. This hill was two to three miles west of their base on Hill 55.

Hathcock shivered slightly from the coolness of the morning's heavy dew, which soaked through the front of his uniform.

While Hathcock and Land lay behind their leafy blind, a lone Vietnamese sniper stepped carefully along the edge of the stream. The man wore a black shirt and pants with the legs rolled up past his knees, and he was undoubtedly heading back to his unit's underground headquarters beyond the bomb-scarred hill. He stepped slowly and paused, sniffing the air for cigarette smoke and listening for any unnatural sound.

"Hathcock," Land whispered. "You take the scope for a while. I'll give you a break off the rifle."

"Five more minutes, Sir. I got a feeling that Charlie is gonna step out any second."

"You'll have that feeling all day until you get a shot out. And when he shows himself, you'll say, 'See, I told you so.' Carlos, you're not psychic. Let me take the rifle for a while."

"Sirrrr," Hathcock whispered, "Just five more minutes."

Land said nothing but put his eye back to the rear optic of the M-49 scope through which he scanned the clearing and the lane that led to the hilltop.

"Hathcock. Give me the rifle," the captain said after waiting fifteen minutes more. "I'm tired of looking through this scope. I need the relief, if you don't."

"Yes, Sir. I'm sorry," Hathcock said softly, taking the rifle from his shoulder and slowly passing it to Land.

Just as the captain grasped hold of the weapon, and before Hathcock had released his grip from the small of the stock, both men saw a lone dark figure creep from the trees along the stream and step into the open, two hundred yards away. It was easy to recognize this soldier's specialty by the long wooden stock of the bolt-action rifle that he carried across his back—obviously a sniper.

"Give me the rifle, Hathcock," Land said, pulling the weapon toward himself, trying to loosen Hathcock's grip.

"I'll get him, Sir. Turn loose."

"No, Carlos. I'll shoot him."

Hathcock pulled hard on the rifle, forcing Land to grunt, as he fought to win what had now become a tug-of-war. And rapidly the struggle between the two men escalated into a full-blown wrestling match.

"God damn it, Carlos. Let go of the rifle."

Hathcock let go. Land shoved the butt into his shoulder and put his eye to the scope in time to see the fleeing enemy sprint into the tree line and disappear, before the captain could get a shot away.

"Shit!" Land said, looking at Hathcock, who was futilely trying to resist laughing. The captain began smiling too. "You dumb ass. He got away. Now we gotta pick up and move. He'll be back with help."

Carlos blinked and a curious expression came over his face, "Captain Land, what if we sat tight? We got our six o'clock covered by that patrol that dropped us off. If that gook wants to come back with his friends, who's to say we can't shoot ourselves a bunch of them. And, what if he brought back his boss. You know who she is."

"Get on the radio, Carlos," the captain said firmly. "Tell that patrol to close up on our rear and sit tight, and be ready for anything. In the meantime, I think we'd be better off at the other end of this clearing. We can set up in those low bushes on that rise along the edge. They might come back with mortars or rockets, and I don't want to be hanging out where old Nguyen saw us last.

"You're right about that woman. She's gotta believe there are a couple of bozos out here, after that little show of mature professionalism that we put on. She just might come out here lookin' to capture herself a couple of easy pigeons."

The two snipers cautiously crawled along the edge of the clearing, through the short palms and on to the upper reaches, where a thick stand of grass and elephant ears covered their movement. A slight rise in the earth made an ideal bench-rest for their rifles. They adjusted the camouflage around their position and settled into their new hide.

By noon, nothing had crossed their line of sight. The patrol that lay hidden far to their rear along a low ridge remained silent, too.

When the Viet Cong sniper reached the network of tunnels and underground chambers that housed his unit's head-quarters, his commander—the woman who hunted Marines at Hill 55—met him at the door. He told her of the two enemy soldiers whom he saw fighting at the edge of the clearing and urged her to hurry back and get them. The woman was hesitant. Where there were two Marines, there could be many more. She had planned an ambush for that evening and to reach the place where it would be set up, she would need to go over or around the hill in front of which the two Marines had shown themselves. After some thought, she decided not to cancel the evening's ambush. She would decide whether they would go over or around the hill when they reached it.

Gnats and other flying, biting insects swarmed in the shade beneath the low plants and palms as the sun heated the humid afternoon. The air hung still in a hot house doldrums that left the two Marines stewing beneath the foliage, helplessly suffering from the bites of the hungry bugs that swarmed over them. Sweat seeped into Hathcock's eyes and dripped from the tip of his nose, while an army of tiny pests crawled around his neck, inside his ears, and on his eyelids and nostrils. Hathcock remembered hearing that the Japanese in World War II had a word for days like this—it translated as "buggy-hot." He lay motionless. Any sudden motion could draw attention from an unseen enemy.

"Sir," Hathcock whispered to his captain, who lay next to him suffering similarly. "You okay?"

"No," came the captain's sharply whispered retort. "I've just about had it. We don't pick up a sign by sixteen-hundred and we're gone."

Hathcock didn't want to complain, but the bugs were getting to him, too. He felt certain that an army of black ants had found their way into his trouser leg and now waged battle on his loins. The reassuring comment from the captain made their stinging more tolerable.

Just then, Hathcock saw a sudden motion among the broken tree trunks at the crest of the hill. "Skipper. Look. Just at the top."

The captain shifted his spotting scope slightly to his left and immediately saw the black-clad man, crawling on his knees through the maze of dead wood with an AK-47 in his hand.

"Don't shoot, Carlos. He ain't alone."

"Sir?"

"Look at the rifle. If he was a sniper, he would be carrying a long stick, not an assault rifle. Bet you money that he's a scout."

"Reckon he belongs to that woman?"

"Odds look promising. We're in the middle of her stomping grounds."

"I keep thinking how good a whole lot of folks would feel if we nailed her. After that night back at Hill 55, I haven't been able to get the idea of her out of my head."

"Don't go gettin' your hopes up. It's likely we won't get a clear shot at her, even if we see her. And, don't forget, she hit An Hoa last night, and that is way over the other side of Hill 55 from where we are now. She could just as likely be laying back there now, looking to catch herself another young boy to skin."

"I know. Still, it don't hurt none, wishin'."

"While you're wishin', just keep your sights on old Nguyen Schwartz out there a snoopin' and a poopin'."

Land had guessed correctly, the Viet Cong soldier was a scout. He had left the tunnels two hours ahead of his patrol in order to disclose any enemy ambushes on, or around, the hill. If the hill was clear, he would wait just below the crest and signal his comrades to approach.

The little man spent more than an hour crawling on his knees and elbows through the heavy fall of splintered tree trunks that lay criss-crossed and tangled, like a heap of gigantic pick-up sticks.

"He's definitely scouting," Land concluded in a soft whisper to Hathcock. "Probably looking for us. Let him look."

The black-clad man moved back to the hill's crest and disappeared on the other side.

"Sir," Hathcock said. "We either let another one get away, or we've got outselves a whole stringerful of fish fixing to strike the bait."

"He'll be back," Land said.

Hathcock looked at his watch. It was nearly 5:30 P.M., an hour and a half beyond the time they had planned to leave this blind. He wondered how long his captain would persist in the wait. He only hoped he wouldn't give it up prematurely.

The November sun now stood just above the mountaintops that rose along the western horizon. It had turned from bright white to yellow and now deepened to a burning orange ball. Long shadows stretched below the trees.

"We're losing our light, Carlos," the captain said. "It's time we pulled in our lines."

"Sir, ten more minutes. I got this feeling that any second . . ."

"Carlos," the captain said, but the sight of a dim silhouette emerging at the hilltop stopped him. "The hilltop. Something's coming."

Hathcock looked through his scope and saw the outline of several figures emerging over the hill's crest. "I can't tell, Sir."

"I can, Carlos," Land said, looking through the more powerful spotting scope. "They're VC. Check out the one that just squatted off to the left, just below the rise from the others."

"It's a woman! She's pulling at her britches leg."

"She's taking a piss, Carlos."

"Is that her? Is that the Apache?"

"It's her," the captain said, now certain from his recollection of the photos and sketches that an intelligence officer at the division command post had shown him. "Carlos, hand me that radio handset. I think that our best chance of hitting them is with artillery. Read me the coordinates off your map."

The answer to their radio call came quickly. The first shell exploded directly at the junction of the trail and the road, killing three of the seven Viet Cong there. Two ran down the trail away from where Hathcock and Land lay hidden. The woman, who was still squatting when the first shell exploded, fell on her face. Two shells exploded behind the first, and a VC soldier ran down the trail, toward the two Marines. The sound of more incoming artillery sent him leaping for shelter among a jam of logs.

The woman scrambled to her feet and, in sudden panic, ran down the trail, and down the hill, directly toward the two snipers hiding in the low palms and grass. She remembered how trouble always seemed to plague her on this hill. It was where her unit had had its headquarters before the bombers had laid it flat. She was running hard in panic, her heart pounding, and tears streaming from her eyes.

Hathcock tightened his grip around the stock of his Winchester rifle and centered the scope's reticle on the woman's chest. "Hold it. Don't rush the shot," he reminded himself. "Keep the cross hairs centered. Wait. Wait. Get her at the turn."

Higher up the hill, the soldier who took cover jumped from the logs and began to sprint down the trail, trying to catch his leader. He realized that she ran, not away from the danger, but straight toward it. This was where he had seen the two Marines wrestling, near the turn in the trail that his commander now approached.

He screamed for the woman to stop, but she kept running. Her temples throbbed with blood, and the shouts of her comrade seemed muffled and unintelligible, as though they came from a drowning man, pleading with his last breath beneath the water's surface.

She looked back and, as she did so, Carlos, coming to his natural respiratory pause, let his finger complete the roll of the rifle's trigger. The recoil sent the Unertl scope sliding forward in its mounts as the bullet cracked across the open land, crossed the narrow stream, and shattered the woman's collarbones and spine, sending blood and gristle spraying over the low, green ferns that lined either side of the trail.

The Marine sniper pulled the scope back to the rear position, cycled his bolt and centered his sights on the woman's body heaped in the center of the trail. The next bullet ripped through her shoulder and into both lungs, scrambling vital organs to a pulp.

The man who followed her reeled on his toes when the first shot blew the woman off her feet a few yards ahead of him. In leaping steps, he sprinted back up the hill. A single shot that Carlos aimed squarely between the man's shoulders killed him instantly.

An enormous smiled passed across Hathcock's face. Land threw his arms around his sergeant's shoulders and shook him hard, "You got her, Carlos! You did it!"

Hathcock laughed in jubilation and then, suddenly, he pounded his fist angrily on the hard-packed earth, and said, "Ya, we did it. We got that dirty bitch. She ain't gonna torture nobody no more!"

10

Rio Blanco and the Frenchman

AT THE NVA compound far to the west of Hill 55, the squat, stockily built old commander rose early. He had not slept well. The forces that he commanded had not enjoyed the success that he had anticipated, and the tension this caused gave him a grizzly's disposition.

Today he hoped for good news.

When the old man walked into his office and sat behind a table covered with papers, a soldier stepped through his door carrying a leather pouch containing intelligence reports and dispatches from the regiments under his command. As the soldier left, an officer came to attention before the general and informed him that the commander of the guerrillas who had so successfully harassed the enemy near Da Nang had been killed, with four of her men, by snipers. The same snipers about whom she voiced concern a month before.

Her death was a sharp loss. Guerrillas of the National Liberation Army were now reluctant to go on patrol in the country where they encountered these snipers, one of whom was gaining recognition for the white feather he wore in his hat, as well as for his marksmanship.

This woman, who had begun as a Lao Dong party worker in the north, meant much to the old warrior. He had the determination, and he believed he had the means, to see to it that her assassins did not go unpunished.

* * *

Far to the east of where the NVA commander sat brooding, Hathcock walked briskly into the sniper school's command hut.

"Sir," he said, "me and Burke, we want to go back out."

"Funny you should come waltzing up here so chipper," Land said. "You get wind of something?"

"Could be, Sir. You tell me."

"You ever hear of Rio Blanco?"

Hathcock had. He constantly kept attuned to all the operations throughout southern and central I Corps, and he knew that Rio Blanco was big. But he liked to antagonize his captain.

"John Wayne movie. Right, Sir?"

"John Wayne my ass, Carlos. That was *Rio Bravo*, and you probably know more about Rio Blanco than I do."

"Oh, no, Sir! I just heard the name, that's all," Hathcock said, trying to sound innocent.

Land rested his arms across the desk and cleared his throat, "Rio Blanco is a major operation that will clear out a wide valley over by Hill 263. The river Song Tro Khuc runs right through the middle of it, and word is that Charlie has a reinforced regiment, or larger, down there.

"Division is massing Bravo, Charlie, Delta, and Mike companies out of 7th Marines, plus two and a half batteries from 11th Marines—a MAU-sized outfit. They will link up with the ROK Marines Dragon Eye Regiment and the Lien Ket 70 Division from the ARVN. They aim to kick ass."

Wilson, who had been sitting at the table with Land, looked at Hathcock and rolled his eyes. The sniper smiled and said nothing.

"Gunny Wilson and I have been putting together a roster of twelve snipers to take down there. The four we leave back here will check in with Top Reinke over at his hooch and operate with 1st Battalion, 26th Marines while we're gone."

Hathcock stood at the doorway, with a long expression on his face. He knew they wouldn't leave him behind, but he needed to hear it.

"We leave at zero six, day after tomorrow," Wilson said firmly. "You be sure the troops are up and packed, Sergeant Hathcock."

"Aye, aye, Sir!" Hathcock said, saluting with his palm turned outward in crisp British fashion.

Two days later, when the sniper team arrived at the 7th Marines command post on the afternoon of November 20, the operation had already begun. A busy major greeted Land and told him that it made no difference to the command where he disbursed his snipers, as long as they remained north of the river.

"General Stiles* will be in and out of this command post, so you might do yourself a favor and establish your CP on one of these fingers just down the hill so you can be close, if something pops. The ITT and CIT folks are set up where they can overlook the operational area from their CP, and they have room for your guys, too. You might consider that."

Land thanked the major and led his snipers down the hill to where he could see the counterintelligence Marines' shaved heads shining in the afternoon sun. "That's right, Major," Land sarcastically thought to himself as he walked away from the command post, "put all the oddballs in one spot where you can keep an eye on 'em, and at the same time, keep 'em out of sight."

"Gunny Wilson," Land said aloud.

The gunnery sergeant jogged down to where Land walked. "Yes, Sir."

"You, me, Hathcock, and Burke will stay up here. I'm farming the other eight snipers out to the four companies down there on the operation. They'll work in direct support of the companies. We can keep ourselves busy around the hill."

Hathcock was walking on the heels of his captain, mouth shut and ears wide open. Already the wheels were turning. He liked this country. He had patrolled it from trucks as an MP and knew that as a sniper he could do some real good.

A skinny and weathered old farmer in his fifties, who looked a hundred, worked in a cane field below Hill 263. He kept his head down and swung his hand scythe through the tall stalks, cutting down the crop that he had planted a full growing sea-

*Brigadier General W. A. Stiles, USMC, Commanding General, Task Force X Ray.

son ago. The man did not want to appear out of the ordinary to the Vietnamese government troops who walked past him while he worked. Sweat trickled down his face, hidden beneath the large, round straw hat that he wore. The perspiration came not so much from heat or work, but from the fear that turned in the pit of his stomach.

Had the passing soldiers talked to him, they would have known at once that he had something to hide. He was such a frightened man.

During the days that Hathcock had patrolled the fields as an MP, riding atop a truck with a mounted .50-caliber machine gun in hand, this man had waved to the Marines as they drove past. He was a simple farmer whose life revolved around the large cane field and two flooded paddies in which he alternated growing rice and lotus. He measured his wealth by his family and by the one water buffalo that he shared with a neighbor, who in return shared with him a cask of rice wine.

The war had already taken his son, but his son's widow and children remained with him. His wife had passed away in her sleep ten years ago. Now his daughter, her two children, and his son's widow and her four children were the family who looked upon him as father, protector, and provider.

In that past summer of 1966, he did not speak of politics. It was a subject about which he knew little. He could neither read nor write, nor could anyone else in his family. They were farmers, not scholars.

There were those in his village who did speak of politics and war. They spoke of Ho Chi Minh and his dream of once again uniting Vietnam. But would a united Vietnam make his cane or rice or lotus grow? Would a united Vietnam return his dead son or his wife to him?

He worked in the three fields, planting and harvesting his lotus, sugarcane and rice. That was his life. He counted on nothing more.

During that summer, the Viet Cong came for rice and pigs and to lecture the villagers. The old man stood in the crowd and listened to them for a while and then walked away.

The Viet Cong commander noticed him leaving. That night the Viet Cong killed the old man's water buffalo and threatened to kill his family and burn his house if he did not cooperate.

The Viet Cong left for him a Chinese-built K-44 rifle. It was covered with rust, and the stock was cracked from the top of the hand guard to the trigger housing. His bullets would do well to strike anywhere near a target at which he aimed, even if he had been a marksman. Each night, the Viet Cong left twenty rounds for him to shoot at the Americans who camped atop the hill. When the Viet Cong returned, they took the twenty empty brass shells.

At that darkest time of morning when the moon had set and the sun remained well below the horizon, he took the rusty rifle, with its broken stock and badly worn barrel, to the edge of his sugarcane field. There, he hid behind a dirt bank and rested the old gun over it. Aiming at the hilltop, he fired twenty shots, one after the other.

Cloaked by dawn's black shadows, the old man collected the spent brass and hurried back to his hut, where he hid the rifle beneath straw mats and dropped the empty shells into a pot inside his tool shed. Once this chore was done, he walked to the fields and worked—hitching himself to a heavy wooden sledge, or plow, that he could pull only inches at a time through the deep mud. These were implements that his water buffalo had once drawn with ease.

On November 21, Captain Land sent out his eight snipers at 3:00 A.M. to rendezvous with the four rifle companies. He, Wilson, Hathcock, and Burke stayed on the hill.

Hathcock had pointed out to Land the fields that lay along the river and told how he used to watch for smoke rising from tunnels that the VC had dug beneath the dikes. Despite the fact that many of those same fields, which lay directly below the hill, were considered under control of friendly forces, the snipers knew this country was rich with Viet Cong.

Hathcock sat down on an ammo case.

"Skipper, what's the plan of attack?"

"Gunny Wilson and Lance Corporal Burke will move down to the river's edge. You and I will spend the day scoping the world from on high. We're gonna watch for smoke signals. We have to come home with a few scalps on our belts so we can stay in business. There are people at places like Quantico and Camp Pendleton who are trying to get snipers organized as a regular part of every infantry battalion in the Marine Corps. This is our chance to sell the program by showing that one man with a rifle can do as much damage as a company on patrol."

Hathcock said nothing. He knew that sniping was highly cost-effective in terms of materials and lives. He also knew its impact on the enemy. Snipers denied the enemy leadership and access to communications and heavy weapons. But mostly, snipers demoralized the enemy. Made them quit. Made them hide and not want to fight.

"Sir, I can't imagine anybody not wanting to make snipers a regular part of the battalion. Just think if every company had a platoon of snipers who doubled as scouts. How could anyone not want that?" Hathcock asked Land.

"They don't want to consider that you, in a single month, killed more than thirty enemy soldiers, confirmed. Forget probable kills. Compare your success—one man—against an entire battalion's during the same period.

"Operation Macon started back on the fourth of July down near An Hoa. That's real hot Indian country. Third Battalion, 9th Marines worked extra hard clearing the area around the industrial complex. They lost twenty-four Marines from the time they started until the end of October, when they wrapped it up. In the four months that Macon lasted, they confirmed 445 enemy dead. That is a little more than 110 per month. It's a damn good result for a battalion. They're proud of it, too.

"From mid-October to mid-November you confirmed thirty kills, nearly a third of what an entire battalion accomplished patrolling day and night.

"Look at October alone. Operation Kern netted seventy-five VC kills and cost eight Marine KIAs. Operation Teton nailed thirty-seven VC and two Marine KIAs. And Operation Madison blew hell out of Cam Ne hamlet—looking for a VC battalion—and got nothing, not even a sack of rice.

"In the first month we've been in business we have more than sixty kills. That's between seventeen people, and most of them students.

"What if those battalions had snipers working ahead of their operations, or keeping security around their camps. I think the results would have been much more impressive and would have had longer lasting effects against the enemy. Lord only knows how long Charlie keeps on ducking and dodging after we've worked an area.

"If we sell the sniper system, battalion and company commanders won't want to go to war without a sniper platoon to keep the boogeyman out of the bushes."

Hathcock looked Land in the eye and smiled. They both knew that if the Marine Corps could be convinced of the value of sniping, they were the ones to do it. Just then, rifle fire began to crack.

The bullets struck the rocks well below where Hathcock sat, but the surprise sent him diving headlong into the dirt. He heard shot after shot splattering against the rocks.

The old man who lay at the edge of the cane field fired his twentieth round and gathered the empty brass.

Land glanced at Hathcock in the gray light that now filled the hillside as November 21 dawned. "I know one place to start hunting tomorrow."

Wilson and Burke returned from their day's stalk with little more than a few blisters. They had not had a good hunt. They had seen Charlie, but by the time they got authorization to shoot into that sector, he had strolled right on by.

Land looked disgusted, "I swear these rules of engagement get my goat. One place there's a free fire zone. Shoot anything that moves. Next place you can't shoot at all unless you get permission."

Resting his head on his pack, Hathcock sprawled out to sleep on the bunker's dirt floor. He thought of how he preferred to work away from the crowd, shooting into free fire zones—places he called Indian country. He felt as though he had just dozed off when Land's strong hand firmly gripped his arm.

"Carlos. Time to get up."

Carlos jerked at his captain's touch. He had slept with a coiled spring's tension, leaving him stiff and sore. Stretching felt good.

Nighttime left a dampness on everything, including the

aching snipers who crawled down Hill 263 into the area that the captain had cleared with operations. The zone included a large cane field that waved in the predawn breezes.

. The gray morning felt chilly as the two snipers built a dummy position a hundred yards to the right of their hide. They counted on it drawing any fire, should Charlie have friends. Land calculated that when they fired, the bullets passing the elbow that jutted out from the hill, just above the dummy position, would cause a crack from the bullet's supersonic wake. Charlie would look to where he heard the loud pop of the speeding projectile as it passed the dummy position, rather than the more distant and less discernable .30-06 muzzle blast from the heavy semivarminter barrel.

The old man awoke late this morning. He, too, had slept poorly. He had seen strange-looking soldiers that his neighbor told him were Korean. His neighbor told him to be careful, these Koreans were not like the Americans—they killed with unquenchable thirst.

The farmer looked across the dark hut at the sleeping children and at the rapidly brightening sky that shone through the window above where they lay. It reminded him that he must hurry.

He crept to where the straw mats covered the rifle, and, with shaking hands, he rolled them back and took the weapon from its hiding place. In the shed where he stored his plow and hand tools, he lifted the lid off a pot and removed a fresh box of shells, left during the night by the phantom guerrilla who prowled through the village while all others slept. He never saw who left the shells, but they were always there each morning, and the spent rounds were always gone at night.

Because the early morning light now exposed him, the old farmer chose a hidden route through the tall, green stalks of cane. He slowly crawled to the earthen barrier that held back the rice paddy's water.

Hathcock took the first watch behind the rifle. He scanned along the dike, searching for a target. As he panned the edge of the cane field, he noticed a dark figure crouched low.

"We got company," he whispered to his captain. "He just

hunkered down behind that dike next to the cane field. It sure wasn't a farmer. I saw a rifle."

"When he raises his head to shoot," the captain answered, "drop him."

The world seemed extraordinarily quiet to the old man, who nervously shoved the muzzle of the badly worn Chinese rifle over the top of the dike. He pulled the rifle's butt into his shoulder and fixed his eyes to the hilltop where he saw dark figures silhouetted against the gray morning sky. His hands trembled as he gripped the stock and rolled his finger around the rusty trigger.

"Get the task finished," he thought to himself as he jerked the trigger.

The sudden explosion from the rusty barrel sent an echo across the valley to where the two snipers lay beneath their camouflage.

"Can you see him?" Land asked Hathcock, who now squirmed behind the long scope atop his Winchester.

Carlos said nothing. He saw the top of the old man's gray head, his temples, his ears, and his one open eye behind the sights of the rifle. The target that the old man presented at five hundred yards lay hidden behind the reticle as Carlos concentrated on the cross hairs' intersection.

Slowly, he increased pressure on the trigger so as not to disturb the sight's alignment on the old man's temple. He watched through the scope and saw the gray puffs of smoke clouding above the old man's rifle.

Above where the farmer and the snipers lay, Marines jumped behind sandbags, swearing at this constant aggravation. Before the operation, the firing had bothered no one, since the Marines who normally camped on the hilltop rarely ventured to the side where they had heard shots each morning since the summer.

A fourth and fifth shot belched from the rusty rifle, yet Hathcock did not rush his. He waited for the pressure to overpower the resistance of the trigger's spring.

"Break, damn it. Break!" Hathcock strained in a whispering breath. It seemed as though the trigger would not release the firing pin and send his round ripping across the rice field and into the head of the man who continued firing the rifle.

"Get aggressive on that trigger, Hathcock," Land said, waiting for the rifle's report. He looked at his sergeant's face, twisted in a grimace. His left eye hidden beneath a wrinkled brow and his teeth showing between his curled and twisted lips. Land glanced at the rear of the Winchester's bolt and saw the problem.

"Try it with the safety off."

A flush of blood filled Carlos's face. He remembered flicking back the safety when he cleaned the rifle the previous afternoon. He'd neglected to return the small lever to its ready position when he finished.

Without removing his cheek from the side of the rifle, Hathcock lifted his right thumb to the small lever on the bolt's tailpiece and flicked it to "ready."

He narrowed his concentration to the reticle and the target beyond it. It seemed as though he had just begun to apply pressure to the trigger when the sudden explosion in the rifle's chamber sent the weapon recoiling into his shoulder. Hot gas blasted down onto a square canvas patch that he laid beneath the rifle's muzzle to prevent a dusty signature that would give away his position. The bullet cracked from the barrel, arched past the lower elbow of the hill, and struck the target.

In that same instant, the old man jerked his final shot, as half his face and the portion of his head above his right ear exploded in a crimson spray. The bullet's impact separated the man from his rifle and hurled him backward into the field. His suddenly lifeless body leaped skyward, violently kicking and crashing through the sugarcane.

"Damn!" Land said, grimacing.

Several Marines who sat behind the sandbags on the hill's finger heard the sniper's shot. They peeked over the top and witnessed the gory sight of the man's dead body reeling in uncontrolled acrobatics—whipping, kicking, jumping.

Hathcock watched through his scope, tracking the nearly headless body as it flopped and crashed through the cane field. Several of his head shots had ended in similar displays of dancing dead, but this was the most gruesome. The sight repulsed him, and he turned his head away.

The old man's body came to rest nearly thirty feet into the

field from where Hathcock's bullet struck it. The body had torn down a wide circle of cane before it finally quit kicking and thrashing. His blood glistened on the broken green and purple stalks.

Two wailing and sobbing women ran down the rice paddy dike to where the body lay sprawled in the sugarcane. The snipers had moved out of their hide and stood among the trees, watching the man's family.

That evening, back at the hill, the four snipers discussed the event.

"I took a look at the rifle that old fart had," Land commented between bites, as the four Marines spooned their way through cans of C-rations and canteen cocoa, "it was a worthless piece of crap.

"Reminded me a hell of a lot of my first kill. You remember, don't you J.D.?"

"Yes, sir. I kind of felt sorry for that dumb asshole, too. I wonder how much the VC pays these gooners to go out and bust caps like that?"

"Obviously not enough," the captain said wryly.

"Their rifles are what gets me. This fella's was just about like that farmer's I killed back at 55. This one here had a split stock, and that old boy had a wore out M-1 carbine, with the stock broken in three places. Shit! The bastard tried to hold it together by wrapping it with wire. And the barrel was worn completely smooth. Why, it didn't have a land left in it."

"War is hell," Wilson commented, stuffing his mouth full of beef and potatoes. "So is this can of beef and rocks."

Hathcock sat quietly eating ham and lima beans, watching and listening as the major who met them when the operation began now squatted next to the captain and talked softly.

"We need your best shooter," he said. "Got word from the Division CP."

"Something big?"

"I don't know, Captain. I'm just passing the word."

"Can I send two?"

"I don't see what it would hurt, but again, that's a shot Division will have to call."

"Okay, Sir."

The major left and Land looked at Wilson, "You sit tight. I'll take Hathcock and Burke over to Division. While I'm there, I'll try to get the lowdown on this mission. I've got a hunch we may be gone a few days."

"Skipper, if you're still on this mission when the operation here wraps up, I'll get the troops back to five-five. Don't worry. I'll take care of everything."

"I expect to be back, but you continue to march.

"Hathcock, you and Burke grab your packs when you've finished your supper. Meet me at the G-2 tent, they may have some information on what's going on."

With his rifle and pack shouldered, the captain stood, dusted the seat of his trousers, and walked up the rise toward the cluster of tents. Hathcock excitedly shoveled big spoonfuls of creamy beige beans into his mouth, swelling out his cheeks, as he hurriedly chewed and swallowed them. Burke followed Hathcock's lead, as he rushed to choke down the remainder of his can of beans and franks.

Wilson looked at the two Marines gulping and wolfing, "You two are gonna smell real sweet, come tomorrow when that crap starts working in your guts. That business will keep a couple of minutes longer while you eat at a normal speed. There's no point in ruining your insides so you can hurry up and go wait over there."

With their cheeks bulging, the two snipers nodded, agreeing with Wilson's logic. But the excitement of going on a special mission made them want to hurry. Both men wanted to discover what venture could be so mysterious that the major who brought the word to them was not privileged with full details.

"Come on, Burke," Hathcock urged, as he pulled one pack strap over his left shoulder and slung his rifle over his right. "We gotta get up the hill and not keep those folks a waitin'."

Burke stood and crammed the empty tin cans back in the small square C-ration box, "Gunny, you mind getting the trash tonight?"

"No problem, John. You two keep your heads down."

"We will," Hathcock said, waving at Wilson.

Hathcock would not see the gunnery sergeant for a month.

The two snipers walked to a cluster of tents and sand-bagged positions where they met their captain walking away from the tent that looked like it housed the operations complex.

"Hathcock, you and Burke follow me. A chopper is turning right now, waiting for us."

"What's the word, Sir," Burke asked, as he walked hurriedly behind the captain. Hathcock, too, stretched his legs at the rapid pace. Something big was happening, and they were about to become the star performers of whatever it was.

"I don't have all the details yet. But they want us to kill a man. A special man. And he needs to be killed now. Once we get to the departure point, they will give us more information."

Adrenalin suddenly pumped through Hathcock's heart and left him light-headed with the urgency and importance of what he was about to do. He knew that it had to be something that only a trained sniper could accomplish. That left him somewhat frightened, yet overwhelmingly gratified and impatient to taste this adventure.

A jeep met the helicopter on the small pad and rushed the three Marines to a complex of buildings and radio towers. Hathcock had no idea where he was or whom he was about to meet.

Inside a green structure that appeared similar to the Quonset huts in which Hathcock lived at boot camp, a colonel greeted them. He shook Land's hand and asked, "These the men?"

"Yes, Sir. Sergeant Hathcock is one of the best long-range shooters in the United States. Lance Corporal Burke is one of the best people in the bush whom I've ever known. The two of them are the best sniper team in the country today," Land said, sensing that it did not impress this Marine.

"Sergeant Hathcock. I need you to kill me a man. What do you say to that?"

"Yes, Sir. Who?"

"A white man."

"Sir?"

"A white man. He's helping the enemy, and it is extremely important that we stop him immediately."

"Can't the Vietnamese government just arrest him?"

"No," he said, quietly sizing up the sniper who stood in front of him. "This man," he continued, "is a Frenchman in his early fifties, slightly bald, with shaggy hair. He's six feet tall and heavyset. He usually wears khaki trousers and a white bush shirt—you know the type with the patch pockets on the chest and on the waist. He will be walking up a trail near his house, early tomorrow morning. You will shoot him at a clearing that he will cross. After you kill him, leave. Don't engage anyone. Don't waste any time. Just run."

"Why do you want him dead, Sir?"

"You don't need to know, Sergeant," the colonel replied. "We will fly into that area before daylight. You will move into your hide and be there before it gets light."

"Aye, aye, Sir," Hathcock responded, snapping to attention.

The three snipers turned to depart and the colonel called to Land. "Captain, you stay back. I have to speak with you some more on this."

At three-thirty the next morning, the three men were up and ready. A tall, slim captain led them to a Huey helicopter. Land, speaking to Hathcock and Burke, said, "This bird will take us to an LZ,* where you two will walk a little less than five klicks to the hide. I will remain at an observation point with a recon team, who is up there. Once you shoot, leave. Hurry back to the LZ, and the chopper will bring you back here."

Both the snipers wondered why it was so necessary to kill the man immediately, and Burke was only putting their thoughts to words when he turned to Land and said, "We're stopping this guy from doing something, aren't we. Otherwise, they would be killing him a whole lot differently."

Land looked at the lance corporal and offered no response.

*Landing Zone. A cleared area where a helicopter can land. Smaller than a Landing Sight, which is large enough for several helicopters to land.

He himself knew little more of the mission, other than the two snipers must depart the area immediately after the assassination. He would wait and catch a second helicopter to a debrief sight.

"Perhaps there," Land thought, "I'll find out what's so special about this man."

Skimming the treetops and hugging the terrain's contour, the single-engine helicopter beat its way across miles of dark jungle, rushing the snipers to their ambush site. The moonless, black sky merged imperceptibly with the treetops and ridges, and Carlos wondered how the pilot kept from crashing into them. Unobtrusively, he bowed his head and prayed.

The flight lasted less than half an hour, giving Hathcock and Burke an hour and a half to steal their way five kilometers, unseen, and hide in a position that would allow a clear, five hundred-yard shot.

Carlos had no idea where he was. His captain had marked the route to the hide on a small, plastic-covered map that someone had cut from a larger section. It made him feel uncomfortable, not knowing which direction he should retreat toward should things go sour. If something happened, he hoped that the Huey would stay long enough for him to get aboard.

The moonless night left the jungle so black that the two snipers had to feel their way down the gentle slope from the landing zone to a small stream that flowed down a long, wooded draw, or gully, that would lead them to their hide. It was a simple route, but the darkness made it a dangerous one. Charlie could be hiding, waiting.

Neither Marine spoke. Every move they made was slow and deliberate; every action, thought out and mentally rehearsed. "Where's Charlie?" Carlos silently asked himself. "Where do we escape if he discovers us now." Every night sound seemed amplified in the darkness. The air. The moisture. The taste and smell. All became part of Carlos's world as he moved silently—one step, then the next.

At 5:30 A.M., the sky began to show the orange streaks of sunrise. The two snipers crawled on their stomachs as they left the cover of the trees and ferns growing along the stream and moved toward a hump of earth covered with tall grass. It was their objective, and beyond it the wooded draw opened into a grassy valley.

A trail, easily visible from the hide, crossed the clearing. Here, Hathcock thought, this Frenchman on a morning stroll would meet his end. What had he done? How had he helped Charlie? What act closed his account with life?

The wait began.

On a hilltop two kilometers away, Captain Land joined a cluster of cammy-clad men who sat in an outcropping of rocks, peering through binoculars, watching the clearing and the trail.

A man with a bushy mustache and long sideburns, wearing tigerstriped camouflage utilities typically worn by ARVN soldiers, sat with his ranger hat's brim turned up in Gabby Hayes fashion and concentrated his vigil on one spot of the valley far below him.

"Either your man is real good, or dead, back in the woods. I never saw a sign of life from the time it was light enough to see down there. He's well hidden or not there," the man said in a cold tone.

"He's there," Land said. "When that Frenchman heads down that path, you'll see. The bastard's good as dead."

"You better hope so. Otherwise a couple of pilots will be wishing they were dead."

"What are you talking about?"

"This Frenchman. He's a professional interrogator for Charlie. One of the best. I think he's a little funny too. You know, sadistic sex, likes little boys. They say the bastard gets his rocks off fuckin' up people."

"Where you get all this?"

"Just take my word for it. That son-of-a-bitch is bad. Charlie has a couple of our pilots down there waitin' to meet ole Jacques. We don't want ole Jacques to get there—he knows too much about these guys."

"Why don't you go in and take them? You know where they are?"

"Can't. Your man is the key to this. He has to kill the cat."

"Spooks," Land thought to himself.

The sun turned the countryside yellow as it now cleared the hilltops. Hathcock rested on his stomach, his heart beating rhythmically against the earth causing his rifle to pulse with each surge of blood that pumped through him. Burke hid to the right and trained his watch to their rear, looking at the jungle's edge and the slopes that surrounded their escape route.

Patiently, the two Marines waited: Watching the air. Smelling and tasting. Hearing the birds distantly call. Hearing the bushes and grass rustle from the breeze that grew stronger as the sun climbed.

Three hours passed.

"Here he comes," the man in the tiger stripes said, as he saw a distant figure wearing tan trousers and a white shirt enter the clearing, far to the left of where the snipers hid. "Shit! There's Charlie, coming to greet him."

Far to the right of the sniper hide, below the base of the hill from where the observers watched, a Viet Cong patrol emerged from the forest and now walked casually into the clearing, toward the Frenchman.

"Gonna be a ruckus," Hathcock thought to himself as the seven Viet Cong appeared on the right. Far to his left, he also saw the Frenchman, hands in his pockets and a pipe in his mouth.

"Well, I hate to shoot and run, but you know how it is," Hathcock said, amusing himself with the situation. He tapped Burke with the toe of his boot. Burke tapped back. Ready.

It was an easy shot. Hathcock placed the reticle on the man's shoulders and squeezed the trigger. The crack of the rifle shot sent the Viet Cong diving for cover. Hathcock did not waste a second round. The man went down hard. The explosive impact of the bullet, which is the real killing factor with a .30-06, would almost certainly have destroyed his heart and lungs.

Before the Viet Cong patrol could react, Hathcock and Burke had turned from the hide and now low-crawled through the grass, toward the narrow stream and the trees that stood on the other side.

"We're gonna have to jump and run," Hathcock told his partner. "They might get a couple of shots off at us, but we got no choice. I'm not gonna get boxed in up that draw."

"Say when," Burke replied, snugging his rifle across his back and crouching like a sprinter in starting blocks.

"Now!" Hathcock grunted, leaping to his feet and bounding across the stream with Burke at his side.

Both Marines dashed to the trees, and as they disappeared behind the forest's green curtain, a shower of bullets riddled the grass.

"Up the hill!" Hathcock ordered. "They'll look for us to follow that draw. But we'll go straight to the top and follow the ridge back to the LZ."

"Good job," the man in tiger stripes told Land, giving him a congratulatory slap on the shoulder.

"It's not over yet. My guys still have to get back to the LZ."

"Nothing you can do about that, Captain. They'll make it."

The Viet Cong continued chewing the forest's edge with their automatic fire. Meanwhile, the two fleeing snipers charged up the hill. At five hundred yards, it was easy to recognize that the snipers were Americans. They saw both men well—even the white feather in one man's hat.

"Christ sake!" Burke heaved in horse breaths. "This hill . . . didn't seem . . . this high from down . . . there."

"Just . . ." Carlos gulped, trying to talk, "think about . . . Charlie! You know . . . he got a . . . pretty good look at us! Better keep running! Don't . . . stop!"

The two Marines ran the five kilometers back to the helicopter in twenty minutes—it would have been a major accomplishment on flat ground and without the added burden of rifles.

As they charged into the clearing where the helicopter sat, they saw the rotor blades start turning. The Huey's crew had heard the gunfire and now anxiously waited, ready.

The chopper was lifting from the landing zone as the two snipers fell into the doorway, where the crew chief grabbed both men by their collars and pulled hard, dragging them aboard as the treetops began rushing beneath the aircraft's skids.

Hathcock rolled on his back, blinking sweat from his eyes as it streaked through the green greasepaint that covered his face. His chest heaved and his head pounded. With his hand, he felt Burke's shoulder and arm at his side, and smiled triumphantly. All was well.

11

Sniper on the Loose

MID-AFTERNOON HEAT kept the comfort level at "unbearable" for many who worked on the dozens of helicopters on the flight line beyond the row of green Quonset huts, where Carlos Hathcock and John Burke slept. Yet for the two snipers, the comfort level had reached a mark that they had not experienced for months—"wonderful." The two Marines rested atop cotton- and spring-filled mattresses mounted on metal bed frames—real beds. They were nothing fancy, the same type of racks that had graced their barracks back State-side, yet their comfort was indescribable after months of sleeping on wooden-and-canvas cots or on the ground.

After cleaning their rifles, both Marines had scouted the area and found the shower and head facilities, behind the Quonset huts. There they took full advantage, washing their bodies and clothes.

Also during their tour of the air facility, they discovered the hut that housed the service club. Inside, an American civilian wearing khakis and a St. Louis Cardinals baseball cap took a six-pack of cold beer from the old, LP, gas-operated Survel refrigerator, which stood in the corner, hooked to a squatty, silver fuel cylinder. It was covered with decals ranging from Flying Tigers Airways to the Dallas Cowboys. And in the center of the rust-stained and chipped cooler, fastened with two-inch-wide masking tape, hung the centerfold photograph of *Playboy Magazine's* "Playmate of the Year."

"Drink up," the man said, pitching the cardboard package to Hathcock and slamming the refrigerator door shut, leaving the old monster rocking on the unlevel floor.

"Ain't got no cash," Hathcock said, ready to hand back the beers; they were so cold that in the moment he held them they already began to condense water on their sides.

"You the Marines who got ol' Frenchy?"

Hathcock looked at the man suspiciously, "Yes, Sir. We shot a fellow that they told us was a Frenchman. You involved in the operation, too?"

"Not really. I do some flying around here. Let's say you did a lot of folks a big favor by zapping that frog. I owe you at least a cold beer or two."

The man walked back to the formica-covered, plywood bar where Hathcock and Burke now sat, tearing open the six-pack. He slapped Burke on the back and threw down what was left of his beer.

"You boys enjoy. I've got a date down south."

"Thanks for the beer, it's my favorite kind," Hathcock said, with a broad smile.

"That right?" the man said as he hooked a pair of gold-framed sunglasses on his ears, their large, dark green, tear-drop-shaped lenses hiding much of his expression. "Yes, sir. Yellow beer."

Burke yucked and chuckled and shot his elbow into his sergeant's shoulder. He waved at the man, "Thanks a lot, Sir. You ever get to Hill 55, look us up."

Hathcock followed with the invitation, "We ain't quite got the luxury up there, but we'll make do with something. We're down on finger four, if you ever get up that way."

The man waved back, as he closed the screen door.

For the next hour, the two Marines sipped the cold beer and played on a pinball machine that blinked multicolored lights behind a glass painting of scantily dressed women with ray guns shooting wart-covered monsters.

By 3:00 P.M., both men had returned to the Quonset hut and lay snoring on the racks, wearing only their utility trousers.

Outside, helicopters flew nonstop, with the sound of their blades rhythmically pulsing—whomp, whomp, whomp.

Monsoon rains drenched Hill 263, as a single Huey helicopter skimmed the treetops and raced toward the landing zone. Inside, Hathcock sat, belted to a web seat, looking at the dark green jungle blur past, while he clung to the rifle that he rested, butt first, between his feet.

The crew chief stiffly leaned out the open doorway, a gunner's belt strapped around his waist, and pushed his shoulder into an M-60 machine gun,* which he had suspended on thick, nylon-shrouded, rubber cords that he anchored to the helicopter's upper framework. He laid into the gun with the full weight of his body, jutting out of the doorway at a thirty-degree angle, suspended by the cords like a marionette dangling in the rotor blades' down-wash.

The Marine grasped the top of the heavy, black machine gun's short, nylon stock with his left hand and rested the right side of his chin against his knuckles. His right hand clutched the gun's pistol grip, with which he pulled the weapon into his shoulder and maintained his balance.

As the light utility helicopter zigzagged along the ridges, sporadic small-arms fire popped from beneath the trees. And with each assault from the ground, the pilot banked the Huey sharply on its right side, circling above the assault, tilting the

---

*The M-60 machine gun is an air-cooled, belt-fed, gas-operated automatic weapon. It fires the 7.62mm (.30-caliber) ball, tracer, armor piercing, and armor piercing incendiary cartridges (standard service ammunition for field use consists of ball and tracer cartridges in a 4 to 1 ratio). It is able to provide a heavy, controlled volume of accurate, long-range fire that is beyond the capabilities of standard individual small arms. The weapon fires from the open-bolt position and is fed by a disintegrating belt of metal links. The gas from firing one round provides the energy for firing the next; thus, the gun functions automatically, as long as it is supplied with ammunition and the trigger is held to the rear. The weapon is 43.5 inches long and weighs 23.2 pounds. It has a maximum range of 3,725 meters and a maximum effective range of 1,100 meters. It effectively extends grazing fire (knee high) up to 700 meters. The machine gun has a 100-round-per-minute sustained rate of fire (6-8 round bursts), a 200-rounds-per-minute rapid rate of fire (10-12 round bursts) and a cyclic rate of fire of from 550 to 600 rounds per minute.

open door to the point that the gunner lay out in the air directly above the fire. The rotors beat the air loudly, mixing with the chopping sounds of the rapid bursts that the Marine fired, showering the jungle and the hidden enemy with red tracers.

The helicopter drifted toward the ground and tilted its nose skyward as it settled onto its skids. Hathcock felt the tension that had built in the forty-minute flight disappear. He stepped quickly away from the noisy aircraft and sloshed his way through the grass and mud to a clear area away from the helicopter. He turned and pulled his bush hat back on his head to shield his face from the rain that fell in heavy sheets.

Once the three Marines stood clear of the landing zone, the Huey broke its bonds with the muddy ground. Shuddering slightly, the aircraft dipped nose down and raced away, disappearing quickly behind the trees.

Gunnery Sergeant Wilson met the three snipers at the hilltop and updated his captain on the status of the snipers—all were well, and each had kills. But what Wilson and several other Marines at the observation post really wanted to discuss was the job that the three Marines had just completed—this special mission.

For more than an hour, Hathcock and Burke sat cross-legged on the dirt floor of the snipers' command post—surrounded by curious Marines who jammed in to hear—telling them about shooting the Frenchman, and unable to answer the paramount question: Why? Why did the spooks want him dead? Yet it was this unanswerable question, this dark secret shrouded in cloak-and-dagger mystique, that made the adventure a zesty, gee-whiz tale. From that first telling in the bunker on Hill 263, the story rapidly circulated, growing in drama and speculation as it spread.

From time to time Hathcock wondered what deed the Frenchman had done, or was about to do, that warranted this special mission to kill him. Captain Land had some insight based on what the curious man in tiger stripes had mentioned concerning the downed pilots and the Frenchman's mission to interrogate them, but he heard nothing to confirm that, so he kept the hearsay to himself.

Operation Rio Blanco lasted three more days, ending at

6:00 P.M. on November 27, 1966.

The United States Marines, the Republic of Korea Marines, and the Army of the Republic of Vietnam forces, by their combined action, accounted for more than five hundred enemy dead, yet the Viet Cong and North Vietnamese continued to appear throughout the region along the Song Tro Khuc. Several units remained behind to mop up. Captain Land left four snipers at the Hill 263 observation point to assist, with Sergeant Carlos Hathcock in charge of them.

Very quickly the demand for sniper services surpassed Hathcock's ability to meet them. He kept both two-man sniper teams on patrols and small operations day after day, recording their activity in situation reports, much of which he copied directly from his sniper log, and sent them every other day to Captain Land.

Since Hathcock was the fifth man, he assumed the risks of working alone and accepted the overflow requests for himself.

After ten days of constant patrolling, Hathcock saw the wear showing on his Marines They looked like baggy-clothed zombies, with tired red eyes sunken deep, beneath drooping brows. He began taking their patrols, telling them to stay on the hill and rest.

On December 14, Hathcock stood in front of the low, sandbag-walled bunker that the snipers had been using as their headquarters for the past twenty-four days. His men stood in a semicircle around him, their packs loaded and weapons at their sides. Today he was sending his four Marines home to Hill 55.

"Burke, tell Captain Land that they still need me down here. I'm sending you guys back because you're wore plumb out. You might make a mistake out there and get yourselves killed. Besides, it's gettin' to be Christmas."

Burke looked at his sergeant and matter-of-factly said, "Sergeant Hathcock, you don't look too good yourself. Reckon this might be a mistake?"

"I know what I'm doing, Lance Corporal!" Hathcock said sharply. "It ain't your place to question me. You just pass the word to the captain."

The reaction bit deeply, yet Burke somehow expected it

from his tired boss. He had come to greatly admire Hathcock, and he knew him well.

"I apologize for being out of line, Sergeant Hathcock, but I just don't want to see nothing bad happening to you. You know, we're supposed to take care of each other. Marines take care of their own. Right?"

"Yeah, Burke."

"What would it hurt if you kept me back here. We're a real good team, Sergeant. You said it yourself. I could sure be a help to you."

"You'll be a bigger help getting to Hill 55. And all I'll have to worry about is myself. You just get these Marines back safe."

Burke nodded morosely. "We'd better be going, huh."

"Yep. You tell the captain I'll keep him posted. I'll get back soon as this mess clears up down here."

The four Marines, packs and rifles strapped across their backs, walked away from the bunker where Hathcock stood.

"We'll be thinking about you, Sergeant Hathcock, when we're sleeping in them new cots and partaking of that Christmas cheer," Burke said, waving.

Hathcock waved back. "That's okay, me and Charlie gonna have our own little celebration. You boys keep your heads down, ya hear."

Burke gave him the thumbs-up sign.

"Where the hell is Sergeant Hathcock?" Land snapped, as the four snipers came up beside him. He was standing behind a bunker on Hill 55 with a scope-sighted, .50-caliber machine gun trained on the flatlands beneath.

"Sir," Burke said, standing at rigid attention, "Sir, Sergeant Hathcock had some more work to finish. He's okay. He said he would keep you informed."

"I expected to see him and you back here a week ago. Now you tell me that he's off on his own, completely unleashed. Hell, now he has total freedom down there."

"Sir, don't be mad at him," Burke said, trying his best to defend the sergeant. "He's doing a lot of good down there."

"Burke! Bullshit! I know how thick you and Hathcock are. You'd do anything to defend him. But, he's wrong! Gunny,"

Land said looking at Wilson, "you better get in touch with someone right now. I need to know what that skinny little shit is up to—today!"

Hathcock had known the captain would not be pleased to see the snipers return without him, but he had developed a rapport with several unit commanders. They let him call many of his own shots, planning sniper operations. And with each operation that he planned and brought off, his reputation grew. He liked that.

Enjoying a status shared by few other enlisted Marines, Hathcock's ego thrived, even as he became more gaunt and weathered. However, he remained mentally sharp and demonstrated increased cunning against the enemy with each outing. No matter how bizarre the plan or dangerous the mission, his opinion meant much to the Marines who daily dropped him off on patrol and picked him up again at its completion. He had sold "snipers" to them.

Christmas passed and the new year was one day away when Hathcock marched outside the security wire with a patrol that would drop him at a bend in the Song Tro Khuc, where he could move and cover two wide zones that had opened to free fire.

Enemy contact had increased in this area, well to the west of where he usually worked. Now he embarked into that no-man's-land to observe and count the enemy as well as to harass them with his fire. He would remain overnight and return on his own.

At a bluff that overlooked the bend in the river, Hathcock constructed his hide where he could watch his rear and flanks, as well as observe the river country below. He had three quick exits, should the enemy bear down on this position.

The afternoon passed into the evening. Under a clear sky, the moon shone brightly on the river and its marshy banks. Anyone who moved along that route could not pass without his seeing him.

With it too dark to take aim and shoot, he spent the night observing through his twenty-power (M-49) spotting scope several long boats filled with soldiers, sliding silently past him. "Coming back by the boatload. Lots of gear, too. Bet they're headed to those tunnels below the hill."

When dawn broke, he watched the last boat slipping downstream in trace of the all-night procession. It was a much smaller craft, built like a dugout canoe. It appeared as a black dot, but as it drew nearer, he could distinguish three seated figures. The man at the bow and the man at the stern each paddled, while the man in the center simply sat with his arms folded and his head turning casually, watching the quiet banks as he drifted past them.

As the boat neared, Hathcock put his rifle's scope first on the man paddling at the bow—a Viet Cong soldier wearing a black shirt and black shorts. He had a carbine across his back. But it was the man in the center—the man who did nothing but ride—who interested Hathcock.

Holding steady on the slow-moving boat, the sun's orange light exposed the red collar tabs on the gray uniform that the man wore. As he came nearer, Hathcock recognized the large red star above the bill of the man's cap. "Chinese. I'll be damned."

Hathcock had no idea what rank the man held, so he watched through his scope and held his fire until he could clearly see the gold star and clusters of braid on the large, red, collar tabs. "I'll make a note of that. Maybe CIT can tell me what this guy is."

He watched as the boat came abeam him, and as the small craft passed, Carlos tightened his grip around the Winchester's stock and squeezed the trigger, sending a shot ripping into the back of the Chinese soldier's neck, knocking him out of the boat.

The two Viet Cong who guided the small boat down the river bent low in the craft and paddled as hard as they could toward the far bank.

The two men powered the boat over the reeds and salt grass that grew in the shallows along the river's edge. The soldier who crouched in the rear rose up. Just as he jumped into the water and the boat struck shore, Hathcock sent a shot across the river that shattered the man's spine and sprayed his terrified comrade with blood. That soldier leaped from the boat into the reeds.

Hathcock cycled the rifle's bolt and pulled his scope back through its mounts. But as he sighted through the scope, he saw only a flicker of the third man as he disappeared into the thick brush that lined the river.

In the Song Tro Khuc's main channel, where the current pulled strongest, Hathcock could see the Chinese soldier's back and shoulders above the water. Taking careful aim, he sent a bullet into the man's back, making certain that this advisor's last testament to the Viet Cong would be a warning to beware of the whispering death.

Hathcock silently slipped from the hide and crept through the jungle toward a mark on his map where he knew friendly forces now waited.

"Happy New Year," Hathcock called out, startling a day-dreaming Marine who was manning a forward outpost.

"What the fu--! Where in the hell you come from, man?" the Marine called back.

"That's, where in the hell you come from . . . Sergeant!" Hathcock said with a broad smile, showing a line of white teeth contrasting against the camouflage paint that covered his face. "You got a radio?"

"Sure. You a sniper?"

"Yep. I spent the night observing Charlie moving a lot of men and equipment downstream. And I killed what looked to be a Chinese officer."

"Chinese? Shit!"

"What net you on?"

"7th Marines. Just talk and the regimental CP will answer."

While Hathcock spoke with an operations officer at the regimental command post, Captain Land talked with the 1st Marine Division's operations officer, Col. Herman Pogge-meyer, Jr.,—his boss. Land was getting short. His orders home had arrived.

"Captain," the colonel said, "you've done an impressive job with the snipers. General Nickerson is extremely happy with the program and sad to see you go. But you need to go home. I want you to stop in and see the G-2. He'll show you one good reason why you should not consider extending in-country."

What the intelligence officer showed Land shocked him a little and concerned him a lot. "God damn it, Hathcock!" he roared.

A newspaper story that had appeared in the *Sea Tiger** extolling the greatness of "Hathcock and company" had fed the enemy vital information about the 1st Marine Division's sniper school, its officer in charge, and the sniper with the most scalps—the one who wore the white feather—Sergeant Carlos Hathcock. The Viet Cong had issued a leaflet based on the story.

Land stared at the black-and-white leaflet, written in the Vietnamese language, to which the intelligence officer had attached a translation. A pen-and-ink sketch on the left half of the front page depicted a perfect likeness of Hathcock, complete with bush hat and white feather, and on the right, a perfect likeness of himself, square-jawed and steely eyed.

The translation stated that the two Americans were wanted by the People of Vietnam for the murder of hundreds of innocent women and children. They offered the pay that a middle-class city worker would make in a period of three years as a reward for either man—dead or alive.

Captain Land handed the leaflet back to the captain who had custody of it.

"You know, Charlie has a standing reward of eight dollars a head on any sniper. What you're looking at is several thousand bucks for each of you two. If I were you—and I thank God I'm not—I would get in the bunker in the center of the compound and not come out until the Freedom Bird took me back to the world."

Land smiled. "I've got work to do, Captain. Good day."

Seeing the leaflet made Land feel naked. He wondered who might be watching even now and walked near cover, consciously avoiding the open.

Hathcock must be warned. He had no way of knowing that Charlie wanted him bad enough to pay literally a king's ransom for his head.

---

*Sea Tiger was a weekly newspaper published by the Informational Services Office of the III Marine Amphibious Force, Vietnam.

"God damn that Hathcock!" the captain swore. He walked to a pickup point, where he could catch a truck from Hill 327 back to Hill 55.

A helicopter rushed Hathcock to a debriefing at the 7th Marines command post, while Captain Land bounced and jarred in the back of a "six-by" truck headed south. Several officers crowded around as the sniper read from the notes that he had jotted in his log book during the night.

"Are you certain he was Chinese?" a lieutenant asked. "Could he have been North Vietnamese or Laotian?"

"Could have been any kind of Oriental Communist, Sir," Hathcock said. "But he looked to me like he was wearing a Chinese uniform. It was gray, or light brown—I couldn't be certain because of the color of the early morning light. However, he had that big red star on his hat and those big red and gold tabs on his collar. I have no doubts about that."

A husky gunnery sergeant, with a bulldog wearing a Marine campaign cover tattooed on his forearm, said, "Sir, what the sergeant described is a Chinese officer. Probably about like our field grade—perhaps a colonel. From an intelligence standpoint, I'd like to examine that body and what he had in his pockets."

"I want that body," a major said, taking a pipe from his mouth and blowing a cloud of cherry-scented smoke through the command post tent, where they grouped around Hathcock. "Call for some helicopters to sweep the river. Put out a reward to anyone who can lead us to where that body may be snagged up."

"Odds are the VC already got him," another major said. "We can offer twenty thousand piasters. Those gooners will turn in their mothers for that. But I wouldn't hold my breath."

"Sergeant, good job. We'll write this up as two probable kills and send your report to division with the sitrep."

The Marines walked outside. Hathcock was already planning another mission.

Late that afternoon, Captain Land climbed down from the bed of the dirty truck in which he had ridden to Hill 55. His body ached and his head throbbed from the long, rough ride, but throughout the whole trip back he had thought only of what to do about his sniper who had spent the past month walking patrol after patrol, working himself to physical exhaustion hunting the Viet Cong, and now who had been billed as one of the Communist enemy's most-wanted men.

"Gunny Wilson!" the captain bellowed as he walked toward the snipers' headquarters. The angry shout echoed through the compound, sending heads turning and wide-eyed faces peering from behind screen doors. The captain never broke his stride as he walked inside the sniper hooch and slammed the screen door behind him.

Gunnery Sergeant Wilson hurried into the small building. Captain Land was rummaging through the large file drawer, looking for a bottle of aspirin.

"Gunny, what's the latest on Hathcock?" Land said.

"Sir, the last report in on him is two probable kills this morning. He claims one was a high-ranking Chinese officer —possibly a colonel."

Wilson hesitated and then added, "He's patrolled daily since the other snipers came home. The gunny I talked to told me that Hathcock will come in with one squad and catch another going out and fall right in with them, without even taking his pack off. That gunny's concerned."

"Me too. Did you know that the NVA and Charlie both have a bounty out on Hathcock and me? A big one? Several grand?"

"No, Sir."

"I think it's time for our Sergeant Hathcock to pack up and come home. I want you to go and get him—put him under arrest, if you have to—but bring him home. I want him standing tall in front of my desk by tomorrow afternoon."

"You want me to arrest him, Sir?"

"That's right, gunny. I want you to hog-tie the little shit, if you have to. He'll kill himself out there, I'm certain. The dummy won't stop unless I lock him up or Charlie puts a bullet in his head. I'll be go-to-hell if I'm gonna lose him now. You go and make your travel plans right away. See if you can get air—maybe a Marlog* flight."

---

*An acronym formed from Marine Logistics, used to describe daily resupply/administrative support flights.

At daylight Wilson sat staring out the open door of a CH-46 helicopter, looking over the shoulders of an air crewman who stood behind a .50-caliber machine gun, gripping the two wooden handles and swinging it from side to side as the aircraft shuddered its way to Hill 263.

This daily mail and logistics flight would sit on the ground there only long enough for the crew to unload a few sacks of mail and some boxes of resupply items. Wilson hoped that the gunny in the operations shop there had been able to reach Hathcock before the sniper departed for the day. If Hathcock was waiting at the landing zone, according to instructions, they could fly back on this helicopter. If the gunny had missed Hathcock, it might mean remaining there an extra day.

Hathcock was waiting when the helicopter landed. He had known that the clock had run out from the way the gunny in the operations tent talked.

"Hathcock!" Wilson yelled inaudibly, beneath the whine and roar of the two gigantic rotors that churned through the air above him, as he walked down the rear ramp. He saw Hathcock standing and waving, his baggy uniform whipping in the wind.

Waving him aboard, Wilson turned and disappeared inside the belly of the huge bird. Grabbing his pack and clutching his bush hat in his right hand, Hathcock trotted up the ramp after him.

Wilson tried to talk to Hathcock, but the engines' loud roar drowned out his attempts, and he sat silent for the rest of the trip.

"Gunny, what's going on?" Hathcock asked, as the two Marines walked from the landing zone at Hill 55.

"Sergeant Hathcock, you're under arrest. That's all I can tell you. The captain came back from Colonel Poggemeyer's mad as hell."

The gunnery sergeant's words knotted Hathcock's stomach. "What have I done?" he thought. "Did I kill somebody I shouldn't have?" He thought of the Frenchman. Perhaps the captain, Burke, and he had fallen into a well-planned scheme of murder, where they were left holding the bag.

The two Marines walked toward finger four where their

captain stood behind a sandbag wall, scanning the fields and hills below.

Hathcock remembered presenting himself to his battalion commander for nonjudicial punishment seven years before in Hawaii. In that case, he lost a stripe for slugging a lieutenant in a bar. They were both drunk, and the officer started it. But striking an officer is striking an officer—drunk or sober. Hathcock clearly understood why he got busted then.

But this. What had he done now?

"Sir. Sergeant Hathcock reporting as ordered, sir!" Hathcock barked, as he stood at rigid attention before the captain.

Land eyed his sergeant and felt a sharp pain—Hathcock looked worse than he had imagined. The 24-year old Marine almost looked like an old man, gaunt and hollow. He had shrunk so much that his camouflage uniform bagged off his shoulders and hips. His boots were scuffed white, and his dark red eyes had sunk deep in their sockets.

"God damn you, Hathcock!" Land said, "What am I going to do with you?"

"Sir. I don't understand what I've done wrong. I have done my best to support that operation, and they are real sold on snipers now."

"I left you down there with thirty-two kills to your name, and you come home with what? Sixty-two or sixty-three confirmed! That's thirty more on your own. You did one hell of a job. But you did something stupid."

"Sir?"

"You forgot one of the most important aspects of leadership that I know. You totally neglected the welfare of your men."

"I sent those men home after two weeks, Sir. I went out on patrol for them when they looked too tired to work. I didn't neglect them, Sir."

"You neglected one."

After a silent pause, Hathcock concluded, "Me?"

"That's right—you. Hathcock, you don't know when to quit. You put yourself into situations that are impossible. You hang your life out on the ragged edge and gamble against all the odds. You overload your ass and then won't stop. What the hell you weigh now?"

"Sir, about a hundred forty-five or fifty."

"Maybe when I left you there. I don't think you could tip the scales at more than a hundred twenty-five pounds now. You're out there living on a can of peanut butter and a handful of John Wayne crackers."

Hathcock half smiled, "Sir, it keeps the buzzards off my back."

"Shit yeah! for a day or two, but not for a month. The buzzards wouldn't waste their time with you now!"

Land folded his arms and looked up and down at his sergeant, who remained at attention, and then the captain shook his head. "Hathcock, I put you under arrest because that was the only way I could be sure to get you back here. You look like hell. You probably haven't slept more than a couple of hours a night in the past month. You've lost so much weight that your clothes are falling off you. How can you do that to yourself?

"If I hadn't pulled you out, how long would it have taken before you fucked up and let Charlie kill you? Hathcock, I'll be damned if I'm gonna write Jo a letter, telling how you got yourself killed!"

Hathcock's face betrayed his disappointment. He hadn't realized that the chances he took would wound the captain as deeply as he now realized they had, and he spoke up strongly: "I'm as sorry as I can be, Sir, and I feel awful that I destroyed your confidence in me. I was trying to do the best job I could, and I just totally forgot about myself. I ain't making any excuses. I'll take whatever punishment you order, but I want you to know I'm sorry."

"Sergeant Hathcock," the captain said, with official sternness, "You are restricted until further orders. You may go only to the head, the mess hall, and to chapel services. You step outside this wire, and I'll have a stripe. That clear?"

"Yes, Sir."

"That starts now! Get to the hooch. Square away your gear. And get some sleep!"

"Aye, aye, Sir." Hathcock said, taking a rearward step with his left foot, executing a drill-perfect about-face, and walking briskly toward his quarters.

Land reached into his back pocket, pulled out a dirty black wallet, and withdrew five dollars.

"Gunny Wilson, I want you to go buy a case of beer and take it to Sergeant Hathcock. When he runs out of that, come see me. If I don't keep him drunk and sleeping, he'll manage to worm his way out on the next operation—I know the way he maneuvers. His body has to get some rest."

12

Nguyan Stalks the Hill

A HAND SLOWLY parted a patch of tall grass on a knoll that rose in a cluster of small peaks along a low ridge beneath Hill 55. In that gap between the thick grass stalks, a rifle barrel surrounded by a wooden hand guard slid forward and stopped. A stocky Oriental man wearing a dark green, long-sleeved uniform, snuggled behind the rifle, pulling its butt into his shoulder. He blinked away small drops of sweat and peered through the weapon's telescopic sight at the sleepy encampment atop the hill five hundred yards above him.

In the early morning's stillness, he trained his rifle at the squat silhouettes of sandbagged bunkers, set low on the hillside. He could see the dirt walkway that led between the bunkers and branched to three long tents with plywood sides and sandbags stacked around them. Tracking his scope's sight-post* up the pathway, he followed it far to the right to a small plywood structure with a sloping roof—the privy. There he took aim and waited for nature's morning call to summon his next victim.

Hathcock awoke with a jerk. The popping sound of a bullet impacting outside his door startled him. He made no sudden

*The Soviet-built, 3.5-power PU and 4-power PE scopes commonly used on the M1891/30 Mosin-Nagant sniper rifle used a pointed aiming post rather than a cross-hair reticle.

moves, but opened his eyes and rolled off the cot onto the floor in a push-up position. The single shot told him that there was a sniper lurking somewhere outside the wire.

"Welcome home," he thought to himself. He shoved an ammo carton filled with empty beer cans to one side and quickly low-crawled toward the front of the hooch, where he heard the moans of a wounded Marine. He grabbed his rifle and a cartridge belt, on which hung a first-aid pouch, and pushed his way outside the door. There on the dirt walkway leading past his hooch lay a man, a gunnery sergeant, blood soaking through his shirt.

Ignoring the danger, three Marines and a Navy Corpsman scrambled across the open ground to where the Marine lay. The Corpsman carried a large, green canvas bag filled with medical equipment and quickly went to work on the casualty as Hathcock and the other Marines crouched around him, ready to assist.

Opening the man's shirt, the Corpsman exposed the wound, which had opened the Marine's belly. "Hang in there, Gunny," the Corpsman said as he pulled a canteen from his cartridge belt and began dousing the man's drying entrails with water.

Among the tall weeds and brush that grew on the cluster of knolls below Hill 55, the sniper slid swiftly down a draw, covered by a canopy of broad-leafed trees. Then he dashed to the base of the low-lying hills. There the trees grew next to a narrow canal that fed water to the many rice and lotus fields that checkered the valley. The sniper slipped into the water and let it carry him away. He drifted downstream, hidden by grass growing along its banks, to a place shielded by the jungle. There he climbed out, unseen.

On the hill, the battle to save the gunnery sergeant's life continued.

"I can't move. I think I shit my pants," the wounded Marine said, fighting back sobs.

"I can't tell, Gunny, so don't worry about that. You just keep yourself awake."

The gunnery sergeant blinked in the sunlight that bore down on his face, and Hathcock seeing this, moved over the man's head to block out the blinding rays.

"Doc's taking good care of you, Gunny. He'll get the

bleeding stopped and fix you up. Just keep awake."

The wounded Marine tried to speak, but his strength was fading. He mumbled in whispers, "I gotta go home now. Gotta go . . ."

"Hey, Gunny!" Hathcock pleaded, a lump building in his throat. "Hang on—you'll make it!"

Hathcock stared into the Marine's eyes and watched his pupils grow wide and transparent, like two black, glass marbles. It seemed as though the man's soul drained from his eyes, leaving only empty clear pools where life had been.

"He didn't have a chance, Sergeant," the Corpsman said. "His liver was gone. You know him?"

Hathcock looked at the Marine and shook his head, "No."

An hour later, Hathcock sat in the doorway of his hooch sipping a warm beer, still thinking of the Marine's death and of how quickly life can vanish.

"Carlos!" a familiar voice called.

Captain Land walked toward the hooch and Carlos stood.

"Yes, Sir."

"Let's talk."

The two Marines walked inside the sergeant's quarters where Hathcock sat on the corner of his cot, and the captain pulled up a large wooden box and sat on it.

"Thanks for the beer, Sir. Gunny Wilson said you bought it for me. I shared some of it with a few of the guys last night," Carlos said, shaking the crate filled with empties and smiling.

"No problem," Land said. "Too bad about that gunny getting killed out here."

"Yes, Sir. I've been thinking about that for the past hour. It never gets better, does it?"

"I don't think it does."

Hathcock gulped down the last swallow of beer and tossed the can in the box. "What about this sniper?"

"Don't you even think about hunting this guy," Land said firmly. "You're restricted, and that's that. Besides Top Reinke has a half-dozen teams out hunting him right now."

Hathcock looked at the captain expressionlessly.

"You understand?"

"Yes, Sir."

"All right. As for the sniper, he started pot-shooting us about three weeks ago. He hit a staff sergeant about a week ago, and got two men out on the wire a week before that. He's good. Real good."

"Sir," Hathcock said, "I think if you let me and Burke team up, we could find that hamburger."

"No, we'll get him. But that's not what I came to talk about. I had an interesting visit at division headquarters the other day. I saw something that you might want to see for yourself."

"What's that?"

"Your picture and mine on an NVA 'wanted' poster. They've probably dropped thousands of them across the country. Looks like ol' Nguyen of the North wants us real bad. They offered a big bounty for our heads—equal to what a Saigon or Da Nang middle-class worker would make in three years' time—several thousand dollars."

"I reckon they mean business," Hathcock said, raising his eyebrows.

"Reckon so, Carlos. My orders are in, and I'll be gone in a couple of weeks. Going on Inspector-and-Instructor duty up near Boston. You have until what, April?"

"Yes, Sir."

"I want you to slow down."

Hathcock smiled.

"I'm not going to tell you to crawl in a hole and hide, but you need to be aware of how serious they are about killing you. They want your head awfully bad, to offer that kind of money for it.

"Another thing is that from all the sniping and booby-trap incidents we've had in the past month, I'm guessing that the enemy has a whole sniper platoon down here now. Remember that they know who you are, where you live, and what you look like."

The captain stood and looked down at Hathcock, who sat on the cot, staring at the floor, visibly frustrated.

Land tilted back his head, rolled his eyes, and said with a loud sigh, "Okay, Hathcock. I'll let you go down on the finger during the day and observe. Who knows, you might luck out with a shot at this guy. But don't you dare leave the hill. The positions out on the finger are as far as you go. Got that?"

Hathcock looked up, smiling. "Yes, Sir. Don't you worry one bit. I'll be here in the hooch or down on the finger."

Land looked back at his sergeant as he walked out the door, "Just be sure you get your food and rest."

The following morning, while the sun still lay hidden beyond the foggy horizon, Carlos Hathcock silently crawled behind a blind of bushes and grass on the far end of finger four. Months before, he had constructed the hide by digging a small hole in which he could lie and bench his rifle over two sandbags. From it he could watch the rice fields below and the hills that flanked them.

More than twelve hundred yards directly ahead of him, a small thatched hut sat near a stand of tall trees. Near the hut a high stack of straw and grass stood with its top covered by a large canvas tarpaulin. Through his scope, Hathcock could see the dark doorway and a woman walking outside, carrying a large jug.

A thousand yards to his left, a less-prominent hill rose from the forest, and on its peak, overlooking the countryside, stood a small, one-room temple, crowned with a bell-shaped top, that had large, oblong windows. The entire shrine was made of stone tinted green and black with moss and mold.

Across the fields and hedgerows to his right, several small hills rippled up from the flatness of the surrounding farmland. It was from there that this sniper who killed the gunnery sergeant had fired the fatal bullet. Every time he shot from that cluster of knolls, the Marines on watch responded with concentrated machine-gun and mortar fire, yet he survived each attack. The dead space between the series of hills gave him several sheltered channels through which to escape and allowed him many avenues in which to maneuver to a variety of exits.

As Hathcock scanned the wide panorama of low hills and rice paddies, Captain Land and Master Sergeant Reinke, green greasepaint on their faces, climbed toward the small stone temple atop the peak at Hathcock's left. They hoped that the shrine's different sighting angle would expose the enemy sniper while he climbed to his hilltop hide.

A misty fog lay like a humid blanket over the deep green jungle that covered the hillside through which the captain and the master sergeant struggled. Tangled humps of slick, moss-covered roots covered the ground. They grasped low branches and saplings and pulled their way up the hill hand over hand, while their feet slipped and slid beneath them.

Long beams of light shone down between gaps in the forest's canopy revealing the humid air in smoky swirls of mist and fog. Ahead in a clearing, lit by the orange light that shone at an angle through the trees, stood the small stone temple, bathed in glimmering moisture from the dank air that hung over the hill.

Land turned and motioned for Reinke to come close. "I'll check the inside," the captain whispered into his assistant's ear. "You stand out here and be ready in case somebody jumps out. It's too close in there for the rifle, so I'm going in with my .45. You just be ready."

Reinke nodded and crept to the side of the building, where he crouched on one knee and held his M-14 ready to snap into his shoulder and fire.

Land crawled next to the shrine and leaned his rifle against the wall, inadvertently causing an audible click as the barrel struck the stone. He drew out his pistol, which he carried in a holster that he wore at an angle on the back of his belt, and prepared to make his entrance.

The captain felt confident with the pistol. As well as being a Distinguished Marksman, he was a Distinguished Pistol Shot, winning many interservice and National Rifle Association championships. More than that, Land had excelled in snap-and-shoot combat pistol competition. Clearing one small room ought to be no challenge for his expertise.

With his pistol raised, a vision of John Wayne entered the captain's mind as he lifted his leg high and slammed his foot against the temple's thick wooden door. The heavy door swung open, and he stepped inside with a turn, pistol first.

During the night a black-clad Viet Cong scout had slipped into the temple, where he planned to spend the day observing the Marines on the adjacent hilltop. While he waited, the guerrilla relaxed on the floor and fell asleep.

The click of the rifle's barrel against the wall had alerted him to the company outside. He was silently creeping up a narrow set of stone steps that led to the upper portion of the shrine when the door suddenly banged open and the green-faced Marine stepped in, waving a pistol.

Land saw the soldier leaping up the steps with his AK carbine in hand, and for a second his mind went blank. Then he scrambled out the open doorway, and, as he did so, he blindly fired three shots in rapid succession through the temple's doorway.

Wide-eyed and visibly shaken, the captain cautiously peeked back inside and found the Viet Cong soldier sprawled on the floor, shot twice. Land stood and turned toward Master Sergeant Reinke.

"Sir," the top said, with his eyes twinkling and a grin on his lips, "you sure came out of there a whole lot faster than you went in."

"Reinke . . . just don't say another word," the captain grumbled.

Hathcock raised his head when he heard the three muffled pops faintly echo across the valley. He immediately turned his twenty-power spotting scope, which he had mounted on a small tripod that he had set on the end of the sandbag, toward the shrine. Turning the rear eyepiece with his fingers, he brought into focus Land and Reinke, who, having realized that the gunshots had alerted the VC and removed any possibility of their staying at the temple, were just disappearing into the dense jungle.

He scanned the treetops, looking for a gap through which he might catch a second glimpse of the two snipers as they moved away from the shrine. But, after several minutes of searching and seeing nothing but jungle, he turned the scope back toward the hut that stood more than three-quarters of a mile away.

Now the sun bathed the pointed, thatched roof and the hard-packed dirt that surrounded the small house. In the yellow morning light, Hathcock watched as the woman, who appeared to live alone, placed a wooden stool outside the doorway and set a small table near it. A young girl dressed in a white blouse and black pants, who had come to the woman's hut while Hathcock had his attention trained on the shrine, sat on the stool and removed the straw hat that she wore.

The middle-aged woman studied the girl's face, lifting her chin and tilting her face to the right and left with her right hand. She turned from the girl and took a waxed string from a box that sat on the small table and looped her right thumb and forefinger in one end and her left thumb and forefinger in the other.

Pulling the string tightly between her hands, she began to roll it up and down the girl's cheeks, under her chin, and over her forehead, catching fine facial hairs on the spinning string and plucking them out as they tangled around it.

From the distance that Hathcock watched, he could only tell that the woman was rubbing something across the girl's face. And even from the distance of more than twelve hundred yards, it was obvious that this woman provided certain beauty services for her neighbors.

When the woman finished, she patted the young girl on her head and walked back into the hut. The girl put her straw hat back on and walked down a trail that led along a rice paddy dike to where other huts and sheds stood.

Hours of boredom carried the morning to the early afternoon and Hathcock continued watching the hut and hills below his outpost. He saw several brightly colored chickens with long green tails and ruffles of orange feathers around their necks strutting and scratching in the dirt near the tall haystack. The chickens fascinated Hathcock and held his attention as they pecked and pawed at the debris that littered this farmyard.

"Bingo!" Hathcock said to himself suddenly and picked up his rifle, which he had rested to the right of the spotting scope. While watching the chickens claw through the dirt, searching for tiny bits of food, he saw two men slip from behind the tall trees that grew to the left of the hut and trot quickly inside its doorway. Both were dressed in dark green uniforms and carried long rifles.

When they emerged again, both men had removed their shirts and had set their rifles out of sight inside the hut. One man patted the woman on her shoulder and sat on the stool, while the other man squatted nearby. As he squatted there in the dirt, he waved his hands and shook his head in active conversation with the others.

The men were stocky and muscular, and Hathcock recognized them clearly as NVA. Probably they were snipers, he judged, because of the long rifles that they carried. Possibly they were the very snipers that had killed the gunnery sergeant.

Looking through his rifle scope, Hathcock judged the distance and moved the elevation knob to raise the strike of his bullet. He could see the mirage boiling up from the rice field and leaned to his left to peek through the spotting scope and get a better look at the heat waves.

Giving the rear eyepiece a quarter-turn to the left, Hathcock brought the mirage into full focus and could see it angling first to the right, and then boiling straight up, and then angling to the left. "Little bit of a fishtail," he told himself. At more than twelve hundred yards, the shifting wind, even though a very light breeze, made this one of the most difficult shots a marksman could attempt.

Waiting until the mirage leaned well to the left, Hathcock set his rifle scope's reticle on the chest of the man who sat on the stool having his hair trimmed by the woman. He took a breath, exhaled, and squeezed the Winchester's trigger.

The rifle's crack sent a flock of dark brown and black birds flying skyward from the thick brush that grew on the hillside below the hide where Hathcock lay. He drew back his bolt and chambered a second round, watching the first strike the thick, straw roof of the hut and skip skyward.

The woman and two men heard the shot strike the hut's roof and immediately leaped for cover behind the tall pile of straw and grass. They knew that the haystack would block them from the view of the rifleman atop the hill and hoped that it would stop his bullets, too.

Before Hathcock could settle his aim on any of the three, they had vanished from sight. "Damn it," he said under his breath, turning the knob on the right-hand side of his scope four clicks, moving this next shot down two minutes of angle, slightly more than twenty-four inches from where he had zeroed the last one.

"Well," he told himself, "it's a stab in the dark, but what

can I lose?" Steadily, he positioned the center of the scope's
cross hairs on the middle of the haystack, and after one last
check to see that the mirage leaned well to the left, he sent a
second round cracking down from the hill, across the rice
fields, and through the haystack.

Like frightened animals, the two men scurried from behind
the haystack, bolted across the wide yard, and disappeared
into the stand of tall trees, leaving their rifles and shirts inside
the woman's hut. Hathcock chambered a round and drew his
scope to the rear for a third shot, but nothing else moved.

"I must have nailed her," he said to himself, taking a closer
look at the scene through the twenty-power spotting scope. He
continued watching, waiting for the two men to return for
their rifles and shirts. But that hope quickly turned sour when
he looked to the right of the hut and saw a Marine patrol
hurrying toward the haystack.

They had been on the other side of the community of huts
where the young girl had gone earlier, and had heard shots.
They saw the unarmed woman lying in the dirt behind the
haystack and hurried to give her assistance. They thought that
the woman had been hit by a stray round.

When Hathcock saw the Marines rushing down the dike,
one by one, thirty yards apart, he knew that he had struck the
woman with his shot. "I better get up the hill to counterintelligence and ITT," he told himself. "If that woman is alive, that
big, ugly gunny will want to talk to her."

He screwed the lens cap on his spotting scope and slid it
back into his pack. Scooting out of his hide, he slung his rifle
over his right shoulder, grabbed his pack by the straps, and
hurried up the trail from the lower edge of finger four. He
walked to a hard-back tent near the center of the compound,
where he found the gunnery sergeant whose job it was to
interrogate prisoners of war and enemy suspects brought to
Hill 55.

Many of the Marines assigned duty with the counterintelligence and interrogator/translator teams had shaved their heads
and had grown long handlebar mustaches. The gunnery sergeant was much taller than Hathcock and was very broad
across the shoulders. Hathcock felt intimidated by his menac-
ing appearance and thought that if this Marine and his kind

caused that much uneasiness with him, they surely must devastate the Vietnamese suspects whom they interrogated.

"Gunny," Hathcock said, heaving and panting after running up the hill from his hide. "I need to talk to you about something that just happened down off finger four."

The fearsome Marine wore a flack jacket and no shirt beneath it. He carried a helmet in his right hand and dipped his head as he walked outside to meet Hathcock, who ran the final few steps up the dirt pathway to the gunnery sergeant's hooch. "What did you see, Sergeant?"

"It ain't exactly what I saw as much as it is what happened," Hathcock said huffing. "I watched this woman cuttin' what looked like two NVA snipers' hair, and I took a shot at 'em. I shot a little high, so the three of them ran to this haystack to hide. I put my second round into the haystack, and I believe I hit the woman. Meantime, the two NVA hot dogs got away in the tree line."

"What makes you believe they were NVA?" the Marine asked, leaning slightly down to make eye contact with Hathcock.

"They wore dark green uniforms and carried long rifles—looked like Mosin-Nagants. Those two hamburgers left them in her hooch with their shirts when they flew the coop."

"Hmm," the gunny said thoughtfully. "What else?"

"A patrol walked into the scene and picked up this woman. I need to know where they're taking her, because I don't think that they realize what she is. Those Marines never checked out her hooch or anything around it. They just snatched her up and hauled her off and never saw the uniforms or the rifles."

Palming the helmet in one hand, the interrogator shoved the camouflage-covered, steel pot on his head and began walking briskly toward the operations center. "Come on, Sergeant. We better get a lead on these guys."

In less than five minutes the two Marines had a report from the patrol who had found the woman. They sent a fire team back to the thatched hut to search for the weapons.

Thirty minutes later, word came on the radio that the fire team had found nothing. They claimed that this probably was someone else and that she had been hit in the neck by a stray round. She was just too far away for it to come from Hill 55.

"Gunny, I shot her," Hathcock said, narrowing his eyes. "She is a collaborator. Those two hamburgers doubled back and grabbed their rifles and shirts. There is one sure way to prove she is the woman who was cutting those ol' boys' hair."

The gunny looked at Hathcock and started to walk back to his tent. "Okay, Sergeant. How's that?"

"When they take her to the aid station, have one of your own men standing by while the doctor pulls that slug out of her neck. If it's my woman, the bullet that they pull out will be a 173-grain boat-tail Sierra."

Hathcock lay on his cot, leaning his head and shoulders against his pack as he read a letter from Jo and listened to Glen Campbell singing "Gentle on My Mind." The screen door slamming shut, followed by heavy footsteps, distracted his attention from the home thoughts and music.

It was the mountain-sized gunnery sergeant. He stood twirling his long handlebar mustache with his right hand as the low-angled sunlight shone off his head. "She's yours, Sergeant Hathcock. The doc pulled a boat-tailed bullet out of her neck. I'll talk to her tomorrow. I just came by to let you know, and to say thanks. She may know quite a bit. If these gooks talk to their barbers like we do, we might get real lucky."

Hathcock smiled, "Hope so, Gunny. If you think of it when you interrogate her, you might ask her about a platoon of NVA snipers. Captain Land thinks they're operating a full platoon down here now. If she knows something, give me a holler. I'd surely appreciate knowing anything about that."

The big Marine nodded to Hathcock and clomped on through the hooch to the back door.

"Thanks again, Gunny."

"Anytime, Sergeant. Anytime."

The gunny let the door slam shut as he stepped outside. He wheeled on his toes, crunching small rocks beneath his heavy boots, and looked back through the screen at Hathcock. "One hell of a shot, Sergeant. Right at three-quarters of a mile, maybe more. You make many like that?"

"A few, Gunny."

"What's the secret? Luck?"

"No secret," Hathcock said, still lying on his cot. He raised his hand in the air and crooked out his trigger finger. "Maybe a little luck, but mostly good trigger control, proper alignment, and allowing for just the right windage."

"How do you get just the right windage?"

Hathcock looked toward the gunny and with a straight face said, "I watch the clouds . . . how fast they're moving. I look at the treetops and bushes. I take a good look at the mirage, that tells me a whole lot. Once I settle on direction and velocity, I take a swag and come up with minutes of windage."

The gunny cupped his hands around his face and peered through the screen at Hathcock, who sat up on the cot smiling at him. "What's a swag, Sergeant Hathcock?"

Hathcock narrowed his eyes, cocked his head to one side, and in a serious tone said, "We use it a whole lot in long-range shooting."

"Oh yeah?"

"Uh huh. Swag . . . Scientific Wild-Ass Guess."

13

Sniper Counter Sniper

FOUR REPORTERS HUSTLED to stay abreast of Captain Land as he led them to a bunker built on the military crest* of Hill 55's finger four. He purposely rushed them past the hard-back tents, where several bare-chested snipers sat on ammunition crates watching this media parade.

It was mostly because of the third reporter that Land hurried the group past the snipers. This correspondent carried a tape recorder slung across his shoulder and held a microphone in his hand. He spoke into it as he walked, turning his head every direction, apparently describing each vision that confronted him. His presence made Land feel uncomfortable.

As the group passed the lounging Marines who gathered outside to watch the "exhibition," Land shot a cold glance at his men, warning them that this was not the time nor place for a bravado show.

The little party came up to where the low profile of a bunker stood overlooking miles of hills, hedgerows, rice fields, and jungle. "Gentlemen," Land said, stepping atop the bunker and pointing to a heavily sandbagged machine gun nest to his side, "this is our longest-reaching sniper weapon, the M-2 .50-caliber machine gun . . . effective out to three thou-

---

*The highest point on a hill that allows maximum visibility and fire coverage while at the same time offering maximum cover and concealment from the enemy. Usually below the topographical crest.

sand yards. You may notice, on the upper right-hand side of the weapon, we have mounted a telescopic gunsight. That is an eight-power sight made by the Lyman Gunsight Corporation. It is one of three primary scopes that we use on our sniper rifles. We also use a very similar-looking eight-power scope made by the Unertl Optical Company and a variable, three-to-nine power scope made by Redfield.

"Either of the Unertl or Lyman scopes will fit on the machine gun by way of the detachable mounts that we designed and had specially made right here," the captain continued as the men gathered behind the big gun, taking turns looking through its sight, trying to imagine what it might be like to shoot someone with it.

"My snipers will go on missions and carry a set of mounts in their packs. When they get to the operational unit, it is a minor task to attach the mounts to any M-2, .50-caliber machine gun available. A sniper easily fastens the mounts to the big gun and removes his scope from his rifle and attaches it on the machine gun mounts. After that, it is a simple job of leveling the gun and zeroing the weapon to whatever distance that he expects to engage the majority of his targets.

"In this way, our Marines can carry their normal sniper equipment and still offer a battalion commander the benefit of extra long-range sniper fire."

Absorbed in the tour, the two photojournalists amongst the four reporters jockeyed around the machine gun and snapped pictures of it and Captain Land as he stepped off the bunker and stood in front of the sandbag wall, over which the machine gun's barrel tilted. Concentrating on his lecture Land forgot that standing outside the sandbags' protection exposed him to any enemy sniper who might be watching.

"What's this thing that looks like a level?" the man with the tape recorder asked, pointing to a device that hung from the tripod on which the machine gun sat.

"That's a Gunners' Quadrant. And you're right, it is a kind of level."

Just as the reporter knelt behind the big gun for a look through the scope, a rifle shot cracked across the valley from the cluster of low knolls to the right of finger four.

The bullet struck the hillside just below Land's feet, splitting a small rock and blasting away a chip the size of a quarter, which ricocheted off his shin. Land leaped, thinking that the bullet had hit him. He dived over the top of the bunker and rolled to the other side.

The photographers scrambled behind the sandbags, and with their motor-driven cameras singing, they took aim at two Marines who scurried to the big gun and quickly trained it on the knoll and released a rapid burst of fire into its several peaks.

As he did every time he shot from that hide, the sniper slipped through the covered escape route and floated safely down the narrow canal at the base of the knoll.

While the reporters huddled around the two Marines who fired the machine gun, getting names, ages, and home towns, and taping comments to go with the "sound of battle," a colonel unobtrusively watched the demonstration from several yards away, safely behind cover. As Land turned to see who had joined them, he recognized the man—his boss—Colonel Herman Poggemeyer.

The colonel frowned sharply at Land and motioned for the captain to come close.

"Sir," the captain said, walking near the colonel. "Everyone appears to be okay. It was awfully close."

"Captain," the colonel said, "step up the hill with me, away from this crowd."

Land said nothing but followed the colonel and felt a sudden tightness fill his stomach.

"What kind of example of leadership do you call that?" the colonel growled angrily. A long pause followed while the captain stood, braced for the storm, looking straight ahead and saying nothing. "I'm surprised at you, Captain—exposing yourself to fire so that a bunch of reporters can get some good pictures? What about those Marines back there who depend on your being around to lead them? What on earth got into your head? What about those people waiting for you back home? How could you needlessly risk leaving a family without a father! There will be no condolence letter to your wife. That's because you will not leave your quarters until you rotate.

"Captain Land, you're restricted. You may go to the chow hall, head, and chapel. You will sit down tonight and write your wife a letter. Tell her you will be home in a couple of weeks—alive. Is that clear, Captain?"

"Yes, Sir!" Land barked in the same manner as he had done to his sergeant instructor at Officer Candidates' School.

The colonel held a folder filled with papers and opened it, pulled out several that he had stapled together, and waved them in the captain's face. "Do you see this?" Poggemeyer said, speaking with increasing vehemence. "I came here to tell you that I had recommended you for a Bronze Star. But you can forget that now!"

As he lashed out those final words to the captain, he tucked the folder under his arm, took the award recommendation in his hands and, ripping it in half, threw it at Land's feet.

Captain Land did not move. He stood rigidly fixed at attention while the colonel turned from him and stormed away.

When Colonel Poggemeyer returned to his quarters, he reconsidered what he had told the captain. A man of his word, he did not recommend Land for a Bronze Star, but at a ceremony at South Weymouth, Massachusetts, some time later, Land received the Navy Commendation Medal with Combat V.*

Land walked to his hooch, sat at his desk, and wrote his wife, Ellie, a letter. The remainder of the night he worked on a turnover file that he would give to Maj. D.E. Wight, his replacement. He told no one that he was on restriction.

"Sergeant Hathcock," a voice shouted outside the quarters where Hathcock lay on his cot, looking at a map that detailed the terrain surrounding Hill 55. "Sergeant Hathcock. You in there?"

Hathcock yelled, "Come on in, Gunny. What ya got?"

"That woman, she may be full of shit, and then again she may not be. But take it for what it's worth."

Hathcock sat on the edge of his cot and took a can filled with cigarette butts off an ammunition crate; he offered it as a

---

*A metal letter V worn on the medal's ribbon. It is awarded with some medals to denote that they were awarded for valor in combat rather than for meritorious action or service.

seat for the huge gunnery sergeant, who had interrogated the woman that Hathcock had shot in the neck.

"Go on, Gunny. What's this woman full of it about?"

"I don't doubt that these NVA told her this, and it may be a lot of brag. You know, the way we sometimes build up things to get folks' attention. But I think there is a root of truth to what she says."

"To what?" Hathcock asked impatiently.

"She said that there are a dozen snipers—a whole sniper platoon—down here now from North Vietnam. They trained at a place up there that supposedly looks just like Hill 55. She said they have a compound, complete with bunkers and sniper hides, exactly like this here. They probably know the land as well as you do."

"That makes sense. The way they've been picking people off around here, I was thinking they had some inside information," Hathcock said, wrinkling his lips and nodding his head philosophically.

"Well, the best part is this," the gunny said, resting his forearms across his knees and leaning toward Hathcock. "They want you."

"Figures," Hathcock said, without showing the shock that the gunny thought the news would evoke. "Captain Land told me they've got a bounty out on me and him. He saw a leaflet that they dropped all over creation. It figures that these hamburgers would have me at the top of their list. What about the skipper?"

"She didn't mention him. All she could talk about was Long Tra'ng—White Feather—and how they had all taken a blood oath to not return home without your little trademark and scalp."

"They don't scare me none, Gunny. I don't care how hard those hot dogs think they are, there ain't none of them hard enough to get me."

"You're not Superman, Hathcock. You're not invincible."

"Oh, no! I never said I was. Oh, they could kill me. I could let down my guard and they would kill me in a heartbeat. But the harder they hunt me, the harder I get. There ain't none of them who know how to move and hide like I can. And there sure ain't none of them who can outshoot me. That's what I mean, Gunny. I'm just a whole lot better than they are, and that gives me the advantage."

"You may be better. And again, they may have an ol' boy who is better than you."

"And . . . ?"

"Well, that woman told me there is one sniper in particular who is doing the majority of damage to the Marines walking around on the hill. He's the man who killed the gunny outside your door. All this guy does is live in the jungle. He eats rats and bugs, weeds, lizards, and worms—shit like that. She said this guy catches cobras and vipers with his bare hands and eats 'em raw so that he'll have their spirit in him."

"Eating garbage and living in the mud don't make you smart. You have to be smart in the first place. I can see where living in the wild and learning the ways of nature can improve this guy's chances, but I've spent a lot of time crawlin' around the woods, too."

The gunny stood and slapped Hathcock on the back of the head. "I know your reputation. But this fella has one, too. Take it for what it's worth . . . keep your head down."

Hathcock walked the gunny to the door, "I figure this fella has a fair aim, considering the long-range shots he's notched. But, no matter what he does, if he keeps shooting at us from the same little knoll out yonder, we'll get him. It's just a matter of time."

The last of the lingering monsoon showers fell as Captain Land packed his sea bag. Outside his hooch, the rain pattered on the orange mud and collected in hundreds of puddles throughout the hilltop compound. The blue day matched Land's mood. He had not left the hill since the colonel restricted him. For a while he thought that his boss might ease off, but now with only three days remaining in-country, he knew that the colonel's word was firm.

Hathcock now looked nearly like his old self. His face was full and his eyes clear and twinkling. The rest had put him back on his feet. He had remained restricted to the hill until a few days earlier, when the captain cleared him to go back to the bush on a day-to-day basis. And each evening, Hathcock made a point of checking in with Land. He did not wish to spend another day on restriction.

"At the tone, the time will be 5 P.M.," a voice announced over the radio that played softly in the captain's hooch. He leaned down to turn the volume up, following the short blare of a 500-hertz tone. Every hour, on the hour, Armed Forces Radio Da Nang broadcast five minutes of news.

Land listened as the voice told of increasing numbers of American troops now committed to the escalating war in Vietnam, as President Johnson proclaimed that this conflict would not be lost at any cost. Richard Nixon had begun his campaign for the presidency and vowed that he would bring an honorable end to the war. Meanwhile, young men burned their draft cards and others waved North Vietnamese flags in protests that sprang from Boston to Washington, D.C., and from the University of California at Berkeley to Allens Landing near Houston's Old Market Square, where fighting broke out on Love Street when a Vietnam veteran attacked a demonstrator, ripping the Communist flag from his hands. The veteran was jailed for assault. Dr. Timothy Leary's followers were dropping LSD, and stories of "bad trips" that ended in space walks from hotel windows added a punchy finish.

". . . for details, read the *Pacific Stars and Stripes*," the voice concluded as the newscast ended for another hour. "Sounds worse at home," the captain grumbled, as a voice began singing to a slow rock beat.

Land jerked as the sound of a rifle shot, followed by a scream, "Corpsman! Corpsman! The captain's hit!" echoed throughout the encampment.

Leaning out his door, he looked at the crowd huddled thirty feet away from his hooch and saw two feet kicking, toes up, in the mud.

Land thought of Hathcock and Burke, who had gone out to set up below the cluster of knolls, hoping to get a clear shot at the sniper. Instead of walking to where the corpsman frantically worked to save the wounded Marine's life, he hurried to a sandbagged observation point and looked far below at the ruby stream of tracer bullets pouring into the lower hilltops.

He searched the low valley and along the rice paddy dikes for a sign of his snipers. He was afraid that they might have ventured out of their positions and been caught in a line of friendly fire. For the next hour of lingering daylight, he waited to find out what had happened to the two sniper teams he had put out.

Hathcock had told him what the woman had said to the interrogators, and it was then that the captain made the decision to keep Lance Corporal Burke and Sergeant Hathcock teamed. This combination of his best snipers gave Hathcock a better chance at surviving, but more important, it pitted the most lethal tandem possible against the phantom slayer who this rainy afternoon had shot another Marine on Hill 55.

When darkness fell, Land walked to the sniper school headquarters where Master Sergeant Reinke and Gunnery Sergeant Wilson sat in the dark talking about the new M-40 rifle, a .308-caliber, Model 700 Remington that had just arrived in country.

"Where're the two teams?" the captain asked softly, as he felt his way inside the darkened hooch.

"One team is in, but there is no word on Sergeant Hathcock and Lance Corporal Burke yet, Sir." Reinke said in the darkness. "We're gonna sit and wait. I don't think we could do them any good wandering around the jungle in the dark. What with the clouds blocking the moon and the rain falling so hard now, I think that they may be holed up for the night."

"I agree," Land said, repressing his own emotional need to go out and search for his men. He felt a strong bond with all his men, but especially with Hathcock. The captain had watched him mature from a seventeen-year-old, trouble-prone private in Hawaii to an exemplary sergeant in Vietnam. More than that, Carlos was a friend.

"Here's where he got out," Hathcock whispered to Burke. It was so dark that the corporal held tight to the sergeant's pack straps as they drifted and paddled along the edge of this canal that fed water into the many rice paddies below Hill 55. Rain beat the broad leaves above their heads, like hail on a barn roof. The two men stirred, sloshing the water as they climbed from the canal where the grass lay parted and broken. Here, the North Vietnamese sniper had crawled out earlier and now made his way to his jungle lair.

During the afternoon, the two Marine snipers had hidden below the knoll where their quarry had fired the fatal shot across to Hill 55. After the retaliatory fire had ceased, Hathcock and Burke moved around the hill searching for a fresh trail; they found skid marks in a muddy slide that was sheltered by a growth of dense foliage and that led from the upper reaches of these low hills to a narrow canal.

The entire route lay in dead space, secure from machine-gun fire, and it allowed the enemy free entrance and exit from the area.

It was simple, yet cunning, Hathcock thought. Float in and float out, always out of sight.

The two Marines had found the place where the enemy sniper climbed out of the canal, and now, as they followed his soggy trail, the rain beat relentlessly down on them.

"We'd better find a hide and hole up for the night," Hathcock whispered into Burke's ear. "Up among that bunch of fallen trees might keep a little rain off our backs."

Burke nodded, and the two pushed their way into the brush and dead wood and burrowed against a log covered by broad-leafed plants. The rain dripped in, but the direct downpour fell away from them. They opened a can of C-ration crackers and cheese spread and ate in relative dryness. Here they waited until daylight.

The rains passed as darkness gave way to dawn and narrow shafts of orange light beamed down through the jungle's canopy, illuminating the steam that rose in smoky swirls from the wet forest floor. During the night, Hathcock and Burke camouflaged themselves with leafy twigs and vines, draped and fastened through loops and buttonholes on their uniforms and hats. They painted their faces, hands, and necks shades of light and dark green, with sticks of dull makeup that they carried in their cargo pockets and jokingly called mascara.

Silently, the two men moved out of their hide and followed the trail of broken stems and tread marks in the mud. The rain had washed the footprints to only faint impressions, which required a tracker's skill to spot. Yet the combination of broken plants, skid marks, and faint footprints provided a clear trail.

"Burke," Hathcock mouthed to his partner soundlessly.

Burke came close and Hathcock whispered in his ear. "This trail is too easy. If I was chasin' some VC scout, I wouldn't worry. But this is an NVA sniper—maybe even the best of them. He wouldn't leave a clear trail by accident."

Hathcock dropped to his knees, and Burke followed his lead, crouching low too. "From here on out," he whispered to his partner, "we go worm style."

Hathcock and Burke crawled up the trail. After each silent, precisely limited motion of an arm or leg, they paused to survey their surroundings.

Smelling the air, tasting it, searching for any scent that might give away another man, the two Marines scouted for a sign that would reveal their quarry. Hathcock's eyes shifted quickly from corner to corner; he looked for anything out of place or changed by man. His ears followed the track that his eyes took.

He saw nothing but green stillness in the damp morning, smelled only the mildew and rot of the jungle, felt only the grit and slime as he crawled, sniffing, tasting and observing. The distant sound of jets followed the rumbling thunder of their bombs. He heard a fire fight in progress, far away on another hillside. The slow rhythmic chop of a .50-caliber machine gun echoed across the distance. Hill 55? Another sniping?

The thought passed as quickly as it came, and Hathcock continued his single-minded stalk. Slowly and deliberately he pushed forward, reading the trail, cautious that as he stalked this quarry, that quarry might, in fact, be a cunning hunter stalking him.

Near the top of the ridge and not yet visible to the two snipers, a small, hand-dug cave, lined with grass and covered with brush and vines, stood empty at the end of the trail. Inside it, a grass bed lay matted flat from the weight of a man sleeping there for a time. But no one had rested there for several days.

On the other side of a shallow gully, on a steep hill where thick vines and tangled brush covered the granite boulders that cropped out from the earth, a sniper hid. He watched a six-foot clearing that he had carefully hacked out in front of the cave at the end of the trail. And as he had done each time before, after killing a Marine on Hill 55, he patiently waited in ambush. He knew that it was only a matter of time before a Marine would pick up his trail and follow it to the small hole and the narrow clearing near it. The sniper hoped that the Marine who stalked him, and who slowly closed on his bait, would be the sniper who wore the white feather—Hathcock.

White rays of midday sun bore straight down on the jungle floor, raising steam from the damp mulch that covered the ground where the two Marine snipers slowly crawled. Several hours had passed since the mild morning sun's orange beams had tilted at sharp angles through the forest's canopy, waking the day.

Now as the tropical temperature rose in the January afternoon, Tiny flies and gnats swarmed in the greenhouse-humid air that hung in sweltering stillness beneath the trees. The hungry insects smelled the body fluids oozing from the two snipers' pores and attacked them, biting and sucking sweat and blood. And as the tiny gnats and flies landed on the Marines' wet necks and began to gnaw, they drowned in perspiration and collected in little black balls along the wrinkles on the men's necks. They attacked the corners of the two snipers' eyes and crawled into the creases of their mouths. Hathcock and Burke ignored the discomfort and pushed up the hill.

Every few yards, Hathcock raised a pair of binoculars and scoured the ground ahead. He searched for trip wires or any sign indicating hidden pressure peddles that would release the explosive charge of a mine or booby-trap. He searched for alterations of the foliage that would allow his enemy a clear shot. The two snipers moved forward over thick ferns and wet, rotten leaves.

Hathcock suddenly froze. Raising his binoculars, he focused them on the small, grass-lined burrow twenty feet away. Burke lay still.

The afternoon sun shone brightly through the trees, sprinkling bright spots of light across the forest floor. Small saplings and twisted vines wound their way between the larger trees, filling every available area in which they could grow. Yet at the cave, the forest seemed almost garden-neat.

Had the burrow's resident cleared it away for his comfort? Hathcock carefully eased himself closer, trying to see how far

the clearing extended laterally and how much exposure it offered. He could not tell for certain, but he did know that if he
had made the burrow as a hide, he would have left the front
yard piled with twisted growth. He would have made alternate
escape routes from it, too. It seemed strange there was but one
way in or out of this small hole.

"I don't like it," Hathcock thought to himself. He drew out
a plastic-covered map that he had folded into a six-inch
square, with this hill at its center. Tracing the hill with his
finger, he found the slight hump near its crest where this cave
lay and noticed the tiny draw at its right.

Lifting his binoculars, Hathcock tried to glimpse the ridge
that faced the other side of the draw through the thick forest.
"He's over there," he thought, although unable to clearly see
the other side. "He's bound to have a direct line of sight to
that cave."

Without a sound, motioning Burke to follow, Hathcock
moved off the trail to his right and began to make a wide
circle around the cave. He pushed through the tangle and
thorns around the hide and over the hill's top, where the draw
came to a head.

Across the draw, the dark-faced sniper lay still, covered
with ferns and vines, ready at his rifle. He sampled the air,
sniffing and tasting, wary of the possibility that his enemy
might detect the trap and sneak across the draw to where he
hid.

By mid-afternoon, Hathcock and Burke had moved to the
top of the draw where it flattened into a saddle on the ridge.
As the two men pushed forward, they began to notice many
birds pecking and scratching through the leaves. Above them,
on lower branches, other birds sat and twittered. Below in the
draw, more birds gathered. Hathcock took a closer look with
his binoculars and saw what had attracted the many birds—
rice. Someone had scattered rice throughout the saddle, and
now birds and other forest creatures feasted on it, and by their
presence created a natural early-warning system that would
alert the Communist sniper to the arrival of an intruder.

The man deserved respect for his cunning. Hathcock knew
that successfully stalking this enemy would require a change
in strategy.

The saddle and hilltop where the two Marines waited offered a clear vantage across the saddle and down the draw. From the place where the birds pecked for the rice, he could get a clear view of the draw below, as well as relatively clear fields of fire through a number of routes that his quarry might take. But Hathcock also knew that it would offer his enemy the same open field toward him as well.

The two Marines found a rest where a rock protruded up from the ground. To the right, a dead tree lay on its side, falling apart with rot.

Once positioned, Hathcock took a branch and tossed it into the flock of birds. The sudden stir of wings flying up to the higher branches in the forest echoed down the draw to where the small, brown man lay behind his Mosin-Nagant rifle, peering through its short 3.5-power scope. His eyes shifted sharply to his left. A wild pig or big cat might have sent the birds skyward, but another person might have done so, too. The sniper pushed his way over the vine-covered rocks and quietly headed toward the saddle.

He followed the sloping ridge to the draw's head, but rather than moving across the saddle where Hathcock and Burke lay, he went down the far side of the hill and picked his way through a thicket of thornbushes on the Marines' right flank.

Hathcock lay quietly listening to the sounds of the forest, hearing a bird's song carried on a breeze that quaked through the treetops and rustled the leaves. He could hear a slight wheeze in Burke's lungs as his partner breathed in slow rhythm, two feet away. "The kids's probably caught cold from sleepin' in the rain," Hathcock thought. And as his eyes shifted toward Burke, a sharp crack echoed through the brush to their right.

Without a word, both Marines shifted to their left. "He circled around us!" Burke whispered hoarsely, as he quickly pushed his way behind a tree.

"Shoot the gap, Burke!" Hathcock whispered back. "He's closing right in on us."

The two Marines scrambled down the saddle and into the thick cover that the draw offered. Once behind its shield of tangled stalks and vines, they dropped to their bellies and began to quietly crawl up the ridge where the enemy sniper had passed on his trek to their former hide.

The crack and thud of the two Marines scrambling into the draw told the NVA sniper that his quarry had flown. When his sleeve had snagged on the thornbush and snapped its branch, he had known the chances were that they would hear. Still it was frustrating. He crept up the hill and examined the spot where the Americans had lain. Then he looked across the low saddle and surveyed the field of fire that his enemy had covered. It looked good. He would settle into the hide and wait and see if Hathcock and Burke came up the ridge and entered their own killing zone.

Meanwhile, the Marines pushed an inch at a time through the low vines and bushes to where the ridge met the saddle. They were at the opposite end of their former field of fire. Sweat beaded Hathcock's face and dripped off the end of his nose as he looked across at the rock behind which he and Burke had hidden. Where had the enemy crawled?

From their opposite ends, all three men watched the clearing, waiting for the next move.

Burke swallowed hard to clear his scratchy throat, now irritated and dry. He reached to his hip and quietly unfastened his canteen pouch, allowing the green plastic bottle to slide out. Hathcock watched the young Alabama native press the open canteen to his lips and drink. The green camouflage, which had once covered Burke's face, now eroded off his jaws by the rivulets of sweat that dripped from his chin, revealing his naturally bronze complexion and the redness that flushed over his cheeks.

As Burke slowly swallowed the water, he squinted his eyes with each gulp, reacting to the soreness in his throat. He glanced to his right and saw Hathcock watching him with concern. Burke cracked a toothy smile and, with liquid smoothness, slipped his canteen back into its pouch.

Hathcock knew that his partner was coming down with something and that the risk of his coughing or sneezing increased with time. It was risk enough for him to take the drink of water.

"He's got to be here," Hathcock thought to himself after searching every conceivable hide and seeing nothing. From his low, prone position, he could only see the flat front angle that the rotten log and rock presented. Despite the fact that he and Burke had vacated them only a half-hour earlier, they represented the best cover from which to control the openness of the saddle. But there was no sign of a muzzle or sight protruding from behind either object. "Where could he be?" Hathcock asked himself.

A large tree grew to the Marine sniper's left and offered enough cover to allow him to raise himself to a sitting position and possibly see behind the rock and log. Grabbing around the tree with his right hand and clutching his rifle with his left, Hathcock began to work his way up the tree's trunk to where he could sit and point his rifle scope at a high enough angle to see if his adversary had indeed moved into the two Marines' vacated hide.

Hathcock had almost positioned himself and was about to work his legs into a cross-ankle shooting stance when the ground gave way beneath the edges of his boot soles and he sat hard, crunching twigs and leaves with a noisy plop.

The brown man who hid behind the rotted log peered through his rifle's scope and saw the sudden flash of movement—the head of a man, wearing a hat with a white feather.

He had the American who could make him a wealthy hero clearly in his sights. And like the old fisherman who, after trying time after time to hook that grandfather trout, finally sees the great silver-and-green fish nipping at his lure, only a tug away from catching him, suddenly yanks too soon and misses his catch, the dark-faced man jerked his rifle's trigger, bucking his shot wide and low.

The sudden crack of rifle fire sent a surge of adrenalin through Hathcock's system. He raised his rifle and put his cross hairs on the log, where he saw the dark green flash of the enemy sniper disappear behind the foliage that cloaked his hide. "Damn!" Hathcock said under his breath, and then he looked down and noticed his partner lying motionless at his side, with an expression of wide-eyed alarm on his face.

"Sergeant Hathcock! I'm hit!"

"Where?"

"My butt. He shot my left cheek! It's bad! It's burning like a hot iron, and I can feel the blood running all over my legs!"

Hathcock dropped on his belly, crawled to where he could examine the wound, and then said sharply, "Burke, get up! That ain't blood, it's water. The bullet just grazed your hip and blew the bottom out of your canteen. Let's go! He's getting away!"

Both snipers could hear the brush breaking as their enemy crashed his way through the woods. They, too, jumped to their feet and hurried along the hilltop to a ridge that sloped down the windward side and overlooked a broad, treeless gap that extended down the hill. Beyond the gap, another ridge sloped to the forest below, and there Hathcock saw a gully where the runoff from the rain had eroded a route of escape for their enemy.

"Get down," he told Burke, as they crawled to the edge of the tree line, near the top of the ridge. "Bet you everything I own that he's in that gully."

Resting on his elbows, Burke scanned the full length of the gully with his binoculars, while Hathcock lay at his side, prone behind his Winchester, looking for the slight flash or motion that would reveal his quarry.

They watched the long gully for an hour without seeing anything, yet Hathcock felt certain that their man had not fled, but hid in waiting for them.

Hathcock was angry. His sudden movement had put them in this predicament. It was his turn to shoot now, and he wouldn't quit until he had taken it.

The sun lay low in the afternoon sky, sending its light down the hill at Hathcock's and Burke's backs and casting long shadows across the wide, grass-covered gap that sloped toward the gully where two almond-shaped eyes squinted behind a pair of black binoculars.

The enemy sniper slowly searched each tree trunk and bush for the white feather. "The arrogance of such a thing will cost this man his life," the sniper thought, as he picked apart the cover opposite him. "I will teach you to flaunt yourself. It is the humble man who wins here, my friend."

As he trained his binoculars again at the top of the hill where the trees met the crest of the gap, something caught his eye, something small, yet bright, fluttering in the shadows. The little man squeezed his eyes shut and looked again through his binoculars, squinting to see through the blinding rays of the low sun. "I think, maybe, I have found you, my young warrior with the white plume."

In a smooth and deliberate motion, the North Vietnamese sniper raised his rifle from the gully and tucked it into his shoulder, steadying it with his left hand, which he rested on the ground above the trench. He concentrated on the pointed sight-post inside the scope, but his target disappeared in the sun's glare, causing him to tilt and cant the weapon as he tried to pinpoint the Marine through the small scope and kill him.

"What's that?" Hathcock said, catching a flash of light in his scope.

"What's what?" Burke responded in a hoarse whisper.

"There, again. Down in that gully. Something's flashing down there. Reflecting the sun. Something shiny."

"Reckon it's him?"

"I can't tell, but something is sure sparkling in the sun. You got your field glasses on it?"

"Yeah."

"Make anything of it?"

"No. It's like somebody shining a mirror in the sun. I can't tell anything."

"Hold tight, Burke. I'm gonna gamble a shot."

Carefully, Hathcock centered his scope's reticle on the glimmer of reflected sunlight. He released his breath and let the cross hairs settle on the target, and, as they settled, his .30-06 cracked down the hill, echoing through the wide, tree-less gap.

"Holy shit, Sergeant Hathcock! You got him," Burke said as the glimmer disappeared and revealed the now dead man whose body had bounded against the opposite side of the gully when the bullet struck.

Hathcock smiled at his partner and said, "One shot—one kill."

Although there was no sign of any other enemy, the two Marines avoided open areas and took the extra time to move along a covered route to where the dead soldier lay in the gully.

Burke reached the body first. He looked at his sergeant and said, "Nobody is gonna believe this unless they see it. Look at that. You put that round straight through his scope!"

Hathcock took the Russian-made sniper rifle from his partner and looked into the hollow tube of a telescopic sight that had had the glass blown from it as his bullet passed down its length and entered the enemy sniper's head through his eye.

"Burke, I just had a scary thought. What's the only way a person could make a shot like this?"

Burke looked puzzled. "What do you mean, Sergeant?"

"Stop and think about it. He had to be sighting his rifle right at me in order for my bullet to pass clean through his scope and get him in the eye like that."

"Why, then he almost had you!"

"Yeah, Burke, when you get down to it, the only difference between me and him is I got on the trigger first."

With the last remaining daylight, Hathcock sat next to the man's body and marked the exact position of the kill on his map. He would pass the information to headquarters, should they want to recover the body. As for the rifle, its lensless scope and bloody stock were a grim reminder to Hathcock of how close he had come to losing this duel, and he carried it away with him.

"Damn you, Hathcock," Captain Land shouted in the blackness of the sniper hooch as the two Marines crouched in the doorway at midnight. The silhouettes of the two men stood out in the moonlit sky as the captain rose to his feet and bear-hugged them together. "I haven't slept for two days, worrying about you two! What happened?"

"Got that boogerman for you, Sir," Hathcock said, proudly holding out the long rifle. "Shot him in the eye. Thought you'd like to go back to the World with that problem solved."

"That's one hell of a good going-away present, Carlos, but I'll tell you both, I'm a lot happier to see you two back here alive."

Hathcock put his name on the tag on the bloodstained, Mosin-Nagant sniper rifle and turned it into the command headquarters. He was hoping to save it as a special souvenir, but he never saw the rifle again.

One day later, Capt. E. J. Land departed Vietnam, leaving

Hathcock and Burke. He passed his concern for their safety to his relief, Major Wight.

"Hathcock's a dichotomy," Land told the major. "The man will put himself into the most dangerous situations imaginable, yet once he's out there on his own, he's the most cautious and thorough sniper I've ever seen. The only reason he's alive is because he is so damned good, once he's in the bush.

"Burke's just like him. Hathcock taught him everything he knows. They'll never say no. So watch 'em. Don't let them get in over their heads."

14

Stalking the General

THE LATE AFTERNOON sun shone through the camouflage netting draped over the old plantation house that now served as a North Vietnamese Army division's command center. The yellow light cast spotty shadows through the window and over the old commander who sat behind his tablelike desk, scratching out a note.

His division continued to expand and improve. But the old commander was like the great tiger that lived in these mountains and now limped because of a thorn that festered in his paw. This "thorn" was the increasing number of U.S. Marine snipers and especially the one who wore a white feather in his hat—a symbol that enraged the Communist general because he saw it as an insult to the abilities of his best guerrillas. News of someone sighting the sniper who wore the white feather spread fear among his troops, as well as among the local peasants. Whenever this man was seen, people died.

He gazed out the window, looking through the blotchy netting as the blood red sun stood at the crest of the mountains that arose from the sanctuary of Laos. The setting sun's highlights sparkled from the gold and silver that ornamented the large, red patches sewn on his collar. He thought of the war and the increasing numbers of American soldiers and weapons that now flooded into South Vietnam. And he thought of the increasing number of heavy bombs dropped daily from the bellies of high-flying B-52s.

* * *

As those bombs fell along the Demilitarized Zone and the Laotian border, Hathcock wadded a green-and-white cigarette pack and tossed it into the wooden ammunition box that he had turned into a combination nightstand, stool, and trash container. He lay back on his cot and took a long and deep drag off his last cigarette. The sun now set behind the distant hilltops in the west, and he watched the blazing orange sky turn dark as night fell.

As he lay there, he thought of his conversation with Gunny Wilson earlier that day just after he'd finished writing to Jo; recounting his past six months as a sniper made him realize that many things had permanently changed in his life. The Carlos Hathcock who reported to Maj. George E. Bartlett at 1st Marine Division's military police company nearly one year ago at Chu Lai, and who worked there as a machine gunner and desk sergeant, was a completely changed person from the Carlos Hathcock who spent the last six months on duty as a sniper and assistant chief sniper instructor at Da Nang. When he reported to the "Mustang"* major, himself a competitive marksman, Carlos had never killed anyone. He had never known the heat of combat or the reality of war. Now, he had eighty kills confirmed to his credit and had trained several hundred snipers, more than one hundred of them personally. When he came to Chu Lai, he equated marksmanship to targets. Now he equated targets to living, breathing human beings.

In a few days, he would pick up the orders that canceled his temporary additional duty as a sniper, and he would return to the Military Police Company, his parent command, that would process him for travel back to the World. He came to Vietnam a green kid, twenty-three years old, still immature and full of ideals and dreams. Now, his face bore wrinkles at twenty-four years, his ideals and dreams were tempered by the lessons of combat. And his boyishness had disappeared, drained from his soul at Elephant Valley, Charlie Ridge, An Hoa, and Da Nang. Now he felt old.

---

*Slang term used to describe Marine officers who were commissioned from the enlisted ranks.

Hathcock looked at the letter that he had written to Jo apologizing for not telling her that he was actually a working sniper, not just an instructor. The idea of her reading about it in the newspaper continued to rouse his anger. "Once I got home, I would have told her," he thought. "I just didn't want her worrying."

"Sergeant Hathcock! You in there?" a voice called in the night.

"Yo!" Hathcock called from his cot and raised himself on his elbows to see outside his hooch. "Yeah, Burke, what's up?"

Burke peered through the screen door. "Gunny needs to see you. I think they want you for one more trip to the bush."

Hathcock sprang to his feet like a fireman hearing the alarm sound. "What do you know? They tell you anything?"

"No. Gunny just said for me to roust you up."

Hathcock slipped on his shirt as he walked toward the sniper headquarters where he could see two figures standing outside.

"Looks like some sort of powwow," Burke said in a low voice as they drew near.

A hulking Marine captain who looked as though he could play on any National Football League team's front line stood next to the gunny. Wrapping his enormous paw around Hathcock's outstretched palm, he started shaking it.

"I've heard a lot about you, especially from Major Wight. That's why I made the trip down here to see you. We have a very risky job. And we think you're the only man who can pull it off and survive. I know you're due to go home in a matter of days, so I'm not here to order you. You may accept or reject our proposal. I can only tell you that the need is urgent."

The words "the only man who can pull it off" overshadowed everything else the captain said. No sales pitch was necessary beyond that. Hathcock knew that if they believed that he was the only man who had a chance at surviving this mission, then he must accept. If he rejected the request they'd select a less experienced sniper. A man who had less chance of surviving. He couldn't go home with that on his conscience.

"What's the job, Sir?" he said, folding his arms, ready for some sort of hint at this very dangerous assignment.

"I can't say. You have to accept or reject this request based totally on the prospect that it will be extremely hazardous. The odds of your surviving are slim, so I can only ask you to volunteer.

"If you accept, you will come with me and receive a briefing and a package containing all the information and planning that we've done on this mission. You can then tailor this plan to suit your needs and abilities. You will receive total support."

Hathcock scraped the toe of his boot through the dirt and thought of the short-timer stories about Marines who took one more mission with only days remaining in-country and died on it. To take such a mission violated a superstition. Go on patrol when you're a newbee or a short-timer and you're dead. But, he also thought that the odds stood in his favor more than in any other sniper's, despite the short-timer superstition.

He looked at Burke, standing silently in the moonlight. What if they turned to him or to the gunny or the top? Which friend would he allow to go in his place?

He looked at the captain and took a deep breath. "Sir, I'll go. I wouldn't be able to face myself if I didn't."

The captain put his arm over Hathcock's shoulder and patted him. "I've got a map and some recon photos up at operations, we'll talk there."

The two Marines walked away from the sniper hooch, and Burke watched them disappear in the darkness. A feeling of emptiness suddenly pulled at his soul: he would never go hunting with his partner again. The reality of it struck him as he watched his friend leave. He wished he could go too.

"Oh, Carlos, oh, Carlos, you ain't a comin' back alive from this one! You and your big ideas," Carlos Hathcock said aloud. Johnny Burke sat on a wooden crate scrubbing his M-14's bolt-face with a doubled-up pipe cleaner. Carlos sat on another crate. Between his feet a topographical map and several photos lay spread on the dirty plywood floor of the sniper platoon's command hooch.

"How on earth did I ever get myself into this one?" Hathcock said with a sigh.

"You're the best, Sergeant Hathcock. That's why you wear that white feather, isn't it?" Burke said, looking up.

Hathcock glanced at his partner. "Maybe. But, I ain't so sure about this one. Come here and look at these recon photos. I tell you, this one's suicide."

Burke laid his bolt on a towel and walked across the hooch. Hathcock had drawn an orange line on the plastic film that he had laminated to the face of the map to make it weatherproof. The line represented the path that the patrol, which dropped him off, would take. He was pondering the best route from there to his mission's ultimate destination.

"There ain't a stitch of cover within two thousand yards of that place," Hathcock said, pointing to an aerial photo that corresponded to an area on the map around which he had drawn a red circle. "I've got the tree line for cover up to here," his finger tapped the circle as he spoke. "All I'm ever gonna get at the guy is one shot. I've gotta make it count. Once that round goes, all hell's gonna break loose so the odds for a second shot are zero. I can't gamble on connecting at two thousand yards—it's gotta be eight hundred yards or less. That means I've gotta cover about fifteen hundred yards of open ground without being seen."

Burke knelt on one knee and shook his head. "Sergeant Hathcock, I don't know!"

Hathcock looked at Burke, an unusual expression of worry crossing his face, "I know." He looked back at the map and photos and again leaned his elbows on his knees, clasping his hands together beneath his chin, as if in subconscious prayer, "I've gotta go worm-style across there and hope they don't walk across me."

Burke walked back to his crate and sat down. He picked up his rifle's bolt and began scrubbing its face with a fresh pipe cleaner.

"Sergeant Hathcock, if anybody has the answer, you do. If it can be done, you can do it. But I gotta tell you the honest truth. Goin' into the NVA's headquarters and blowin' away their stud duck takes one hell of a lot more guts than I've got. Too bad you can't tell 'em to forget it."

"Nope," Hathcock replied without looking up. "Ain't my style. Job's gotta be done."

Carlos looked at his watch and softly laid it inside his footlocker with all his other personal items. He would leave everything behind on this stalk.

He took his bush hat with his left hand and gently slipped the wispy white feather from its hatband, dropping it between the pages of his Marine Corps issue New Testament. He placed the cigarette-pack size book in one corner of his footlocker and dropped shut the locker's wooden lid. Snapping the combination lock on the big box's hasp, he tucked on his bush hat, slung his rifle over his shoulder, and walked out to meet fate head-on.

As he walked through Hill 55's complex of deeply dug and heavily sandbagged bunkers, hard-backed tents, and antennae farms, Carlos listened to the new day come alive.

"Goooood morning, Vietnam!" a voice boomed from a nearby radio tuned to AFVN. "It's six-oh-five in the A-M and time to . . . Shout!" Joey Dee and the Star-Lighters' all-time rock and roll favorite, "Shout," echoed through the camp from scattered radios tuned to the Da Nang American Forces Radio station.

A black Marine with a gold-capped front tooth sat on a stack of sandbags next to his rocking and rolling radio. His steel helmet pot, half-filled with milky colored water, sat in the dirt before him. Lather covered his face, and he stretched his neck tight as he shaved under his chin, rolling his eyes downward in order to look in a mirror balanced atop the radio. Hathcock thought about how long it had been since he had stood in front of a bathroom sink and shaved with hot water.

He walked down the hill beyond the bunkers and joined a group of Marines wearing helmets and flack jackets. Each man had two fragmentation grenades and several pouches full of ammunition, balanced by two full canteens hanging on their cartridge belts. Carlos had only his rifle, one canteen hooked to his belt and a KaBar knife. He reached in his pocket and touched the tube of camouflage greasepaint resting there. He was scared.

The walk to the landing zone did not take long, neither did

the flight—due west and well into the high mountains that bordered Laos.

The Marine rifle squad moved quickly taking him to the departure point, and by noon Hathcock sat alone, his back against a tree, surrounded by heavy vegetation. He was preparing himself mentally for what he knew lay ahead. The fear that lay like a heavy animal inside his chest would need some calming.

DAY ONE

Carlos had calculated perfectly, as always in the past, and arrived at the tree line's edge just as the sun set. He covered his exposed skin with shades of light and dark green grease-paint from the tube that he carried in his pocket. Every but-tonhole and strap on his uniform held various-shaped leaves and grass.

Here, at the edge of the open country, he saw the NVA's heavily guarded buildings with their camouflaging and their fortified gun positions. He had no idea where in Southeast Asia he was at the moment and had not wished to ask. The terrain map he had studied had had no place names. From their flight path and the distance covered, he would not have been surprised if he was in Laos or even North Vietnam.

Under the cover of darkness, Carlos retouched his camou-flage paint and exchanged the forest's deep green leaves for the lighter green and straw-colored grass that now surrounded him and covered the vast open land ahead. He drew his can-teen and poured a capful of water. He brought the lid to his lips and sipped, his eyes constantly shifting and looking for signs of movement, his nose testing the air for any smell of other men.

For the next hour, he continued preparing himself, drinking sips of water from his canteen lid and relaxing in the tree line's cover.

Finally, his every move fluid and slow like that of a clock's minute hand, he lay on his side and slipped into the open. His Winchester rifle was clutched tightly against his chest.

His body was in constant motion, but the motion was so slow that a man staring at him from ten feet away would in all probability have seen no movement. He traveled inches per minute and yards per hour. From now until he reached his goal, Hathcock would not eat or sleep and he would drink rarely.

He had had no idea that he would have to move this slowly. The dry grass was about a foot above his head as he crawled slowly on. Hathcock noticed the stars in the clear night sky and prayed for rain. If it came he could move quickly, since the enemy's vision would be obscured and the shower's noise would cover his. Dampness would also soften the crackling dry grass and weeds.

The Marine sniper had crawled approximately thirty feet from the tree line when he heard the first enemy patrol approaching his position. His eyes strained to find them in the moonless dark. He knew they were closing in on him by each crunching footstep's increasing loudness. Hathcock held his breath. The patrol was very near. His lungs burned, and his heart pounded. Sweat gushed from every pore on his body. He was worried they would smell him. Absolutely motionless, he stared back at the trail of bent and broken grass that lay behind him.

Hathcock thought, "If they see me, then that's how. They'll see my trail." His lungs could take no more pain—he must have air. He felt like a pearl diver gone too deep, seeing the water's mirrored surface over him. Too much distance lay between him and the sweet air above. He remembered, as a boy, diving deep and swimming up, and how his lungs ached just as he reached the water's surface. Hathcock relaxed his lungs slowly—silently releasing the captive breath. He longed to gulp a replenishing surge of oxygen, but instead filled his lungs silently and very slowly with tiny puffs of air.

Movement near his feet nearly made him scream. A leg flashed by him. Another and another flickered past. The NVA patrol was now between him and the safety of the trees.

He heard one soldier clear his throat. Another whispered something in Vietnamese. Hathcock thought, "These guys are goofing off. They aren't even looking. They're safely in their own backyard and don't suspect a thing."

As the patrol passed, Hathcock watched them traipsing along beside the tree line, oblivious of his presence. "That looseness just might save my life," he thought. "Boy, will they be sorry," he told himself. A smile crossed his face, and his confidence soared. As soon as the enemy was out of earshot, he pushed on through the night.

DAY TWO

The hour before sunrise has a sleep-inducing effect. Nearly any soldier who has had to remain awake through the night will testify that the worst hour, when fighting sleep poses the greatest challenge, occurs when the night is darkest, coolest, and quietest—an hour or so before dawn.

Hathcock had to rest, but he could not afford risking sleep. In the past months, he had taught himself to nap, yet remain awake, his eyes wide open. He did not know what sort of self-hypnosis made it possible, but he always felt very rested following one of these ten-minute respites.

The flickering light from a small cooking fire caught his attention and brought him out of his catnap. "These dumb hamburgers!" he thought, "Another time and another place, and you would have been mine, Charlie."

An iron pot filled with boiling water and rice hung over the fire. Three NVA soldiers squatted nearby, sleepily waiting for their breakfast to finish cooking. They manned the "Quad-51" machine-gun position on the left flank of the compound. A narrow trail through the grass led from the compound, passed next to the machine-gun nest, made a sharp left turn, and then led arrow-straight to the trees. Lights shone through several windows of the main house. Carlos supposed that it had been a French plantation in years past.

Inside, the short, graying general leaned over a porcelain bowl filled with cold water. A thin white undershirt covered his hairless, sagging chest and wrinkled belly. Baggy white shorts covered his bottom. He wore no shoes but stood on the glossy teak floor in his stocking feet. The old officer's brown uniform rested neatly on hangers hooked to a peg on the door. Gold clusters and braid shone on the uniform's wide, red shoulder-boards and on the broad red patches sewn on his collar.

In an adjoining room that had been made into an office, the

general's aide-de-camp huddled over papers, shuffling them into order for the old man. They would inspect a battalion today. The day before, the general and his entourage had walked the perimeter, inspecting the security of his headquarters. He had found it satisfactory.

Hathcock had seen him, but the old man was too distant from the Marine sniper's firing point. Now the sun fully lit the new day. In the distance, Hathcock watched a white car pull away from the house, drive up the trail, and disappear into the tree line.

"Old man's gone for a while, I reckon," he told himself. "Good. That means that those guys will really slack off."

By late afternoon, Hathcock had put five hundred yards between himself and the tree line. More than twenty hours had passed since he had left the jungle's cover.

Just before sunset the white sedan drove up to the house and stopped. Carlos watched the indistinguishable figures walk toward the door. "Just keep it up, Homer—you and your hot dogs. I'll get you."

The evening security patrol began its first tour of the perimeter. Ten NVA soldiers fanned into a line and began closing toward Hathcock. He stopped his oozing wormlike slither and waited. He watched as the soldiers approached him in the dimming light. "It could have been worse," Hathcock thought, "They could have come before sunset."

After lying flat in the dirt for twenty-four hours, Carlos had attracted a following of ants. His body ached from hundreds of small lumps left by their bites. He wondered if enough ant bites could eventually kill a man. Sweat poured into his eyes as the enemy patrol came on. They were spread on-line with twenty- to thirty-feet wide gaps between them.

"Here I am, gettin' hell stung out of me," Hathcock thought, "my body crawlin' with critters, layin' here can't move—and here comes Homer and his friends. Hell, I'll probably crawl all the way up, never be seen, kill this old muckety-muck, and then when I try to leave, I'll die from all these critter bites. The ants will cart off my bones, and I'll wind up MIA forever."

Carlos watched the approaching patrol. He could see only three of the soldiers now, the remaining seven were on his blind, right-hand side. He watched the three NVA riflemen plod closer and closer.

"If the guy on my right don't step on me, I'll get by this one too," he reassured himself. But the soldiers were looking far ahead, toward the tree line, and they were oblivious to the sniper they had just passed.

DAY THREE

The sun found Carlos Hathcock twelve hundred yards from the compound's headquarters, its doorways and windows now clearly visible to him. He watched as the soldiers relieved and posted the guard. "It's as though they're back at Hanoi," he thought. Over everything hung the calm air of routine.

Throughout the day, he observed couriers filing in and out of the compound, reporting to the man with the red collar. The sniper kept to his steady pace. He could feel adrenalin surging at the thought that tonight he would halt and prepare to fire with dawn's first light.

He thought of how he had succeeded thus far. He also turned his attention to his escape. To the right of where Carlos would eventually lie, a small, almost imperceptible gully ran nearly to the tree line. Once he fired his shot, he planned to slide along the shallow and gently sloping gully and disappear through the trees.

"It's a good thing, Carlos," he told himself. "These hamburgers are so loose here, it'll take them half a day to figure out what happened."

Hathcock squirmed forward a few more inches and then, looking ahead of him, his confidence faded at the same time that his entire body stiffened.

The hunger, which had wrapped his stomach in knots for two days, vanished. The blood drained out of his face and the whole world took a violent spin. He wanted to jump up and run. He wanted to scream. He wanted to do anything rather than continue to lie there and look into the eye of a jade-green bamboo viper that lay coiled in the grass six inches from his face.

Panic ripped through every fiber of self-discipline that Carlos had ever been able to string together. He felt numb as his eyes focused on the deadly snake's emerald head, its ruby-colored eyes evilly slanted above head-sensing pits.

The snake was motionless but the sniper felt his own body shaking. "Gotta get hold here," he breathed slowly. "Oh Jesus! What if he bites me in the face! Control yourself! He ain't bit you yet." He knew this snake was neurotoxic like the cobra. One pop, even a little one, would kill him in minutes. "You've come too far to let a bamboo snake end it all," he told himself as he lay still and watched the viper flick its black, forked tongue from its yellow-rimmed mouth, testing the air.

Almost as though the shaken Marine had never existed, the glossy snake turned its head, whisked silently between broad stems of grass, and disappeared.

After Hathcock's heart slowed to its normal rhythm and the shaking effects of the adrenalin that sent his blood coursing through his temples had subsided, his nagging hunger returned, accompanied by a sudden thirst. "Where's the groceries!" he exclaimed to himself. "Where's the water!"

His hand found the canteen lid, and he began to carefully unscrew it from the flask. Half an hour later, he felt the wet relief of the now warm liquid soaking into his swollen tongue like water on a dry sponge.

Hathcock moved on, wincing with every inch he went. His hip, knee, and arm were covered with blisters from the three days of constant pushing. Shards of pain shot through his side. He had less than two hundred yards left to travel, and compromise began tempting him now.

"You can do it from here," he considered. In all his years of marksmanship competition, his best scores came from the thousand-yard line. "It's been all bull's-eyes and Vs from this distance," Carlos told himself. But in all his years of shooting, never had one shot been so critical.

A second voice told Carlos, "Stick to the plan. Don't change things now. Survival depends on it. Survive." Carlos always listened to that voice. It had kept him alive. "You thought out this plan when you were rested; now you're tired. Gotta stick to the plan—got to."

He pushed on toward where the slight depression came slicing through the grass. It was very much as he had estimated—almost precisely eight hundred yards from the target.

Darkness fell and, as he drew near to his planned firing position, Hathcock's anticipation mounted. He versed himself on everything in these surroundings that might affect his bullets flight. He was constantly aware of humidity, wind speed, and wind direction. The faint sound of men laughing caught his ear. He could imagine the North Vietnamese general and his officers drinking and toasting each other around a dining room table. "That general had better enjoy himself while he still can," Hathcock thought.

The Marine sniper watched as the nightly patrol began another round. "They don't even consider a ground attack," he reflected. "They're more worried about air assaults. Look at the bunkers and holes they've got around here. Everything's covered."

The last guard changed as Carlos Hathcock reached the shallow gully he had spotted on aerial photographs and that he had spent the last three days crawling toward. It was not even six inches deep, but it was wide enough for a man to lie in. The depression, which stretched fifteen hundred yards to the distant tree line, actually began here in the middle of the open field, and at its head there was a slight rise, on the back side of which Hathcock positioned his rifle. He unfolded a handkerchief-size cloth and laid it down beneath the weapon's muzzle so that the gases the rifle expelled from the barrel when he fired it would not raise up dust from the ground and give away his position.

DAY FOUR

When the sun sent its first rays across the wide clearing, the Marine sniper's eyes already blinked through the eight-power scope atop his rifle, searching for his target.

He had estimated the distance correctly—his experienced eyes verified eight hundred yards to the walkway. "I've got to get him standing still with either his face or his back toward me," Carlos told himself. "Don't compromise." He watched for signs of wind—trees rustling, smoke drifting from the cooking fires next to sandbagged gun positions, the waving of the grass and weeds between him and his target. But more important than these, he watched the mirage, how it danced and boiled above the earth and tilted with the wind.

From that he could calculate the wind velocity by dividing the angle of the mirage by four. After determining that, he could multiply the velocity times eight, which represented this particular range in hundreds of yards, and then divide that again by four and have the number of "clicks" or half-minutes of angle he would need for windage.

The sun climbed higher and sweat trickled down the sniper's cheeks. His eyes still fixed to the scope's lens, he felt his neck burn from the overhead sun that baked the ground powder dry and left the grass wilting in its heat.

From somewhere behind the complex of bunkers came the sound of an automobile's engine. The white sedan wheeled around the bunkers and stopped short of the walkway upon which Carlos held the rifle scope's cross hairs. The driver waited with the motor running.

"Here we go," Hathcock told himself. "Get a firm grip. Watch the cross hairs." The general stepped through the doorway, and Hathcock centered the man's profile in his scope. He waited for him to turn face-on. He did, but as the commander turned and walked toward the sniper's sight, the general's aide-de-camp stepped ahead of him. "Dummy! Don't you know that aides always walk to the left of their generals? Get out of the way!"

At every moment since the sun rose Hathcock had refined his attunement to the environment with computerlike detail and speed, judging the light, the humidity, the slight breeze that intermittently blew across his line of fire. He factored in the now-increasing heat and how the rise in temperature would elevate the mark of his bullet by causing the powder to burn more quickly when he fired. The air density and humidity would affect the velocity of his bullet, and the light would change the way his target appeared.

Based on his estimations, he decided to place his scope's reticle on the general's left breast, in case the breeze carried the round eight inches right. The bright sunlight warned the sniper to keep his aim high on the man's chest, but not too high, in case the heat raised the bullet's flight a few inches.

The group of officers walking out with the general departed toward the side of the house. It left only the old man and his youthful aide. Carlos waited. The young officer took his place at the left side of his superior. Hathcock said, "Now stop." Both men did. The sniper's cross hairs lay directly on the general's heart.

Hathcock's mind raced through all his marksmanship principles, "Good firm grip, watch the cross hairs, squeeze the trigger, wait for the recoil. Don't hold your breath too long, breathe and relax, let it come to the natural pause, watch the cross hairs, squeeeeeeeeze."

Recoil sent a jolt down his shoulder. He blinked and the general lay flat on his back. Blood gushed from the old officer's chest and his lifeless eyes stared into the sun's whiteness.

The general's aide-de-camp dove to the ground and began crawling toward a sandbagged gun position. The other officers, who had only seconds earlier left their commander's side, ran for cover.

The Marine sniper slid into the slight gully and, flat on his belly, began pulling himself stealthily along the ground with both arms. His rate of retreat seemed light-speed compared to his inbound time. Still smooth and deliberate, he traveled many feet of ground per minute. He now covered a distance, approximately equivalent to that which he had crawled across in three days, in four or five hours. The fact that no patrol approached him during his retreat told him that no one had seen his muzzle flash. In daylight, at eight hundred yards, that didn't surprise him. The patrols would be out, but they would be searching hundreds of acres. Once he thought he heard one far to his left.

It was almost nightfall when he reached the jungle's edge. Squirming past the outer layer of greenery, Hathcock lifted himself off his knees for the first time in three days. The pain was an excruciating counterpoint to his inner exhilaration. He hurried through the heavy forest. He was wary of mines and booby traps, but going as quickly as he dared, he covered the three kilometers to his preplanned pickup coordinate in a matter of a few hours.

There Carlos sat in a bush and waited, well aware that patrols might be scouring the jungle for his trail. His heart settled to a resting pulse. The songs of birds and other jungle creatures replaced the sound of heaving breath that had pounded in his ears. And as the hubbub settled to tranquillity, he thought of Arkansas and how similar this moment seemed to many childhood days behind his grandmother's house, when he sat in the bushes there—the old Mauser across his lap and his Shetland collie dog panting at his side. He closed his eyes for the first time in four days.

"Sergeant Hathcock," a voice whispered. "I thought you knew better than to doze off like that." The Marine who led the squad that had left Hathcock four days earlier now knelt by the bush where the Marine sniper waited.

Hathcock smiled slowly, not even opening his eyes at first. "I knew you were there," he said. "I heard your squad tromping up the ridge five minutes ago."

"Let's get going. Charlie's crawling over these hills, and we've got a lot of ground to cover between here and the LZ," the squad leader told him. "When we left the Hill, Charlie's lines were burning up. I guess you got that general?"

"Well, he hit the ground mighty hard," Hathcock said, pulling out his canteen and swallowing its last few drops. "Spare any water?"

"Sure," the Marine said, handing Hathcock a canteen and sloshing its contents out the open top. "We better book.* Charlie's mad as hell now. They'd love to get you after today."

Hathcock felt uneasy when the squad leader told him, "Charlie's mad as hell." During the flight back to Hill 55, he wondered if the assassination of the general would only arouse the North Vietnamese and Viet Cong to fight with greater fury.

He would always have mixed feelings about this day's work. As American casualties rose sharply in the weeks that followed, he began to feel that this was one sniper killing that might have been a mistake.

---

*Marine jargon meaning to go or to leave. Until early 1970s, Marines were required to sign out on liberty in the duty NCOs log book as they picked up their liberty cards. From that came the term "Book Out," which was shortened to "Book."

When Hathcock stepped off the helicopter, home at Hill 55's landing site, a group of smiling and whooping Marines met him. Burke stood among them and said, "White Feather made it."

Hathcock smiled.

The giant of a captain who'd recruited Hathcock for the mission slapped him across the back so hard that Carlos wondered if he had dislocated any bones. The hulking Marine put a pot roast-size hand on Hathcock's shoulder and said, "Son, I'm sure as hell glad to see you back in one piece. Lot of us kept you in our prayers. You did one hell of a job."

Walking up the hill toward his hooch, Hathcock felt the great fatigue from the mission finally take hold. He longed to lie down and sleep for days. But his standards were demanding. And despite the fact that this was his last mission—that he would leave Hill 55 in a few days to return to the MP company and on to the World by way of Okinawa—he remained true to them. He cleaned his rifle and gear before he rested.

15

Saying Good-bye

THE PROPELLER-DRIVEN Convair aircraft taxied to a halt in New Bern, North Carolina, at a few minutes past midnight. Carlos Hathcock, a brand-new civilian, discharged the day before at Camp Pendleton, California, sat alone in the back of the plane and looked out the Plexiglas window, trying to see if Jo and Sonny were there to meet him. Floodlights shone from the eaves of the terminal and made it difficult to tell who was whom.

It had been a long flight, and no one on the plane had spoken to him. He waited until the pushing mass of passengers had almost made their way through the doorway on the side of the airplane before he reached under his seat and brought out his green vinyl satchel with yellow handles and USMC written on the side, and walked out of the plane.

As he walked through the gate, he saw Jo standing there, holding their son and smiling, thankful that her husband had survived and had come home so that they could build a new life. Hathcock took his son in his arms and kissed his wife. The greeting lasted a moment and no one took notice of them.

He took his sea bag and vinyl suitcase from the baggage claim and left the airport, bound for his little house on Bray Avenue, a promised job with an electrical contractor, and a new life as a civilian.

* * *

Nearly one month later Carlos Hathcock sat next to Jo on the front porch of his small frame house and held his son on his knee, bouncing him up and down, playing horsy. He thought of the past long weekend. He had taken Thursday and Friday off and had driven to nearby Camp Lejeune where he watched the Marine Corps' Eastern Division Rifle and Pistol matches. There he met many of his old shooting partners from the Marine Corps team. He saw again that side of the Marine Corps that he loved and now missed.

The weekend with his friends had planted a seed of doubt in his mind. For eight years he had put down roots in the Marine Corps and now, as he bounced his giggling son up and down, his thoughts drifted away to the firing ranges, to the comradeship between friends, and to the competition and the possible chance of winning another national championship.

The night that he got home from Camp Lejeune's Stone Bay ranges, Hathcock told Jo that he missed the Marine Corps already. And from the tone of his voice, she knew that the odds of him remaining a civilian and staying out of the war had grown slim. She was well aware that Carlos did not like being an electrician, it had become obvious that going to work each day was an increasing drudgery for him.

"I was safer in Vietnam," Hathcock said sharply, after telling Jo how a screwdriver, hurled by an electrocuted co-worker, narrowly missed his head. "I don't like that job."

"What does that mean?" Jo responded. "You want to go back into the Marine Corps?"

He sat silent for a moment, looking at his son bounce. He felt a tightness in his stomach wrench into a hard knot with her response. "Would that be so bad?" he asked. "I'm a competitive marksman and marksmanship instructor. I'm sure not volunteering to go back to Vietnam."

"Carlos, I knew what you were when I married you. I've never liked the Marine Corps, but I accepted it. Don't feel like you're doing me and Sonny a favor by staying out and being miserable. I want you to be happy. That's what makes me happy."

By summer he and his family had moved from New Bern to Quantico, where he was assigned to the Marksmanship Training Unit and the Marine Corps' national champion rifle team.

Hathcock continued shooting the three hundred Winchester magnum rifle at a thousand yards as well as the M-14 on the National Match Course,* but he also began pursuing the international small-bore (.22 caliber) competition as well, hoping for a chance at the 1968 Olympics.

One day in July, 1967, Hathcock came home from Quantico's Calvin A. Lloyd Rifle Rangers and saw Jo waiting at the door, holding a letter with a Massachusetts postmark.

"Honey, you got a letter from Captain Land," she called.

He trotted across the lawn to the door, smiling. He had not heard from his friend since he left Vietnam. He tore the envelope open as he walked in the door, stopping for a moment to pick up his son and give him a bear hug.

As he settled into an easy chair, the 6:00 P.M. television news came on, and he put down the letter. A reporter spoke from atop a hotel in Saigon. He watched intently, hoping to hear of the 1st Marine Division and the war in I Corps.

During the commercial, Carlos looked at the letter that he had pressed flat on his lap.

Dear Carlos,

I'm glad to see that you made it out alive. At first I heard that you got out of the Marine Corps, but now I see that you have made it to the Big Team. You deserve it, my friend. You earned it.

I can understand you getting out for a while, you were pretty well burned out. I'm sure. I'm glad that you got back on your feet and reenlisted. The Marine Corps needs you.

I wish this letter could be all good, but I'm afraid that I

---

*National Match Course consists of firing twenty rounds standing slow-fire from the two hundred-yard line at an "A" target with a twelve-inch bull's-eye and six-inch V-ring; ten rounds standing to sitting rapid-fire from the two hundred-yard line at an "A" target with a twelve-inch bull's-eye and six-inch V-ring; ten rounds standing to prone rapid-fire from the three hundred-yard line at an "A" target with a twelve-inch bull's-eye and six-inch V-ring; and twenty rounds prone slow-fire from the six hundred-yard line at a "B" target with a twenty-inch bull's-eye and ten-inch V-ring. Total possible score on this course is three hundred points with sixty V's.

have some bad news. I got a letter from Major Wight the
other day. He said that the sniper program is really working
well. Burke got promoted to corporal and went to 1st Battalion, 26th Marines, and took charge of a squad. He was
really proud.

Burke and his men got assigned security duty up at Khe
Sanh and ran into trouble. Carlos, Burke got killed.

I don't know any more about it, but I feel sure that he
died with valor and not from some dumb mistake. After
all, you taught him well.

I know that you thought the world of him. I did too.
Next to you, he was one of the best Marines I ever had. I
feel a great deal of grief for him now, and I can imagine the
sadness you must feel too. He was a good, good Marine.
We will all miss him.

Carlos looked up, and his eyes flooded with tears. He
stepped into his backyard, looked at the setting sun glimmering through the tall oak and maple trees and thought of his
friend. The best partner he ever had. And as he stood looking
toward heaven, tears streamed down his cheeks. "What happened, Burke? What happened?"

Khe Sanh was a series of hills located in the northwestern
corner of I Corps along the Laotian border. Hundreds of paths
and tunnels branched from the Ho Chi Minh Trail and wound
past Hill 881 and Long Vei and through the steep mountains of
the Khe Sanh area. One lone mountain among that cluster of
peaks was Hill 950. There a small encampment of Marines
defended a combat outpost—one of the toughest corners of
the Khe Sanh neighborhood. It was the new home of Corporal
John Burke and his snipers.

Sleep came hard on Hill 950. There were no comforts of
home. If a Marine was lucky, his "rubber bitch" did not leak
and he could spend a quiet night in relative comfort. But the
nature of life in combat does not afford rubber air mattresses
staving off punctures, and thus Burke's leaked.

As he prepared for sleep, he blew it as full as it would hold
and placed a fresh Band-Aid taken from his first-aid kit, over
the pencil-point sized hole. But by 4 A.M. the hard ground and

rocks awoke him, and he would remain awake for the rest of the day. It had come to be a way of life.

The sun set at about 8 P.M. on June 6, 1967, and left the jungle greenhouse hot. Most of the Marines slept outside. Below, in the jungle, the men could hear the screech of birds and the chatter of other creatures. The Marines standing watch listened to the echoes of an animal roaring in the far distant hills. They felt sure it was the sound of a tiger. None of them had ever seen one, but they knew it stalked these jungles.

As the Marines who stood watch that night listened to the distant roar, faint and echoing between the rock walls of the tall mountains, another, more frightening sound disrupted the stillness of the night.

Inside the bunker, the field telephone croaked. Burke snatched the receiver, pressed the black rubber button on its side and gave his name.

"Got noise on the wire," the voice at the other end said. "Several cans rattled."

"Can you see anything in your starlight scope?"

"Nothing."

"Load up and be ready to fall back to your alternate positions. I'll roust everybody here."

Burke felt that familiar tightness build in his stomach. He did not like being on the defensive. It gave one no place to maneuver and only two choices of tactics, to hold or to retreat.

Burke began waking his men. The field phone rang again.

"Corporal Burke," he answered.

"Sappers! Looks like they're trying to blow the wire. I see a lot of people out there."

"Let them commit themselves to the attack, and then turn on the lights with your pop-ups. We'll all open on them when you put up those flares."

Hurrying outside, Burke heard the familiar pop of a rocket-propelled grenade.

"Take cover!" he shouted.

And as he spoke, the grenade exploded in the midst of the camp, wounding several of his men. Burke began dragging them to the bunker. He could hear the heavy bursts of his listening post's M-60 machine gun chewing into the sappers as they hurled their charges to the wire. He hoped it would hold them back until he got help.

More rocket-propelled grenades came whistling into the small outpost.

"Corporal Burke," a Marine called to him in the orange light of the pyrotechnics that now drifted down, burning as they dangled beneath their small parachutes. "Sappers are in the wire!"

Burke knelt next to the bunker and began picking off the Viet Cong who were sacrificing themselves to break a hole in the wire with their satchel charges. Suddenly a grenade exploded in front of the Marine who had called to him. A large fragment of it struck Burke in the hip but the main force of the blast took out the other Marine who was kneeling thirty feet away.

Burke had taught that Marine the way Carlos Hathcock had taught him, and with a shout he ran toward where the man lay writhing in pain, and as carefully as he could lifted him up and began to carry him toward the bunker's doorway. Before he could get the Marine inside, Burke heard the whistle of another grenade, and setting him down he fell across him. The explosion came a second later from somewhere close.

Burke felt the shrapnel tearing into his flesh, but ignoring his own wounds he got up and pulled his partner inside the shelter.

Burke could hear other wounded Marines crying out for help. He listened for the sound of the machine gun, and it spoke, belching a deadly stream of fire into the wire.

As he and another Marine struggled to pull a severely wounded man toward the bunker, a grenade exploded at his heels and sent them all rolling into the sandbags. Burke was bleeding from every limb. He listened for the machine gun. It was silent. Everyone lay wounded, and the end seemed very near.

Stepping into the bunker, Burke picked up an automatic rifle and hung a dozen grenades on his belt.

"What's going on?" a wounded comrade asked.

"Those gooners ain't comin' in here! Don't you worry about that! You just keep those rifles pointed out, and don't hesitate to shoot!" Lifting up his rifle, Burke went out the door.

The Marine charged the dozens of enemy soldiers who were stepping through the tangle of wire and hurled grenade after grenade at them. He held the M-16 in his left hand and with magazines taped end on end, emptied them into the soldiers who fell and scurried and twisted, caught in the wire.

Behind these soldiers, rifle fire erupted, and the familiar sound of rocket-propelled grenades echoed in the night. But Burke kept charging, killing the enemy, and because of his fury, the Viet Cong fled. They did not see Burke fall. They did not look back.

On April 30, 1968, nearly a year after his death, the Secretary of the Navy, Paul H. Ignatuis, acting for President Lyndon Johnson, signed a citation awarding Burke the United States' second highest medal for valor, the Navy Cross.

Even though the weather remained cool and pleasant at Quantico, Virginia, this April afternoon of 1969 burned hot in eastern Texas as Carlos Hathcock drove his blue Chevrolet Bel Aire along Interstate 10 outside Houston on his way to the National Rifle Association's regional rifle matches at San Antonio.

Hathcock looked forward to the San Antonio shootout because it would launch him into the 1969 Marine Corps Matches riding near his crest. If he did well there, he would reach his peak for the Interservice Matches and the National Championships at Camp Perry a week later. Just as in 1965, he saw the earmarks of another big year in 1969. He felt certain of that.

Squinting behind dark glasses, Hathcock strained to see the highway that disappeared into the setting sun. The radio blared a steady flow of country music above the hot, coastal Texas wind that roared through his car's open windows as the speedometer needle pointed at seventy and the dashed white line on the highway blurred past the left side of his car. He had left Jo and Sonny the day before at Quantico, and as he sang "Waltz Across Texas" with Ernest Tubb on the radio and watched the darkening Houston skyline grow smaller in his rearview mirror, he thought of his wife and son at home.

They had endured the long shooting seasons since the summer of 1967, seeing Hathcock only one or two days a week. If they wanted to see him more frequently, they had to drive to the rifle ranges and watch him shoot. Jo had never complained.

She knew that Carlos's shooting could not last forever. He had to do something else, other than compete with the rifle. She prayed for that day to come each time she watched her neighbors at Quantico enjoy weekends and evenings with their husbands.

But, hidden in her thoughts, also loomed the war, and she considered herself lucky compared to her friends whose husbands now fought in Vietnam. Each night on the news Jo watched wounded American soldiers looking into the cameras as their buddies lifted them onto helicopters. She saw the faces of men who, to her, looked too much like her husband.

Tonight, on the news, President Nixon talked of the prospects of peace with honor, yet during this very month of April 1969, as Hathcock drove through Texas, the United States reached its peak of military involvement in Vietnam with 543,400 American servicemen committed to combat there.

While Jo watched the nightly news, the telephone rang. She looked at the clock and reckoned Carlos had finally reached San Antonio. "That must be your daddy," she said to her son as she walked to the telephone.

"Hello."

"Honey. I got here all right, but I have a little bad news," Hathcock said calmly. "I can't shoot down here this weekend. I've gotta come home."

"Carlos, what's wrong?"

"I no more than walked in here and Gunner Bartlett told me not to unpack. I have orders waiting on me at Quantico, and I have to go straight back tomorrow."

"Carlos! Orders where?"

Jo felt the awful emptiness swell in her stomach as she asked. She held her breath as Hathcock tried to sound cheerful about his next assignment. "Well, it's to that big shootin' match across the pond."

"Oh, no, Carlos. You've already been. You just got back. They must have made a mistake!"

"I don't know. I sure didn't ask for these orders, but I don't think it's a mistake. Jo, I'll be home tomorrow night or Sunday morning at the latest. We'll talk about it then. I love you."

"I love you, Carlos."

16

Return to Vietnam

"AIN'T CHANGED MUCH," Hathcock said as he put out his hand to a sandy-haired Marine with a strawberry complexion who stood on the plywood porch of a hard-backed tent on Hill 55. "Looks like they improved the hooches some since '67. I'm Staff Sergeant Hathcock."

Gunnery Sergeant David Sommers took the outstretched hand of the slim-built Marine who Sgt. Maj. Clinton A. Puckett, a man who would later become only the sixth Marine to hold the title Sergeant Major of the Marine Corps,* had assigned him to sponsor. Sommers had already heard much about Hathcock, and he wondered how such a slight looking man could command such a reputation. He had expected a much larger, tougher looking Marine.

"I'm Gunny Sommers, 7th Marine Regiments' career planner and Headquarters Company's company gunnery sergeant. I also keep house in this hooch. I've got you a cot all the way down at the end."

Sommers opened the screen door, and Hathcock stepped inside the hard-back tent, which had a tin roof and long canvas awnings over each window. New metal cots replaced the old wooden ones that he had known two years earlier, and new plywood covered the floor.

---

*The Marine Corps' most senior enlisted Marine. Functions as the enlisted advisor to the Commandant of the Marine Corps.

Hathcock looked toward the end of the hooch and saw his cot. And there, atop his new bed, sleeping in the breeze that blew through the rear screen door, lay a shaggy red dog.

"Yankee!" David Sommers yelled, clapping his hands loudly. "Get off there! Get! Get!"

The dog awoke with a start, sprang from the cot, lunged into the screen door, knocking it wide open, and bounded outside like a startled burglar.

"That dog!" Sommers said frustratedly. I've never seen him inside before. Usually you couldn't get him inside any kind of hooch, even if you threw a steak on the floor."

The slim but hard-muscled gunnery sergeant walked to the cot where the dog had left dirty paw marks and began sweeping off debris with his hand. "Yankee's really not a bad dog," he said. "I guess he's like any other dog . . ."

"Or Marine," Hathcock said, looking back at the front door where Yankee now sat, his tongue lolling out the side of his open mouth and tail wagging across the ground, raising a cloud of dust. Hathcock whistled and knelt to one knee, and seeing the invitation, the dog nosed open the door and trotted to his new-found friend.

"He must sense something about you. Nobody could have gotten him back inside this hooch. I would have taken money on it. That dog is really picky about who he chooses as his friends."

"What you got around your neck?" Hathcock said to the dog, ruffling the fur on Yankee's throat and noticing a military dog tag fastened to a makeshift collar that someone had fashioned from an old belt. As Carlos read the tag he laughed.

It read: "Yankee" on the first line, followed by a row of numbers on the second and the initials USMC on the third line. Sex was indicated by the letter M, religion simply said, "All." But it was the last item that brought on the chuckles— "Blood Type: Dog."

"We'll have to go down to LZ Baldy if he ever gets shot," Hathcock said, grinning. "That Army camp is about the closest source of doggie blood."

Both Marines laughed, and Sommers said, "I don't think Yankee would like it. He'd probably rather try to get by without it."

"Sure a fine-looking dog," Carlos said. "Does he do any tricks?"

"He's full of 'em. But the smartest thing about him is that he knows an attack is coming ahead of time. You hear him start growling, head for the bunker. I don't know how he can tell, but a couple of minutes after he starts growling we'll start getting hit."

Gunnery Sergeant Sommers took Hathcock's sea bag and set it in the corner next to a foot locker. He looked out the door at the heat waves that boiled across the horizon and said, "I guess you know all about Arizona Territory."

"Pretty much. But it sure looks a lot different now. I remember there being a whole lot more trees."

"There were more trees. The war has gotten a lot worse since you were here last. Mostly what you see now is broken trees and bare fields."

Hathcock stood next to Sommers and looked out at the hills and valley below where forests had once flourished thick and green but which now revealed mostly gray skeletons in leafless desolation. "Arizona Territory. That all used to be a free fire zone. We never patrolled over there, just shot across at Charlie."

"We operate out there today," Sommers said. "Still lots of bad guys. Mostly the 90th Regiment and the 2nd NVA division. I think that we do most of our fighting there. One hot spot in particular is a little valley between here and Charlie Ridge. It has more shootouts than a Saturday night western. Troops call it Dodge City."

"1st Battalion, 26th Marines is over there. A good friend of mine, Boo Boo Barker, is with them," Hathcock said.

"Since I've been here, that's where a lot of the action has been."

"How long have you been here?" Hathcock asked.

"I reported to 7th Marines in late November. I didn't really like the idea of coming to Hill 55 because this place stays under constant artillery and rocket attacks and lots of lob-bombs."

Hathcock nodded his head, "I know about lob-bombs. Charlie sets off explosives underneath a satchel charge and lobs the thing in your lap. It's kind of like blowing a fire-cracker under a tin can."

"Right. It seems like every day we get hit. So when I came up here, I was anxious to get with a unit that would be off the hill more often than on it. But Sergeant Major Puckett, bless his soul, wants to keep me up here as the company gunny and career planner. He gets mad as hell when I go off in the bush."

Hathcock laughed, "Career planner in Vietnam? I don't envy you your job."

"That's the way I felt when he told me I was the career planner. Right off the bat, I decided to make the best of it and be just like the career planners back in the World—always out. I got me a boxful of those Mac Marine cards—the ones with 'It's a Good Career, Stick with It' printed on one side and the pay scale printed on the other. I walked down to the LZ and caught a chopper out to the battalions, right in the middle of Operation Meade River."

Sommers started laughing. "I got out there and started passing those cards out to the troops on line. Bullets and mor-tars were flying everywhere, and there I was standing over a hole, handing these two Marines those cards and telling them to come see me. I heard a little zip, zip, zip blowing past my head, and one of the Marines down in that hole gave me a funny look and said, 'Gunny... You're the braaaavest man I eeeever saw!'"

Hathcock roared and Sommers fought to finish his sentence between bursts of laughter. "It suddenly dawned on me that the zip, zip, zip were bullets whizzing past my ears. You should've seen how fast I jumped in that hole. I guess word got around about me because I have the highest reenlistment rate in I Corps now."

"Sergeant Major Puckett must like that," Hathcock said.

"Are you kidding? I thought Puckett was going to kill me. My only saving grace has been the reenlistments. He told me that I must stay close by the home fires. And that's why I stay in dutch with the man. I still get off this hill every chance I can, and he stays mad at me. I want to give you fair warning, I lead the sergeant major's hit parade."

Hathcock laughed. "I usually hold that distinction myself. I guess I'll meet the sergeant major tomorrow. That's when I get to see my new platoon."

"Yeah, you'll see 'em, all right," Sommers said a little grimly. "By the way, I think you ought to know that Colonel Nichols doesn't like snipers. He stays up there in that air-conditioned hooch, and from what I hear, snipers just don't figure in his scheme of maneuver."

"What's the colonel's name again?"

"R. L. Nichols."

"You think he might come around?"

"I wouldn't count on it. Your best bet would be to get after Charlie and win over the sergeant major. If he's on your side, he'll keep trouble off your doorstep. Besides, Colonel Nichols is on his way out. His replacement, a colonel named Gildo S. Codispoti, is already inbound. He's due to take over in a month. Work on impressing *him*."

Sommers looked down the hill at the rusted tin roof of a distant hooch and said, "Part of the reason the colonel has bad feelings about snipers is what you're going to see tomorrow. That platoon is nothing to write home about. But before we get into that, let's get you checked into the company. You'll step into that rats' nest soon enough. You got your orders?"

17

The Tribe

HATHCOCK WIPED SWEAT from his face as he walked from the 7th Marines command post, now on his way to the more familiar finger four where the sniper platoon's hooch still stood. He had spent the morning waiting to see the sergeant major and the commanding officer. When he finally did, he'd been given a typical welcome aboard filled with the standard rhetoric told to all new officers and staff NCOs and culminating with the cliché, "My door is always open. I'm glad to have you aboard." The meeting confirmed Hathcock as the new sniper platoon leader and gave him the license to walk down the hill and begin assuming responsibilities.

It seemed strange to Carlos that the outgoing platoon sergeant had not come to meet him. As he walked down the trail to the low hooch and the bunkers on finger four, he began looking for signs of life—anyone who might tell him where he could find the platoon sergeant.

"Anybody here?" he shouted as he walked close to the old canvas-covered hooch—the same hooch that he helped build two and a half years ago.

"In here!" a voice shouted back.

The place looked dirty and worn now, just like much of the country. Several tears in the canvas hung loosely open and the roof revealed hundreds of small holes, made by years of harassing small-arms fire. As Carlos stepped near the door, he lifted the torn screen with his hand and wondered why no one had tacked it down again. The unpainted door frame was now dark from weather. Black streaks stained the wood from the rusting nails that held the door together—the same nails that Hathcock and Burke had driven in in the fall of 1966.

The door screeched as Hathcock pulled it open on its rusty hinges and stepped inside. The room was filthy. It smelled like a combination of mildew, body odor, and stale beer. Odd gear leaned against the walls and littered the floor. Boxes and bins overflowed with empty beer cans, cigarette butts, and trash from C-rations.

"Where's the platoon sergeant?" Hathcock asked, standing in the open doorway.

"I'm him. What ya need?" the sergeant said, lying on a cot at the rear of the hooch. He slurped a beer and gave a healthy belch. The Marine wore a dirty green T-shirt and cutoff trousers. His jungle boots lay topsy-turvy on the dirty floor, among the cans and men's magazines.

"I'm your replacement."

The sergeant leaned on one elbow. "Welcome to the war."

"You guys just get back from the bush?" Hathcock asked.

"Naw," the sergeant said, gulping more beer. "They don't have any idea of how to use snipers. We just burn the shitters, fill out the mess-duty quotas, and stand perimeter security."

"Where are all your snipers?"

"Out, I guess."

"Where?"

"Don't know," the sergeant said, and opened up a *Playboy*.

"How many men you have?" Hathcock said. He could feel the muscles in his neck tensing. "You do know how many men you have, don't you?"

"About twenty or so, I think."

"How many rifles you have?"

The sergeant shook his shaggy head. "Hell, I don't know. Ask the troops when you see 'em."

"How many scopes you got? How many M-49s you got? Don't you know anything?"

"Yeah," the Marine said spitefully, looking at Hathcock. "You're pissin' me off, hassling me about this shit. Where you comin' from anyway? We're doing just fine. Nobody bugs us and we don't bug nobody. We pull our details, do our time, and go back to the World . . . alive."

"I remember you," Hathcock said. "You were here in '67. I taught you myself."

"Yeah, that's right. I got twenty-one confirmed kills and that's plenty."

"In two years you got twenty-one kills. In six months I got eighty confirmed. In two years you ought to have a hundred. You must have just quit as soon as you got this platoon. You found a good deal, hiding out here, drinking beer, and collecting tax-free pay.

"Well, I don't need you. You go on up to Gunny Sommers and tell him I kicked your butt out of this platoon. Maybe he can find some use for you for the next couple of weeks."

Hathcock took a deep breath and tried to control the anger in his voice. "I'm going out to find my platoon. You be packed out of here when I get back. You got any problems with that, go talk to Sergeant Major Puckett."

Slamming the door shut, Hathcock stormed toward the bunker at the base of the sniper encampment. A suntanned Marine was lying across a long row of sandbags wearing nothing except a pair of utility trousers with the legs cut off at the lower seam of the pockets. He wore sunglasses and was smoking a hand-rolled cigarette. Around his neck dangled a German iron cross and a metal peace symbol.

"You a Marine?" Hathcock asked walking up to the man.

"Yeah."

"You a sniper?"

"Yeah."

"Where is the rest of your platoon?"

"Here and there."

"Can you find them?"

"Sure. No problem. Who wants to know?"

"I do," Hathcock said, narrowing his eyes. "I want you to have them all back here by sixteen hundred today. Will that be a problem?"

"Naw. Most of the guys are goofing off or on work details around the hill. I can get them here in an hour."

"That's even better. You do that."

"You never told me who you are."

"Staff Sergeant Hathcock. Carlos Hathcock. Your new platoon sergeant."

The Marine stood and smiled. "You mean we finally got another platoon sergeant?"

Hathcock nodded.

"We ain't all shit birds, Staff Sergeant Hathcock. You hang tight, I'll round up the platoon."

As the Marine jogged up the hill, Hathcock yelled to him, "Tell them to bring all their sniper gear when they come to my muster."

The Marine waved his hand, acknowledging the last order, and continued jogging in his scuffed white jungle boots.

Hathcock sat down on the sandbags and waited for his platoon.

Less than twenty minutes passed, and one after another, his snipers began to appear. They stood together near the old hard-back tent and kept their distance from the new staff sergeant who wore a small white feather in his bush hat and sat staring quietly at the ground between his feet as if he were by himself. He was no stranger to them. They had heard of Hathcock during training sessions at both Da Nang's and Camp Pendleton's two-week sniper schools. He was one of several Marines that their instructors had cited as frightening, superhuman examples of what they should be striving to attain for themselves. Now the man with the white feather was here and owned them body and soul. Without saying a word, Hathcock had already gained their undivided attention.

Hathcock looked at his watch as he heard the suntanned Marine in the cut-offs shout to him, "Staff Sergeant Hathcock, we're all here—twenty-two snipers, including you."

The vision that met Hathcock's eyes would remain vivid the rest of his life. He had to grind his teeth to keep from laughing. His men stood before him dressed in the widest array of color and costume that he had ever seen. Most of the Marines wore berets, some brown, some black, some red, and others green. One Marine wore a bush hat but had it covered with such an array of pins and buttons that he looked more like a fly fisherman or conventioneer. Many of the men wore wire-framed sunglasses with lenses that ranged in colors from blue to dark green and yellow to pink and cherry red. Their dog-tag chains supported a wide assortment of hardware from beer openers and gold rings to religious medals and protest symbols. Flowers adorned several berets while feathers and beads dressed others.

None of the men wore shirts, all wore cutoff trousers. Their boots showed no sign of ever being polished, and they all needed hair cuts.

"Take off all those ridiculous hats and throw them in a pile right here," Hathcock said, pointing to the ground at his feet. He looked at the tan Marine and said, "You see that generator up the hill?"

"Yes, Sir."

"You see that gasoline can set out there by it?"

"Yes, sir."

"Bring it to me."

The Marine charged up the hill, grabbed the can, and returned, huffing out of breath.

Hathcock shook the little bit of fuel that was left in the bottom of the can on the pile of berets. He tossed the can back to the tan Marine and then removed his Zippo cigarette lighter from his pocket. He flicked it open and set the berets ablaze.

"The only reason that I don't make you strip off those cutoffs is I know you ain't wearing any skivvy shorts, and I don't want you running around here bare-assed naked. But when we hold muster from now on, you will be dressed in a complete utility uniform. I want you looking like Marines, not clowns.

"From now on you'll look and act like snipers. You're no better than any other line troopers so we don't dress any different. But, because you are snipers, those line troopers expect more out of you. They've been told that snipers are disciplined and tough, that they're elite troops. It took a lot of good Marines to develop that respect, and I am not going to let you foul it up.

"The only hardware you'll wear around your necks will be your dog tags, taped together so they don't rattle. If you wear glasses, they'll be the ones issued to you or ones that I personally approve. Get rid of the rest of that garbage. Any questions so far?"

One Marine raised his hand and Hathcock pointed to him, "Yes?"

"Staff Sergeant Hathcock. When we got here, we zeroed our rifles for five hundred yards, but in the past three months, I don't think we got more than a dozen kills between all of us. Now, we haven't been able to go on patrol all that much because of all the shit details we've been pulling, but when we do go, it seems that we miss more often than we hit."

"Good point," Hathcock said. "Right now, I want to get a roster. Tonight I will team you up in pairs. Tomorrow we are going out here and zero all the rifles for seven hundred yards. We will start from scratch. You will be looking like snipers, and I will have you shooting like snipers. Does that answer your question?"

"Yes, Sir."

The flames of the burning berets died in the smoldering ashes, and Hathcock tapped them with the toe of his new jungle boot.

"When we start fresh tomorrow, I want a fresh area too. The rest of the afternoon, I want you to field day this whole finger. I want all the trash raked out of the hooches and bunkers. I want all the porno pictures off the walls and the porno magazines get put in your footlockers or I will make a fire out of them too."

While Hathcock talked to his new platoon, the sergeant who had lain on the cot staggered up the hill beneath the weight of his seabag. Hathcock looked at the departing Marine and felt a flash of sorrow for him. He remembered him as a good Marine and a good sniper, and he wondered what had happened to him.

"One last thing. The cot in the sniper hooch is for the duty. We will man this post twenty-four hours a day, if possible. That sniper hooch is our headquarters, not a lounge or private room. If you have been living in there, you will move out and live in the proper hooches according to your rank. That clear?"

"Now, turn to and get this area squared away."

As the Marines began cleaning up and hauling away the garbage, Hathcock made a list of needed repair materials. He planned to make a stop at the supply tent tomorrow.

The sun set and the 7th Marines sniper platoon continued working, restacking sandbags, tacking down loose screens, and hauling away a year's worth of garbage. Hathcock walked toward his hooch, where David Sommers sat on a chair made of pipe and split bamboo.

"I wasn't sure how you would take that bunch," Sommers said as Hathcock stepped up on the small plywood porch in front of the staff NCO hooch. "I guess you started out on the right foot with them, I've never seen them work so hard."

"Gotta start by giving them some pride," Hathcock said, sitting across from Sommers. "I never saw the likes of that bunch. I've seen hippies that looked better. What on earth is going on, Gunny?"

"Drugs. Marijuana. Heroine. You name it. It's all happening here. Lot of guys on it. We've been on them pretty heavy, but I hear of entire Army units that have refused to go on patrol because of the problems with drugs and booze."

"You think my platoon . . ."

"I don't know. I wouldn't start worrying about that right now. You start fresh with them. My point is to be aware that the stuff is real popular among the troops. Just file it away and keep to your plan. Those troops you have are real good men, they just needed some leadership."

"I got that right off," Hathcock answered. "I just solved a big part of that problem."

Sommers smiled. "Yeah. I sent that sergeant over to the police tent. He'll finish out his last two weeks in-country passing out toilet paper and getting the shitters burned."

"That was a good sniper when I had him back in '67. What happened?"

"He stayed here too long. He's tired, I guess."

"No. I don't buy that. He had twenty-one confirmed kills and quit. When he quit, he quit altogether."

"Too bad," Sommers said. "He's had a shit-bird reputation since I've been here."

Hathcock looked at the gunnery sergeant curiously, "In the conversation I had with my snipers, one Marine mentioned that they haven't had the opportunity to go on operations, that they've been pulling shit detail instead."

Sommers nodded. "That platoon has never produced anything that would give anyone an idea of what they do, other than wander around with deer rifles and pick off stragglers. The sergeant major uses them for whatever has to be done on the hill because they don't seem to serve any other useful purpose. You'll have your hands full changing all of that."

"Gunny, I'm informing you officially that my men are in training tomorrow. That has priority over shit detail. They'll be zeroing their rifles and getting ready to go on patrol."

"I'm all for that. But there're a lot of folks who'll bitch because somebody has to burn the shitters. They won't like filling those quotas that your Marines filled."

"It's their quotas that my men were filling. It's time to balance the books!"

"Staff Sergeant Hathcock, the sergeant major is going to raise hell. It's nothing new for me. Like I said, I lead the sergeant major's hit-parade. I have a hunch that you and I will be competing for that number one spot after this. It's your choice right now. Once you make it, the sergeant major will be on you just like he's on me."

"There's no choice to be made, Gunny. My snipers come ahead of my own pleasure. I've got a hunch that fella I just relieved might have tried to get along and keep everybody happy. He was a good Marine when I first knew him. But you can only compromise so far. I think he chose to keep folks on the hill happy, and his Marines went to hell in a handbasket."

Hathcock stood, "I've gotta go inspect my area and cut the troops loose. You eat chow yet?"

"No. I'll wait for you to get back. We'll go together."

"Sounds good," Hathcock said smiling.

Before the sun revealed any light to the black sky the following morning, Hathcock sat behind a field desk in the sniper platoon hooch. He glanced down a roster of names and from it paired a senior-ranked Marine with one of a junior grade on each of ten teams he organized. He took the odd man, a corporal from London, Ohio, named John Perry. He would rotate these combinations of men and equipment until each team satisfied him. Hathcock compared it to arranging marriages, since much of a team's success depended on the compatibility of the two partners.

The Vietnamese summer, which extends throughout the major portion of the year, drying the monsoon season's mud brick-hard in its blistering heat, had set in long before Carlos arrived in-country during the final days of May 1969. Hot dust now covered this crackling world, its shades of green stripped treeless-brown by the bullets and napalm from a decade of fighting.

As Hathcock sat sweltering in the darkness before another sandpaper day in this dusty, hot land, the afternoon heat of South Carolina June broiled the left arm and face of Staff Sergeant Ronald H. McAbee. With his bare arm propped out the window, he drove his car through the sunny countryside near the house where his wife waited for him to arrive from Texas. He had left San Antonio the day before and slept in a roadside park in Alabama.

McAbee had spent two weeks at San Antonio with the Marine Corps Rifle Team, competing in the Texas State and NRA Regional rifle matches. Like his friend Carlos Hathcock, Ron McAbee departed from Texas with orders for Vietnam. During his tour at Quantico, he and Hathcock had become close friends—like brothers, he would tell anyone who asked.

Ron McAbee first met Hathcock at Camp Lejeune at the end of the Marine Corps rifle and pistol matches in the spring of 1967. McAbee had just finished shooting his .45 caliber "hard ball" pistol in the final day of individual competition when he met Hathcock in the red brick barracks at the rifle range near coastal North Carolina's Sneed's Ferry and Topsail Island. That night they crossed the tall bridge that leads to the beach community and drank Jim Beam bourbon whiskey and water at a tavern there. McAbee was allergic to beer.

McAbee knew that Hathcock was in I Corps, but he did not know where. He guessed his friend would probably be at the 1st Marine Division's Scout/Sniper School, now at Da Nang.

In fact, when Carlos arrived in Vietnam, he had been destined to teach at the sniper school. He had called the 1st Marine Division's operations officer from the Da Nang airport when he arrived in-country. That colonel sent a jeep and driver for this very special Marine. He even offered him the position of senior instructor at the school, but Carlos wanted action, not classes. He told the colonel that he could do the 1st Marine Division more good with a platoon of his own.

Now, as dawn boiled above the South China Sea, Hathcock stood in the doorway of his sniper hooch waiting for his first muster. The fresh start for 7th Marines' snipers.

Already, before others in the encampment above them had stirred, most of the sniper platoon sat below the sandbag wall of their command bunker, talking. This morning they wore a variety of uniforms from pickle colored sateen—the standard stateside Marine Corps issue—to jungle camouflage uniforms with slanted patch pockets. Others wore uniforms cut from the same design as the camouflage but in a solid green color like the sateen utilities. The effort was obvious and Hathcock accepted that for now.

Hathcock shouted, "Corporal Perry!" and a Marine leaped to his feet and snapped to attention in front of the hooch.

"Yes, Staff Sergeant Hathcock."

"Supply have trouble keeping you people in uniforms?"

"Yes. We get one set of utilities at a time. Several of the troops didn't have any, so they borrowed extras that some guys managed to rat hole, or they wore regular sateens. They're all Marine Corps issue, though."

"I can see that. We all need to be dressed alike, or at least close. I prefer cammies. Where's the nearest supply point?"

"On the hill. But they don't have any. If you want real utilities, you have to go down to the Force Service Regiment at Da Nang. But you gotta have paperwork from Division to get anything from them."

"I'll keep that in mind. By the way, you'll be my shooting partner, unless you work out better with someone else."

"That's fine, Staff Sergeant Hathcock."

Hathcock spent the next hour reading the initial pairings of teams and answering questions about how flexible these partnerships would be. He explained that each man could have a combination of partners, no one would be teamed with any one man. But all partnerships must be close. Both members of the team must understand and be able to almost read his partner's mind. This would take time, Hathcock told them.

By ten o'clock that morning, the twenty-two snipers were behind their rifles, outside the wire, shooting at targets seven hundred yards away, zeroing their sights for that distance.

Meanwhile, back at the sniper hooch, the outgoing platoon sergeant flopped on the duty cot. He had gone to see Sergeant Major Puckett, just as Carlos had told him to do if he had a problem with being kicked out of the platoon. The sergeant major took exception to the quick decision by this newly reported staff sergeant and told the sergeant to return to the sniper platoon and work there until he left Vietnam in less than two weeks.

The sergeant major rang the sniper command post telephone, but no one answered. He sent a runner down with the newly returned sergeant, but that man came back with an empty shrug for a response. Finally, at ten o'clock, when the sergeant major received word from the operations office that the sniper platoon was outside the wire, sighting in their weapons, he shouted. "Get me Gunny Sommers!"

Sergeant Major Puckett also heard complaints from the camp commandant—a lieutenant in charge of the order and cleanliness of the regimental area. Half of his detail destined to collect the cans from each of the field toilets and burn them on the downwind side of the hill, had not reported for duty this morning.

At eleven o'clock, a jeep roared to a halt at the small firing range that Hathcock had helped Captain Land construct in 1966. David Sommers casually asked Hathcock, "You ready?" He did not have to say more, Hathcock already knew the trouble.

"Perry, take charge of the platoon and take them back through the wire at fifteen hundred this afternoon, if I'm not back. Spend the rest of the day working in pairs, practicing stalking and movement. Don't get all bunched up and keep your security out."

When the jeep halted at the sergeant major's tent five minutes later, Sergeant Major Puckett stood outside with his arms folded, waiting.

Hathcock stepped up to the sergeant major and smiled. "What can I do for you, Sergeant Major?"

"Be there when I call you, Staff Sergeant."

"I got my platoon up early this morning, getting them ready for operations. We've got a whole lot of work to get done. I've got this here list of supplies I need, and I gotta get authorization to go down to Da Nang to get cammies for my snipers. Sure could use your horsepower. Could you help us?"

"When you leave your hooch, I want you to carry a radio. I had several things happen this morning, and I needed to talk to you."

"I'll be glad to carry a radio. You get me one and I'll carry it. In fact, I could use three or four."

"See the comm chief, he'll sign them out to you. Second thing. Where were your men who had police detail this morning?"

"I wasn't aware of anyone who had police detail, Sergeant Major. Which Marine was he?"

"About a dozen men in your platoon!"

"I only have twenty-one men. That's more than half my platoon. That's a heavy quota. Do all the other units give up sixty percent of their Marines to burn shitters?"

"Don't get smart with me, Staff Sergeant. We have priorities, and your men have not been committed to any action, therefore, they will pull police duty or whatever else that is necessary around this hill. They aren't paid for doing nothing."

"I beg your pardon, Sergeant Major. My men have been working all morning. They will be working long after everyone else has kicked back for the night too. We have a lot of lost ground and training to get caught up on so that we can get back into action. We will pull our fair share of duty. Every man, including myself. With all due respect—"

"Can it, Hathcock! I'll hit the other units for quotas. You will pull your fair share, too. If I find one of your men lazing around the hill, I'll have your hide for it. Clear?"

"Yes, sir."

Hathcock stood at attention and, with all the sincerity he could muster, said, "Sergeant Major, I'm on your side. In fact, I would be honored if you would consider joining us. I'll set aside for you one of the best rifles. I just need your help. I need supplies. My men need working uniforms. You help me get this and I'll give you a sniper platoon that 7th Marines can brag about."

Puckett was a man who had always done what he thought was best for his soldiers, and now, in spite of himself, he had to be impressed. "I'll do what I can for you, if you're serious," he said sternly. "Don't you embarrass me."

Hathcock reached inside the large cargo pocket on the leg of his camouflage trousers and pulled out a list that he had typed early that morning in the dim light of a small lamp. "Here's a copy of my shopping list. I sure appreciate the help." He walked back to the jeep where David Sommers waited and left with him.

All the way down the hill, the two men laughed. "Hell, Hathcock, he'll probably deliver the stuff himself. You sure stuck your chin out, inviting him to become a sniper. The sergeant major's just gunji enough to do that."

"Good! If he's one of us, then he can't be against us."

"Yeah. But he'll still be a pain in the ass. You know, he's got to take care of everybody else too."

"I hope he does," Hathcock said, jumping out of the jeep.

That evening, when Hathcock walked into the sniper hooch, he found the old platoon sergeant reclining on the duty rack, wearing his dirty jungle boots and reading a paperback western.

"Sergeant Major send you back here?"

"Yeah," the sergeant said without taking his eyes from the book.

"You think you can generate enough energy to answer this phone, if it rings?"

"Yeah, no problem."

"For the next two weeks, you're phone watch."

The sergeant glanced at Hathcock and then turned his eyes back to the book.

Hathcock slammed the door as he left and grumbled all the way to the staff hooch where he found Sommers sitting outside, drinking a Coca-Cola.

"Two weeks with that bum! I don't know how I'll do it. I can't stand two minutes with him!"

"Cool off, Hathcock. Look at it this way. The sergeant

major will have someone to talk to when he calls. Who knows, maybe he'll get tired of seeing him lie back there and put him to work."

"Burning shitters? No sergeant's gonna burn shitters. Not even him. But now that I think about it, he may give me the space I need to get these snipers trained and put to work."

Sommers smiled and raised his soda can in a toasting salute. "See, even that dark cloud has its silver lining."

Mid-June heat cooked brown what little green color existed in the elephant grass in the valley below Hill 55. The summer sun sent the mirage boiling in heavy waves above the many empty rice fields that had flourished with tall stands of grain only a year before. Beyond the fields, near the broken trunks of hundreds of denuded trees that prickled the hillside with their shattered, gray skeletons, Carlos Hathcock and three of his snipers trudged in the shimmering heat, carefully following a plan set out by the patrol leader—a corporal who Hathcock was evaluating.

"You seem pretty familiar with this plan," Hathcock said in a low voice to the corporal as they stopped to rest in the cover of several of the downed logs. "You walk this ground very often?"

"Yes. I've done it about three times this week, in fact."

"You took this route three times this week?"

"Sure. I've gotten kills every time too. I thought that today, with four of us, we would hit the jack-pot."

"Or Charlie will hit the jack-pot. You underestimate your opponent, Corporal. That's deadly. Do you think they're going to let you walk out here three times a week and not leave you a little present?"

The corporal was silent.

"Where were we headed next?"

"Down this slope and through that cane."

"That the same route you took the last time you crossed here?"

"Yes. It's a long way from where we're going to set up. It's the quickest way through here."

"You think we ought to go through there?"

"No," the corporal said, "We'll have to go around and follow the contour of the hill, instead. It'll take about forty-five minutes longer."

"Right," Hathcock said. "Now let's walk down to that cane and see what that trail has to offer."

Cautiously, the four Marines crawled over a high, dirt dike below which a tall stand of cane grew green and straw brown. Sitting on his heels Hathcock searched for trip wires. A tense smile spread across his face.

"You see it?" he asked.

"No. Where?" the corporal asked.

"About knee high, all along the edge of the cane. See it?"

The corporal looked closely, and as the breeze rustled the cane back and forth, his eye caught in a flash of sunlight, the fine, black wire stretched across a twenty-five-foot expanse of cane.

Hathcock was watching his expression closely. "All right, good," he said. "Now look on the backsides of these thick stalks. See 'em?"

The corporal eyed each tall shaft of cane from its roots to its leafy, thin top. Suddenly he snapped his head toward Hathcock, his eyes open wide. "Yes!"

Hathcock said in a low voice, "I see at least four grenades tied in right here. That daisy chain stretches across the entire front of this field. Anybody walking through would be blown to pieces against this dike. I wouldn't no more go through there now than I would tap-dance in a mine field."

Unhooking a hand grenade from his belt, Hathcock looked at his men and said, "You men get on up over that dike. I'm gonna roll this down in the field and see if I can't set off Charlie's trap."

The three Marines scrambled up the bank and over the top as Hathcock worked loose the pin with his left hand. He crawled halfway up the embankment and then tossed down the small bomb filled with heavy explosive.

Suddenly, a portion of ground gave way beneath Hathcock's boots. His feet slipped as he scrambled at the top of the high bank, and, as he slid, he yelled. His Marines responded with six hands that grabbed hold of his shirt and pack and jerked him so forcefully that in a second he was airborne. His hundred fifty-pound body flew over the top just as the cane field exploded, sending thousands of deadly steel shards into the dirt bank where he had struggled. The four Marines were showered with leaves and dirt and fragments of cane stalk.

Pale as oatmeal, Carlos looked at the three wide-eyed Marines beside him. "That wasn't too smart either. Thanks."

He looked down at his hands shaking from the adrenalin his body had poured out. "The next time you do something like that get behind cover *before* you throw the grenade."

The corporal looked at Hathcock and said, "I started to say something, but I thought that was the way you did things. A little more gutsy than the rest of us."

"A little more stupid," Hathcock said with a laugh. He was glad to be alive. He stood, dusted off his trousers and took his three snipers on to the point. They killed three Viet Cong that day.

June was a busy month for Hathcock; he sent three sniper teams to work with 1st Battalion, 7th Marines, commanded by Lt. Col. John Aloysius Dowd, who welcomed the opportunity to employ this added dimension of firepower. Hathcock felt honored because Dowd's battalion saw the most action and led the regiment in enemy killed.

During April his battalion killed one hundred sixty North Vietnamese Army troops, fifty-one Viet Cong, and took one prisoner. The second and third battalions killed fifty-eight and eighty-five of the enemy respectively in the same period. In May, Dowd's Marines tallied forty-four NVA killed in action, forty-one Viet Cong, and took two prisoners, while the second battalion killed none and the third killed thirty NVA.

The first battalion seemed to be where the action always occurred, and Hathcock, who had a high opinion of Dowd, was delighted.

While the six snipers operated with the first battalion, Hathcock sent eight others to the division's sniper school at Da Nang. Next month he planned to send four more, and two others after that. By mid-August, he calculated, his platoon would be 99 percent operational.

He faced another problem, however, that would not be so easily solved—rifles. When he reported to Vietnam, he anticipated seeing nothing but the M-40 rifle in use. He saw the first arrivals of the new sniper weapon in January 1967, therefore, it was not unreasonable to expect this weapon—a Model 700 Remington 7.62mm rifle with a 10-power light-gathering, range-finding scope—to be the common denominator among snipers. But what he found when he arrived left him bitterly disappointed. There were vintage World War II era Model 70 Winchesters and M-1D sniper rifles, as well as a couple of M-40X rifles—the test model of the M-40.

The sniper arsenal offered him nothing more up-to-date than the weapons he had left behind in 1967, and in fact, he believed he was handling some of the same rifles he'd fired then. Only now they were a little worse for wear.

"Be nice to have an armorer assigned to the platoon," Hathcock told David Sommers one hot June evening as the two Marines sat on the front porch in bamboo-bottomed chairs.

"You talk to the sergeant major about it?"

"I mentioned it, but he told me that he would be glad to ask for one if I knew where one could be found. I'm out of answers. He did tell me that an assistant platoon sergeant will be coming from division soon."

"That's good news."

"Good or bad. You never know. Kind of like a blind date —you expect the worst and hope for the best. My luck, it'll be an ugly, old, toothless, fat girl."

A week later Hathcock was scratching out notes with his black ballpoint pen on a yellow, legal-size pad. The sweat ran down his shirtless back and soaked into his trousers.

Suddenly the door burst open and two loud feet stomped across the sniper hooch's plywood floor. Hathcock raised his head as he heard the thud of a hundred pounds of personal gear, bound inside a long, green seabag, hit the floor behind him. A familiar voice boomed, "The name's McAbee—Staff Sergeant McAbee. Just call me Mack!"

"Mack!" Hathcock said, twisting around on his stool. "You old horse thief. What in the world are you doing here?"

"Carlos! You the platoon sergeant?"

"Yeah!"

"Hell! I'm your platoon armorer."

To have as his assistant a man who was not only his best friend, but one of the very best high-power rifle armorers in the Marine Corps was a good deal beyond his wildest dreams.

"Look out Charlie!" Hathcock said, laughing and embracing his friend.

"The first project on the agenda is to overhaul all these old sticks we've been shootin' with. You're gonna have your work cut out with them. They're in pretty humble shape.

"What this platoon needs is a set of rifles to choose from like a pro golfer picks clubs—the right one for the right job. Custom-fitted for each man. If you can get our weapons tuned up like that, we'll be the hardest thing to hit this country yet."

"Carlos, you get the parts and machinery and I'll do the rest."

"Soon as you get settled, you're gonna get a truck from 11th Motor T and head down to 1st Force Service Regiment at Da Nang and use their shop. I'll get the sergeant major to grease the skids."

It took three trips to Da Nang before McAbee completed the major work on the rifles. From then on, he passed time at a bench he built in the sniper hooch, fine-tuning each weapon. It was a job that had no end, and he knew it. But with the new glass* jobs and refitted and matched receivers and barrels, suddenly the sniper platoon's kills rose to the level that rivaled battalions.

July ended with the 7th Marines sniper platoon confirming seventy-two kills. Hathcock felt certain it was a record.

For Hathcock and his snipers, McAbee's arrival had turned their lives sweet. His fine gunsmithing coupled with the keen training and leadership that Hathcock provided resulted in a platoon that became one of the best in Vietnam. For their outstanding achievement the platoon received a Presidential Unit Citation, one of the few platoons to ever receive such recognition.

---

*A bed of fiberglass moulded into the rifle stock over which the barrel will freely float. It prevents the stock from warping around the barrel, possibly touching it and affecting the expansion of the barrel as the rifle is fired, throwing off the accuracy of the shot.

* * *

Sergeant Major Puckett had a different view of things. Out of sight meant trouble to him. He felt that Hathcock or his second in command, McAbee, should be available—and accountable—at any given moment. It was a sound command-and-control philosophy shared by most Marines, and Puckett was undoubtedly right in feeling that the sniper sergeant had to take the responsibility of command as seriously as he took the business of getting out in the field and zapping "Charlie."

Hathcock had a hard time sitting in his hooch and pushing papers, remaining by his radio and being always available for the sergeant major's beck and call. Once Hathcock delegated assignments, he and McAbee grabbed their gear and went to the field too. As Hathcock saw it, the sergeant major could always reach him by radio. Most often he would be with Bravo Company, 1st Battalion, 7th Marines.

He had built a bond with that company and its commander, a captain named Hoffman who had reached the enlisted rank of gunnery sergeant and received a battlefield commission. After the war the Marine Corps withdrew his temporary commission and made him a gunny once again. But because this captain "spoke the enlisted man's language," and was a "straight arrow," Hathcock trusted him completely.

While Sergeant Major Puckett fumed because he could not reach anyone at the sniper hooch, Hathcock and several of his snipers spent the first ten days of July working the bush along Western Route 4, between the hamlets of Hoi An and Thuong Duc, supporting Lieutenant Colonel Dowd and his 1st Battalion Marines.

During that brief period, they cleared the area of all enemy positions, and on July 10 escorted the first convoy to successfully pass along this route in more than four years.

July 10 found Hathcock and McAbee peering from behind tall shafts of dry elephant grass, searching a broad clearing. They had moved away from Route 4, looking for signs of enemy movement. McAbee carried the radio and held the handset next to his ear as Hathcock scoured the landscape with his twenty-power M-49 spotting scope.

"Mack, I don't see a thing moving out there. But there is

this little hump six hundred yards out there that I want to stay and watch just a bit. It strikes me a little curious—somehow it just don't fit."

The grassy hump rose from the ground fifty yards from a cluster of trees and much taller grass. Hathcock thought it a likely spot for an enemy patrol to break out. It was the most narrow point in the clearing and seemed to be the most likely place for anyone to cross.

"Perry got a kill," McAbee whispered to Hathcock as the two men lay cooking in the afternoon sun. Hathcock glanced at his watch and noted the time—3:30 P.M.

"How long ago?"

"About fifteen minutes."

"I never heard a thing."

"Yeah, he stayed with Charlie Company when they moved on down by that river. He set up there on a bluff, overlooking that big bend in the river. Perry said he no more than settled in and this Viet Cong laid down his rifle, shucked off his clothes, and started taking a bath right there. One shot put an end to his bath."

"Where's Perry now?"

"He had just moved out when he came up on the net. He's got a patrol covering him, so he's moving out in the direction that the VC he killed came from."

"Look!" Hathcock whispered urgently.

McAbee put his eye to the spotting scope and saw a head rising out of the hump.

"Told you that looked funny."

Hathcock snuggled behind his rifle and laid his cheek against the old Winchester's humped stock. He found his proper eye-relief behind the Lyman 8-power scope that he had selected for this particular mission. Mack had come across with the fine-tuned rifles and now Hathcock did select them like a golfer selects clubs. For this mission, he chose a Model 70 Winchester, shooting a 180 grain, 30-06 bullet, and the Lyman scope for what he called medium range shooting—three hundred to seven hundred yards.

McAbee could hear Hathcock's slow and steady breathing stop, followed by the sudden explosion from the muzzle of the

Winchester. The Viet Cong guerrilla, who had begun climbing out of the hole, suddenly fell on his face. Hathcock waited, staring through his scope. He waited for anyone else who might have been in the hole with the man.

"Look to the left," McAbee whispered.

A man wearing black shorts and a khaki shirt trotted across the open field. He held an AK-47 in his right hand, and when he knelt next to the dead comrade, Hathcock dropped him too. He waited again.

"Here comes another one," McAbee whispered.

"Got him," Carlos said, waiting for the Viet Cong soldier to reach that point where the earth rose slightly and the two men lay dead. The rifle cracked and the third man joined the other two, and Carlos waited.

"Somebody's peeking out of the grass where those two hamburgers came from."

"Got him."

Hathcock followed the soldier, who carried an AK-47, as he cautiously edged from the grass and walked toward the hole. He knelt to one knee, and before he could stand, Hathcock killed him too.

"Four. Any more?" Hathcock asked quietly.

"Yes, looks like three others. They're just sitting on the edge of the clearing trying to see what's happening. With the wind blowing in our faces, I don't think they can figure out where the shots are coming from. That must be their hole, and they're trying to get in to take cover."

"I figured they had some sort of tunnel there. That patrol was headed home." Hathcock waited quietly for ten more minutes, and then the three soldiers rose to their feet and walked cautiously toward the hump and the four dead men.

"Three-round rapid fire," Hathcock said, chuckling as he sighted through his scope. His first shot surprised the group, and the two still-living men turned to flee. A second shot dropped one, leaving him kicking on the pile of bodies. The last man pirouetted in confusion. He was still spinning when the bullet shattered his breast bone, exploding his heart and killing him as he whirled in his death dance.

"Damn! Carlos," Mack whispered in wonder. "I've never

heard of a sniper killing more than seven at a time!"

"I took on a company a long time ago. I don't know how many I killed then. But there was this one sniper I knew back in '66 who killed eleven at one time—all confirmed. I guess that's the official record, if anybody really cares about things like that."

"I guess you're right. You start shooting for record, like it's the Marine Corps Matches or something, and you could go off the deep end. Anybody who enjoys this has got to be crazy."

"Yeah," Hathcock said quietly. "Crazy."

McAbee buried his face in the crook of his arm, and Hathcock watched the big man's body tremble.

"You okay?"

McAbee raised his face from his arm and looked at Hathcock. "I'm ashamed. I was laughing."

"Why?"

"That was the stupidest bunch of gooks I ever watched. They were about as dumb as I've ever seen, walking up there like that." He started chuckling again and Hathcock smiled, seeing the humor in the midst of the ugliness.

"It is kind of funny, come to think about it."

The two Marines moved further up Route 4 and hid on a hill, in a twisted mangle of shattered trees, devastated from heavy shelling and now covered with low, new plants that found sunlight in the absence of the trees' umbrella. There they spent the day waiting for any unlucky enemy who tried to cross the narrow stream that flowed five hundred yards away from them.

"Except for yesterday, this whole operation has been slow as syrup," McAbee said, squinting through the spotting scope, examining the tangled and fallen jungle for signs of a hidden enemy.

"Looky, looky, here comes Charlie," Hathcock said.

A Viet Cong soldier wearing an open white shirt and black shorts walked along the edge of the stream, holding his rifle over his shoulders like a yoke. He walked with a staggered gait, and even at five hundred yards, the two snipers could hear him singing.

"He drunk?" McAbee asked.

"Don't matter," Hathcock said as he sighted through his scope. "He's gonna be dead soon as I crank this round in him."

The rifle recoiled and Ron McAbee expected to see the man drop, but after a jolt that sent the enemy soldier to his knees, he began to run. He ran straight for them, shooting blindly.

Hathcock shot again, and the man dropped but bounced up and again ran, shooting and yelling.

But before Hathcock could shove a third shot into his chamber, McAbee fired his M-14, dropping the man temporarily to his knees. This time the soldier dropped his rifle, but got up again and continued to run toward them, yelling.

Hathcock fired once more and McAbee fired twice, and the man kept coming, blood streaming from both his shoulders and his groin. McAbee could see large chunks of flesh torn away from his chest, yet he kept coming at them.

Taking one long, slow breath, Hathcock took careful aim, laying the center of his scope's reticle on the man's head. Hathcock watched his eyes, flaming and wide. His mouth gaped open, and his arms dangled broken in their joints. Ron McAbee stared through his spotting scope, not believing what he saw. He too saw the eyes—the eyes of a man crazed. Dead yet still alive in his final attack. His mouth wide with a scream that echoed more and more loudly through the once quiet valley.

When the soldier began to climb the slope, three hundred yards below the blind where the two snipers hid, Hathcock sent the seventh shot into the man's face. He stopped at that moment and moved no more.

"He had to be on opium!" McAbee exclaimed. "No normal man could take that many shots."

Hathcock sweated. It was as though he had encountered a devil and in the last moment won.

The next two months weren't easy ones. Hathcock moved with his snipers to the Que Son hills as did the 1st Battalion, 7th Marines. In August, Lieutenant Colonel Dowd was killed in battle, and Carlos, who had regarded him as both a friend and an ally, felt devastated at the loss. On the day of Dowd's death, Hathcock took a bullet in the thigh when the helicopter he was traveling in was fired upon. But the sniper recovered quickly from that and was back in action before the month was out.

18

The Sacrifice

SEPTEMBER IN QUANG TRI PROVINCE feels cooler than September in Da Nang. The high mountain passes that overlook Laos sometimes pick up cool breezes from their lofty altitudes and allow a respite from the uncomfortable 95 percent humidity and 95 degree temperatures of the lower elevations. At a place that Marines named The Slot, one could sit in that cool breeze and watch North Vietnamese and Viet Cong caravans sweating beneath the loads of supplies that they carried over the steaming plait-work of jungle paths that the world called the Ho Chi Minh Trail.

On a rounded hilltop where trees and vines still grew in a green, thick tangle, Carlos Hathcock and Ron McAbee silently slithered their way to a rocky sinkhole hidden beneath the dense jungle's umbrella and surrounded by ferns and vines and slime-covered roots. The monsoon rains of a year ago and the frequent summer showers kept this rocky depression filled with water, warmed by the beams of sunlight that shone between the overhead boughs. Slugs, leeches, worms, algae, and slimy moss made the water look like a puddle of green oatmeal.

Hathcock wrinkled his nose. The watery slime had a distinct odor that Hathcock associated with a neighbor's outhouse near his grandmother's home in Arkansas.

Carefully, he brushed the top layer of lumpy slime away until he saw the black water, clear and almost drinkable, in the

241

small opening he had made. Extending his lips, he put his face down to it and took tiny sips.

"Pew!" Hathcock whispered softly. "It tastes exactly like it smells."

"You done?"

"That's all I can stand."

"You keep watch while I get me a drink too. As thirsty as I am, I could drink piss."

"I think that might taste better."

"I'll try this do-do flavored stuff for now. Here, hold my glasses."

Mack lay over the pool and brushed the slime away to expose the water. He took several sucking gulps and raised his face, dripping wet. After pulling a long string of moss off his tongue, Mack looked at Hathcock and whispered, "It's probably full of liver flukes and we'll be dead in a couple of years."

"You didn't want to live forever, did ya?"

"Yes."

"I hear that a big helping of nuc-mom* will get rid of any case of liver flukes you might pick up in the water."

Mack frowned at Hathcock, "I don't care how hungry we get. I'll eat dog shit before you get me to touch a drop of that nasty crap!"

"Shhhhhh!" Hathcock whispered with a grin, putting his finger next to his lips. "You get loud and we won't need to worry about liver flukes."

Mack put his glasses back on his face, slipping the black elastic strap back around his head. "I gotta be careful with these, they're my last pair. I break 'em and I'm no help at all."

"Keep 'em on your face then."

Hathcock recorded his ninety-third confirmed kill that morning—a lone Viet Cong who climbed a slope, rigging

---

*A fermented soup made of tiny fish, rice, and a variety of vegetables; placed in a sealed jar and buried. It was commonly used by the Viet Cong as a food supply, buried throughout the areas in which they operated. High in protein and carbohydrates, nuc-mom provided the Viet Cong with a rich food supply that they did not have to carry. However, because of its rancid odor and putrefied contents, most Americans considered it a foul substance, not fit to eat.

booby traps along a patrol route. Hathcock called in the position to the Marines on a mountaintop observation post, who verified the kill with their powerful binoculars and plotted the positions of the anti-personnel mines that the man had laid.

When Hathcock and McAbee reached the observation post on that peak a lance corporal met them and handed them a yellow slip of paper.

"Sergeant Major Puckett's looking for us," Hathcock said, grinning.

"I told you so!" said McAbee. "Sergeant major always gets mad when we take off together. You know . . . first and second in command."

"You're the only other man in the platoon who can shoot my zero.* Only one other sniper I worked with could do that. And, just like you, he could almost read my mind. To me, we're the ideal team. I don't want to trust my life to someone else, Mack."

The lance corporal seated in front of a table covered with radios and a spaghetti-work of black wires running to power and antennae, passed the handset across the table to Hathcock. "Staff Sergeant, your sergeant major is coming."

Hathcock put the black receiver against his ear, waiting for what he knew would come.

"Staff Sergeant Hathcock, is Staff Sergeant McAbee with you?" The sergeant major's transmission was weak and Carlos strained to hear.

Hathcock pressed the large, rectangular black button on the handset and heard the powerful lineal amplifier whine as he keyed the radio. When the shrill sound of the radio "powering up" peaked, he answered, shouting, "Yes sir, he's right here with me."

"You two know better!" the sergeant major shouted, trying to be heard.

The crackling message came clear, and Hathcock shook his head. "Everybody else was out, and we had this job—" Hath-

---

*A zero is the sight adjustment necessary for a person to fire a rifle and hit the center of the target in a no wind condition. Since most people differ in build and shooting technique, the windage and elevation adjustment on the rifle sights, or zero, will be different from person to person on the same rifle.

cock could hear the whine of the sergeant major's signal walking over his and knew that the senior Marine had lost his temper. He waited until the channel cleared.

"We're headed home today!" Hathcock shouted.

"Where are you two standing right now?" the sergeant major shouted back.

McAbee looked at the map, and the lance corporal who operated the radios said, "This mountain is called My Dong."

Carlos smiled and keyed the radio. "Right now, we are standing on My Dong."

The next day Hathcock and McAbee were standing stiffly at attention in front of the sergeant major. "I get tired of the wild stories coming in here telling how Charlie finally got you. And how high the bounty is on your head! You're both staff NCOs . . . I want a degree more responsibility out of both of you."

"Sergeant Major," Hathcock said, "Staff Sergeant McAbee is our armorer. We need him out where we operate. And I've got my snipers all paired and that leaves him and me. What do we do, go off separately by ourselves?"

"No. But you don't disappear for a week either. I don't expect you to just sit in camp. But I expect responsible leadership from both of you! The only way you two go to the field together is if your entire platoon is committed and both of you are required to maintain control over that tribe of yours."

Hathcock smiled. At this moment, the sergeant major reminded him of another Marine. A Marine who became so frustrated with his disappearing that he confined him to his quarters to slow him down.

"You got a deal, Sergeant Major."

Both Marines walked directly to the operations tent after shaking hands with the sergeant major and reassuring him that his worries were now over.

"What's going on?" Hathcock asked the operations chief.

The month of September began with 7th Marines still pursuing two NVA regiments that they forced from the Hiep Duc Valley. With the enemy fragmented and scattered to the east and north, 3rd Battalion, 7th Marines, went to Fire Support

Base Ross where India Company conducted a night move to a blocking position northeast of the fire base. Because they made only light contact with the NVA, three companies of 3rd Battalion moved on and began a northwesterly sweep through Nghi Ha Valley. While 3rd Battalion moved northwest, 1st Battalion, along with Mike Company from 3rd Battalion, set up blocking positions along the draws leading into the Phu Loc Valley while 3rd Battalion pushed toward them.

When Carlos went to the operations tent, he found that in two days, September 16, 1969, the operation would end, and 1st Battalion would move back to their area of operation in the eastern Que Son hills.

"We can go there," Hathcock told McAbee. "Our snipers will be concentrated right there. The 90th NVA may be blown away, but the 3rd and 36th NVA regiments, the GK-33, and the 1st Viet Cong Regiment are all prime for the pickin' down yonder. We could organize a regular operation against them."

"You gonna tell Sergeant Major Puckett?"

"Yeah. It's just a short jump down there, and with all our people already working with the battalions, he'll see the logic."

That night McAbee worked late on the rifles while Carlos cleaned both their gear. He was excited about what the operation down south might reveal.

"Reckon Perry can handle things back here?"

"Sure. His team will run local security operations while we're gone."

The September heat kept the night nearly as hot as the day with the humidity lingering at above 90 percent. On these hot nights, most of the Marines slept outside.

Yankee followed at Ron McAbee's heels as the Marine laid a poncho liner and air mattress on top of the sandbags that covered the roof of the bunker outside the staff NCO hooch on the night of September 15, the day before he and Carlos would leave for the eastern side of the Que Son hills. Yankee always slept next to Mack since the six-foot two-inch Marine had arrived. He liked Yankee sleeping at his side because of the dog's uncanny ability to sense incoming fire before any shell impacted. Yankee's low, throaty growl was the big, blond Marine's early-warning system.

As McAbee stretched out on his poncho liner—both of his boots unlaced but still on his feet—he took off his glasses and set them on the row of sandbags that ringed the bunker just below the roof. A stir of air relieved the steaminess of the night and soon lulled both the Marine and the red dog to sleep. Yankee slept with his head resting on Mack's chest.

In the distance the crackle of radio static, muffled inside the operations tent, and the low drone of the generators, scattered on the hill, gave the Marines who stood watch in the towers and along the wire a sense of hypnotic tranquility. A bright moon rose, sending a shimmering silver light over the camp.

During the early morning hours something caused Yankee to stir from his sleep. The silvery moon sparkled in his clear, brown eyes as he pointed his ears and tasted the air with his nose. And deep within him, like the distant rumble of a faraway storm's thunder, Yankee began to growl.

It wasn't a loud growl at first, just a sound of uneasiness that quivered inside his throat, quiet and unheard. But whatever doubt the dog had suddenly vanished, and, sitting up on his haunches, he gave a full, barrel-chested growl.

Mack's eyes popped open. He saw his bedtime companion snarling at the still quiet night, hackles raised and teeth bared. Ron McAbee knew that was no false alarm. He swung his feet down and yelled, "Incoming! Incoming!"

The next sound that Ron McAbee heard was the grinding noise of glass and plastic crunching beneath his boot. He had stepped on his glasses.

"Shit!" he swore leaping off the bunker. He stepped inside the shelter as the sound of explosions shook the camp.

Nothing could make him feel worse than he already felt. Without his glasses he was useless as a sniper or spotter. Without his glasses, Hathcock would have to take Corporal Perry down to join 1st Battalion.

"Here, have a shot," a voice in the bunker's darkness said. It was Hathcock, and he handed a bottle of Jim Beam to Mack.

The two men lay drinking whiskey together while the dust

from explosions swirled around them. The previous afternoon, they had noticed a small funeral procession passing near their camp. It seemed strange to both Marines that the men bearing the casket could only carry the large box (slung on two stout poles) a few yards at a time before having to set it down and rest. The men were outside the wire so Hathcock ran to operations and told the officer on duty.

"It's nothing. Forget about it," the Marine told them.

"You don't care that these gooners are probably carrying rockets or 120-millimeter mortars in that casket?" Hathcock asked.

"We had enough trouble with your partner there taking pot-shots at the tombstone and getting the village chief all riled. Ask McAbee about that seventy five bucks coming out of his pay because of his little shooting spree. Now you want us to go roust a funeral in case there may be rockets in the casket? Are you going to pay the go-min money when the village chief comes raising hell this time?"

"Well, how about if Mack and me go down there and check them out?"

"No!"

They went to their hooch and got the same bottle of Jim Beam they were working on now and spent the rest of the afternoon and evening in the bunker.

"I thought we killed this thing last night," Mack said handing the bottle back to Hathcock.

"No. I thought it might come in handy for another night down here, so I saved it. Want some more?"

"No. That little bit's all I care to drink tonight. You?"

"No. Need a clear head for tomorrow."

"You gotta wait for me to go get another pair of glasses tomorrow. I can get a jeep at first light, drive to Da Nang, and be back here by noon or a little after."

"That convoy is pulling out first thing tomorrow morning. I better take Perry and make sure we get down there."

"Come on, Carlos. There's an afternoon supply helicopter that will go down there, and we can fly instead of ride. Think how sore you're gonna be when you get there, riding in the back of that six-by all that way."

"You think that they can give you a pair of glasses by noon?"

"I'm positive. In fact, I'll call ahead and the doc over at the aid station can read them my prescription over the phone. I'll be back by noon and we'll be down there by the middle of the afternoon. I promise!"

"Okay, Mack. Plan B. I'll wait here and get all our gear double-checked while you're getting your glasses."

Before Hathcock had gotten off his cot the following morning, Ron McAbee had already gone to the motor pool and drawn a jeep. He and three Marines, who volunteered to ride shotgun, raced the nearly thirty miles to the hospital at Da Nang. Mack would be back at LZ Baldy before noon.

Hathcock sat in the mess tent sipping coffee at 7:30 on the morning of September 16. Across from him sat his good friend Staff Sergeant Boone, a counterintelligence Marine. They talked about a patrol that would leave LZ Baldy at 8:30 A.M. and move toward the Que Son area, and Boone invited him to come.

Hathcock turned down Boone's invitation, but after nearly thirty minutes of speculating on what the patrol might encounter, Hathcock began to think better of it. He was already tired of sitting around camp, doing nothing, waiting for McAbee to return. He looked at his watch and realized that he had four more hours to wait for his friend and then two hours to wait for the helicopter.

Boone was halfway out the door when Hathcock shouted to him, "Boone, I'm going. Let me go get Perry and I'll meet you at your hooch."

"Perry!" Hathcock shouted as he pulled open the screen door on the sniper platoon's command hooch.

The junior Marine sat straight up, wide eyed and startled, "What's happening? Something happen?"

"Where's your gear?" Hathcock said, slinging two rifles over his shoulder and strapping down his pack.

"In my hooch. Why? What—?"

"Grab your gear. Meet me back here in ten minutes. Better yet, meet me over at the CIT hooch. We're going on a special patrol."

Ten minutes later, Perry stood next to Hathcock watching a

line of five amtracs* parked with their motors running, waiting for the "all aboard" signal to move out.

"If somebody is gonna take a hit, we need to be where we can help fast. So I guess we ought to get on the middle tractor.

"Hold my rifle while I climb on top. I'll pull up the gear and then you can climb up," Carlos told the London, Ohio, native as the two Marines walked to the third amtrac.

In a minute, both snipers sat with six other Marines. One of them was a first lieutenant who had just arrived in Vietnam. This was his first mission.

"Staff Sergeant Carlos Hathcock," Hathcock said, extending his hand to the officer who seemed more friendly than most.

"Lieutenant Ed Hyland," the Marine said, shaking Hathcock's hand.

"This is my partner, Corporal John Perry," Hathcock told the officer.

"You're snipers?"

"Yes, Sir. I'm the sniper platoon sergeant, and Perry, here, is one of our ace trigger pullers."

"What's with that white feather in your hat? I thought that snipers were masters of camouflage. Isn't that kind of a giveaway?"

"Yes, Sir. I wear it anyway. It's been my trademark ever since 1966. I've got ninety-three confirmed kills and I don't know how many thousands of hours of trigger time, and I've only taken it off my hat once. That was when I snuck into an NVA general's compound and zapped him."

Perry, taken by the opportunity to brag about his leader, said, "Staff Sergeant Hathcock has the biggest bounty on his head in Vietnam. It's more than ten-thousand dollars!"

The lieutenant blinked and Hathcock smiled, "I don't really know how much it is. It's three years pay, whatever that might be.

---

*Amtrac is a shortened term for amphibious tractor. It is an amphibious, armored personnel carrier used by the Marine Corps to carry troops from ships to shore as well as transporting them on land. This vehicle, which operates on treads or tracks similar to those used by tanks, offers limited protection from many forms of small-arms fire and anti-personnel explosive devices.

"This is my second tour. The NVA published a wanted poster on me in 1966, and then last month I got word that they put it out on me again. I haven't seen this new one. I suppose it's still the same. However, now I do know what they call me."

"What's that?" Hyland asked.

"Long Tra'ng and then something after that, but mainly Long Tra'ng."

"White Feather," the officer said, translating the Vietnamese language.

"You speak Vietnamese?"

"I understand some of it. I guess they'd call you Long Tra'ng du K'ich."

"That's it."

"White Feather Sniper," the officer said with a smile.

The amtrac lurched forward and began rumbling down the roadway. Hathcock looked back through the dusty air toward LZ Baldy and thought of his friend. It would be all right. Mack would understand. But he still felt a pinch of guilt as he turned his eyes toward the fields and trees and huts and all the other places where Charlie might be hiding.

The noise of the convoy was so loud that further attempts at conversation ceased. The Marines sat on top of the vehicles, rifles poised, magazines inserted, looking out with caution at a seemingly tranquil world.

Ahead of the column, a mine sweep team carefully cleared the way, giving Hathcock a sense of security. Not perfect security, however. He only felt that when he was on his feet, in his element, stalking the enemy. In the bush he made his own luck. Here, his luck rested squarely in the hands of fate and the amtrac driver.

The amtrac came to a jolting halt, bouncing low on its tanklike treads, causing its three antennae to whip and snap through the air. Hathcock looked back at Corporal Perry and at Lieutenant Hyland who sat next to him.

"I think we're going to follow that trail off to the left," the officer shouted, pointing at some tracks left days earlier by a similar patrol.

Carlos didn't like it. He thought of the hand grenades tied in a daisy chain along the cane field.

One after another, the heavy, armored transports crept off the highway, and as the number three amtrac creeped along the gravel shoulder, starting its turn, Hathcock's entire world disappeared in a booming, ringing, earth-shattering explosion.

Fifty startled Marines scrambled for cover as gunfire erupted from the nearby trees. They saw a forty-foot high column of fire rise from the amtrac on which Hathcock and the seven other Marines had ridden. It filled the air with an acrid pall of billowy, black smoke.

Beneath that smoke, between the flames, Hathcock opened his eyes and saw nothing but blackness and fire. Something heavy pinned his legs. He felt the hair on his neck, his eyebrows, and the top of his head singe and curl. Panic suddenly flashed through his mind and sent his heart pounding—"I'm gonna die!" He had to run. He had to get away.

Hathcock reached for the dead weight that pinned his legs and saw that it was the body of the lieutenant who had spoken to him only seconds earlier. He was already on fire.

"Save him! Got to save him!" Hathcock suddenly thought. And without thinking of his own life, he took the young officer by his flaming clothes and hurled him off the side of the burning vehicle. As he looked at the tangled bodies of the other Marines, who had been whole and well only a second ago, he saw their slow, groggy motion among the flames and instinctively began hurling them off too.

He didn't notice when he threw Corporal Perry clear of the inferno. All the Marines were equally important to him—brother Marines who would otherwise die. He grabbed them randomly and tossed. Privates First Class Roberto Barrera, Lawrence Head, Keith Spencer, and Thurman Trussell, and Lance Corporal Earl Thibodeaux.

He himself was on fire. His trousers were burning, his chest and arms and neck were burning. And as another explosion rumbled beneath his feet and fire belched skyward through the torn and bent hulk that seconds ago was an amtrac, Hathcock blindly jumped through the wall of flames. He had no idea what awaited him on the other side of that fiery curtain.

Hathcock struggled to his feet from the gravel where he fell. He did not hear the clatter of machine-gun fire or the explosions of grenades. He saw the fire towering over him and could only hope to get away from that burning trap before it killed him.

Inside his head he kept asking himself, "Why do I feel wet. I'm weighted down like I'm soaked. Why?"

Hathcock staggered away from the blazing amtrac, holding his arms straight out from his sides. He knew he was hurt, but it was when he looked down at his arms that he realized his injury was beyond anything he had imagined.

Skin hung down from his arms like bat wings, ragged and black, as though draped with moss six to eight inches in length. His heart sank as he stopped and sat on the side of the road. "Will I live?" he asked himself.

"Roll him!" two frantic voices cried. "Quick! Roll him into the water!" Hathcock didn't know that his clothes still burned, and the bandoleer of ammo draped over his shoulder and the six hand grenades that still hung on his cartridge belt were quite forgotten by him.

Suddenly some Marines doused him in the muddy water next to the road. A few seconds later he was sitting in the dirt with his head bobbing and his lashless eyelids blinking over his sore eyes.

A corpsman ran to Hathcock's side and placed a canteen next to his lips. "Drink all this," he ordered, and Hathcock drank. When the bottle was empty, the corpsman pressed another to his lips. "Drink all this too." And he drank. He had finished three canteens of water when a tall black shadow stood over him.

"Can you stand?" Hathcock heard Staff Sergeant Boone ask.

"We try," he answered, blindly struggling to his feet.

Then another voice that belonged to a Marine captain said, "No. Call the chopper down here."

A CH-46 sat on the roadway, beyond where the devastated amtrac burned, and there crewmen, corpsmen, and Marines helped carry the other seriously burned Marines inside it.

"Sir," Boone said, "the chopper pilot says he can't get in down here. We have to carry Hathcock over there."

"Can you walk?" the captain asked.

"Try," Hathcock said.

"You're gonna be okay, Carlos," Boone said. He stood on Hathcock's left, and the captain stood on his right. They put their hands on Hathcock's hips, where his cartridge belt had protected his skin, and held him upright as he struggled each step toward the waiting helicopter.

Hathcock was burned to some degree over nearly every inch of his body. His brick-red face was sore and swelling. His chest and arms and hands and back were opened, crackled, and bloody, and caked black. His legs fared little better, blisters rising on the skin beneath the tattered rags that once were trousers.

As the helicopter lifted away from the land and the war of bullets and bombs, it carried Carlos Hathcock to another war: a war fought with needles and scalpels and chemicals and drugs. A war in which pain was the terrifying constant, the companion of every waking moment—and the enemy.

"I'm still on fire!" Hathcock thought. Every place where anything touched him now felt as though it was covered with white-hot steel. He stood and refused to sit.

"Got to get these clothes off," he thought. "That will help." And he looked at a corpsman who stood in front of him, writing on a tablet. Scissors hung from his pocket, and Carlos pointed a black and bloody bent finger at them, and then at the burned rags that were his trousers. The corpsman went to work.

When the helicopter landed, Hathcock stood completely naked and hesitated to move. He had to find Perry. He had searched during the entire trip and had not seen his partner. "He can't be dead!" Hathcock thought.

As a hoard of doctors, nurses, corpsmen, and Marines filled the helicopter and began taking the injured men away, Hathcock finally saw Perry. He looked well and smiled and waved.

"Sit down, Marine" a voice told him.

Hathcock sat.

"Lay back and we'll go for a ride."

Hathcock looked at the rear ramp of the helicopter where a pile of burned rags that were his clothes slid down to the deck of the hospital ship, USS *Repose*. In the midst of the rags, Carlos saw his cigarette lighter. "That's mine!" he said pointing at the silver-colored Zippo. A nurse picked it up, and Carlos managed a smile for her with his swollen lips.

"Get word to Master Sergeant Moose Gunderson over at 1st Division G-3. Tell him I've been hurt, but I'm okay!" Hathcock said to the nurse. She nodded and he smiled again.

A hand pushed him gently back on the gurney, but when his bloody and cracked back touched the sheet, he popped back up. A hand would push his forehead back and he popped back again, and again and again, all the way to the emergency room where a doctor, masked and dressed in surgical garb, waited.

"How you feel, Marine?"

"I'll be okay, Sir. Got a little hot," Hathcock said, trying to sound as though he was in complete control of his life.

"What do you do?" the doctor asked as he inserted the needle on an IV tube into Hathcock.

Fighting back the urge to shout, Carlos panted, "Scout/ Sniper, Sir. I lead a platoon."

"I think you may be out of action for a couple of days, Marine."

Hathcock felt something happening to his back and arms. He did not look. He did not want to see those parts of him that he would never have again disappear.

"What's going on back there," Hathcock asked.

"Cleaning out a truck-load of gravel," a voice answered from behind him.

"What do you think about giving every corpsman a jeep, Marine?"

Hathcock thought a moment and said, "That would be a terrible idea. I mean it would be outstanding for the corpsmen and those people who needed help. But the logistics of something like that would be terrible. I don't see how..."

When Ron McAbee's driver pulled the jeep to a stop in front of the operations tent on LZ Baldy, a Marine shouted to him, "They finally got Staff Sergeant Hathcock! I think he's dead!"

Mack raced inside the operations tent where the gunnery sergeant, who sat scrawling notes, said, "Hathcock and Perry were on an amtrac that got ambushed. The VC set off a five hundred-pound box mine under it. Blew that sucker sky high.

All the Marines were burned bad—real bad. I don't know whether he is dead or alive. He looked bad when they put him on the medevac chopper and sent him out to the *Repose*. I didn't get any word on Perry, but he's on the *Repose*, too."

"I'm headed out to the ship to see Hathcock," McAbee told the gunnery sergeant, and in two giant steps, the tall Marine jumped in the jeep and roared away, slinging gravel and dirt. Ron McAbee spent the remainder of the day trying to hitch a ride out to the ship. He never succeeded.

A day later, Mack got word from Moose Gunderson that Hathcock was badly burned but alive, and he wrote him a letter.

On the day that Ron McAbee wrote Hathcock, Maj. Gen. Ormond R. Simpson, 1st Marine Division's commanding general, pinned a Purple Heart medal on Hathcock's pillow. The general's aide took a Polaroid photograph of the event.

When the general departed, a nurse took the photo and the medal, and said, "I'll put these in your ditty bag so that you can find them when you wake up." A person dressed in white inserted a needle in Carlos Hathcock's pain-ridden body, and in a moment he was asleep.

He never knew when they loaded him on another helicopter and lifted him to the Da Nang air base, where air force medics put him and the seven other burned Marines on a jet bound for Tokyo. Hathcock never knew that he also spent several days in the hospital at Yakota Air Force Base while the world-famous burn center at Brooke Army Hospital in San Antonio, Texas, awaited his and the seven other Marines' arrival.

And even when he awoke on September 24, more than a week after the terrible fire that would change his life forever, Hathcock did not realize that he was away from Vietnam.

On the afternoon of September 16, (Stateside time) a message arrived at the Navy Annex of the Pentagon, located up the hill, next to the national cemetery, on Columbia Pike in Arlington, Virginia—a complex of buildings where Gen. Leonard F. Chapman commanded the Marine Corps. This message went to the casualty branch of the Marine Corps' manpower division, bearing the names of eight Marines, their next of kin and home addresses: eight Marines burned on an amtrac a day ago, half a world away. And at the top of the list appeared the name Staff Sergeant Carlos N. Hathcock II.

A day later, at 3 P.M., a Marine captain, a Casualty Assistance Call Officer, wearing his dress blue uniform and carrying a message from Headquarters, U.S. Marine Corps, with Staff Sergeant Carlos N. Hathcock's name and condition listed on it, left his office in Norfolk, Virginia, and drove to Virginia Beach. He took the Independence Boulevard exit off Route 44, and drove past the Pembroke Shopping Mall on his way to 545 Sirene Avenue and the house that Carlos and Jo Hathcock bought just before Hathcock shipped out to Vietnam. He had no way of knowing that Jo was out shopping since he avoided telephoning before hand for fear of exposing his grievous message. It is Marine Corps policy and tradition that all such messages will be made in person, without exception.

19

Beating the Odds

THE SEPTEMBER AFTERNOON heat sent Jo Hathcock shopping at Pembroke Mall in Virginia Beach. It was cool there, and it helped to take her mind off Carlos and the dangers he faced in Vietnam.

It was well after 3 P.M. when she walked across the hot, asphalt, parking lot to get into her car and drive the few blocks home. The mirage made the cars look liquid and surreal, and the heat made her head throb.

Traffic was its normal afternoon jam. As Jo waited for the red light to go dark and the green light to flash on, she saw an olive-colored Chevrolet cruise past, just making the yellow light, as she moved out on Independence Boulevard. At the second light, just before her turn, she read the yellow lettering on the trunk, "U.S. Marine Corps." She saw the driver clearly—a captain wearing dress blue and a white hat. "He's no recruiter," she thought. And as the green car made a left turn, ahead of her's, and swayed into the drive at 545 Sirene Avenue, she cried aloud, "My God! Carlos is dead!"

She saw the Marine casualty officer walking toward her door, and halting on her front walk, waiting for her to get out of the car.

"Mrs. Hathcock?" the Marine softly asked.

In a few days, Jo received a message from Brig. Gen. William H. Moncrief, Jr., the commander at Brooke General Hospital,

Fort Sam Houston, in San Antonio, Texas, that Hathcock had arrived there on September 22 and that she could be with him there. She immediately made plans to go.

It was nearly noon when Hathcock opened his eyes. The ship wasn't rolling. He could not move. He cried out from the horrible pain that blanketed him. His legs and arms and shoulders and neck and back, even his ears, crawled and boiled with intolerable pain.

"Carlos?" Jo cried out. "Carlos!"

He turned his eyes toward her and blinked. They were sore and red, and his vision was blurry and tilted. "Jo?"

"Oh, Carlos," she said softly. She had tried to imagine the worst possible image of her husband's burns. She felt that if she imagined the worst that when she confronted the reality of his injury, it would not shock her. But it did. She felt guilty because she could not even recognize the man she had loved for nearly seven years. She stood and looked down at him, "Carlos."

He raised his mummy-wrapped arm and pointed to a table where a green bag sat. Each man had a green bag with black plastic handles, an item similar to the R-and-R bags given to Marines headed for two weeks liberty away from the war.

"Look," he mumbled, pointing at the bag.

"Yes, it's a nice bag. They give that to you?"

"Look," he said again, pointing, "Look inside."

Every effort to speak sent daggers of pain through him. Raising his arm tore open the eschar—the hard crust of scab and dried body fluid—that covered the third-degree burns there, leaving him breathless.

Jo brought the bag back to Hathcock's bedside and opened it. On top she found the blue leather box with gold trim. She opened it and saw the Purple Heart medal.

"The medal is pretty, Carlos," she said holding it up for him to see too.

"Yes," he said in a soft whisper. "Look more."

The only other thing was a small, square photograph. She held it up for Hathcock to see, "This?"

"Yes. Look. Look."

It was the Polaroid photograph that General Simpson's aide took that day on the USS *Repose* when he presented Hathcock the Purple Heart. Hathcock was always proud when a general officer presented him with anything, and he wanted to share that feeling of pride with Jo.

Hathcock smiled as Jo looked at it. She saw the general and saw her husband's burns and bandages. It made her cry. To her, the photo looked horrible. She fought back the urge to scold Carlos for making her look at it, but she restrained herself. "That's real nice, Carlos. Is he your commanding general?"

"Yes," he struggled in a whispering, raspy voice. "He commands the whole division and came to see me."

Hathcock closed his eyes. Jo sat again in the chair. The afternoon drifted away.

Hathcock had been lucky. During the fire his lungs had not suffered any severe burns. The immediate attention that he received from the corpsman greatly increased his survival odds. And the fast action taken to stabilize him on the USS *Repose* gave the doctors good prospects and hope for his recovery. They had set the stage for the burn specialists at Brooke to do the job of rebuilding the broken man, of keeping him alive through the long healing process that severe burns require.

The day Hathcock arrived at Brooke, he had a 102-degree fever, weighed one hundred fifty pounds and had second-and third-degree burns on his head, neck, anterior trunk, posterior trunk, right upper arm, left upper arm, right lower arm, left lower arm, right hand, left hand, right thigh, left thigh, right leg, and left leg. More than 43 percent of his total body area suffered "full-thickness" burns with several areas where that full thickness of the skin had burned completely away (third-degree burns).

With a partial thickness burn, a patient's skin can regenerate from the epithelial* cells lining the skin appendages—hair follicles, sweat glands, and sebaceous glands. Full-thickness burns destroy all these cells and prevent any regeneration. Small full-thickness burns can heal from the skin margins, but

---

*Epithelium: The tissue cells composing the skin; also the cells lining all the passages of the hollow organs of the respiratory, digestive, and urinary systems.

large areas require skin grafting.

They moved Hathcock to Ward 13B. There he made daily trips to the Hubbard tank where he could soak and soften the hard, crusty eschar that covered his burns, while the burn specialists examined them. There they noticed a black spot on his hand, an infection that a biopsy later revealed was phycomycosis. But they felt that this fungal disease did not explain the fever that he could not shake—a fever that rose from 102 degrees on his first day there to 103 on the second and 104 degrees on September 24. They suspected malaria and treated him for it.

To complicate problems, on September 30, before doctors could begin burn therapy, Hathcock developed bronchopneumonia in his left lung. That deferred the therapy until October 6 when the pneumonia finally began to clear.

On October 13, the doctors began the burn therapy—thirteen different operations in which they stripped away the burn eschar and damaged flesh, and applied skin grafts. The operations continued until November 17. Hathcock received eight homografts (skin grafts taken from donors), three autografts (small grafts of healthy skin taken from his own body), and two heterografts (skin grafts taken from animals).

Hathcock's right side suffered the worst and required the greater portion of skin grafting. His grafts included the use of dog skin and pig skin on his right arm and thigh on November 3 and 6.

During this period, Hathcock also developed staphylococcus infections and his red blood count dropped 28 percent. Doctors began waging a battle against the infections and gave him transfusions of 1500 cc's of whole blood. To combat the effects of the pain and infection, they gave him daily doses of narcotics.

For the six weeks that Carlos Hathcock balanced on a tightrope above the abyss, Jo sat at his bedside. She fought his lapses into hallucination and coaxed him back out of the misty black cloud that would have led him into the peacefulness of death. She coaxed him back again and again.

"Mack," he said. He saw Mack back at Hill 55 and there were shells incoming. "Mack! Mack! Incoming!" And Mack kept walking down the finger to the sniper hooch with Yankee, who trotted at his heels.

There was Burke. "Burke!" Hathcock shouted from his dream. Burke had covered his face with camouflage paint and smiled. "Don't let your mascara run," Hathcock heard Burke say. Then he laughed.

"Don't go in there. Stay down! Hathcock shouted from his bed. "My rifle, my hat. Where's my hat?"

"Carlos! Wake up!" Jo shouted, shaking Hathcock's bed. He opened his eyes, yet he still dreamed. He did not see Jo, he saw Mack.

"Mack! You gotta take care. You gotta be more careful!"

She kept shaking the bed. "Carlos! You listen to me!" But he was moaning about Que Son and Route 4.

"Carlos!"

Finally he blinked and said nothing more.

"Carlos," Jo said in a loud voice. "Where are you?"

"Hill 55, Vietnam."

"No! You're at Brooke General Hospital in San Antonio, Texas!"

He blinked, not knowing what to believe. He had just seen the hooches and the shooting and the smoke. It didn't make any sense. He was in Vietnam.

"Repeat after me, Carlos!"

"Whaaa . . . ?"

"You are not in Vietnam!"

Hathcock looked at Jo. It was Jo. He recognized her. He felt the pain. He was alive.

During the lucid moments, Jo would open a letter from one of a hundred friends who wrote to him while he fought for his life, and she would read it. It seemed that everyone who had ever shot a rifle in Marine Corps or Interservice or National Rifle Association competition wrote to him, telling him to get well.

There were letters from Jim Land, filled with lines borrowed from great coaches. He called Hathcock a winner. There were letters from Vietnam—from Moose Gunderson and Boo Boo Barker. And several letters from Ron McAbee.

Mack's first letter told Hathcock how he tried to get out to the ship but could not find a way. In other letters he told Hathcock that Yankee was well and David Sommers too. He told him about the platoon and how it had been a good thing that they had not traveled together that day. This way the platoon did not suffer a break in continuity of leadership. Mack told Hathcock how he pushed the platoon hard—he wanted vengeance. So did the men.

By November 10 Hathcock stopped hallucinating. His infection had retreated, and much of the grafted skin was now healed and showed great promise. His grafts had nearly all taken. The only bad spots were on his right shoulder and right leg. The doctor had removed the animal skin grafts and placed donor skin on the debrided areas.

But the pain continued. He cried out when he saw the doctors coming with the bundles and tools. The pain of debridement sent chills of horror through him. The pealing of flesh and scab from a burn renders a pain that is indescribable.

Hathcock had endured and had suffered not just to survive, but to recover. To become a whole and vital man again. To hunt and to shoot. To become an Olympic champion and fulfill a dream.

On November 10, 1969, Carlos woke out of a sound sleep. Jo was sitting beside the bed.

"What day is it, Carlos?" Jo said happily.

Hathcock thought for a moment and began to look anxious. He did not know. Was it Wednesday or Thursday or Saturday?

But before he could answer that he had no idea, a woman pushed open the door and held a large birthday cake in her hands. It was Mrs. Dickman—Colonel William Dickman's wife. Colonel Dickman was a member of the Marine Corps Reserve's 4th Reconnaissance Battalion and was the officer in charge of their scout/sniper school at Camp Bullis. He had met Hathcock several years earlier at the Texas State and Regional NRA rifle championships at the Camp Bullis rifle range. He had later heard and appreciated the legendary Carlos Hathcock sniper stories too. And because of this kinship, he and Mrs. Dickman took care of Jo and visited Hathcock often.

"Happy birthday!" Mrs. Dickman said.

"Birthday?" Carlos asked. "I may not know what day it is, but it sure ain't May 20."

She said, "Carlos . . . Marine. It's Monday, November 10, and your Corps 194th birthday! Now you ought to remember that!"

Hathcock looked at Jo and laughed. He shared the cake with the other Marines in the ward—Marines like Captain Ed Hyland (promoted in the hospital) and Pfc Roberto Barrera, who had also been in the amtrac.

Hyland, now with only one arm, wished Hathcock happy birthday, and Hathcock returned the wish to him and all the other Marines in the ward.

Captain Hyland wanted to write a recommendation for Hathcock to receive a medal for his courageous action on that burning amtrac. But Hathcock responded with an emphatic no. He told Hyland, "I happened to wake up first. That's all. I did what any of the rest of the Marines on top of that amtrac would have done."

Since Hathcock refused any sort of official recognition, Captain Hyland offered him something personal: a simple pewter mug with names and dates engraved on it. And Hathcock accepted that.

Jo left San Antonio on Friday, November 14, in order to be home for Sonny's birthday that Saturday. Hathcock wanted to go home too.

A few days after Carlos III's fifth birthday, Jo's mother died unexpectedly. Jo was shattered but she dared not call Carlos because she knew he would do what he did the day after Sonny was born: he would get out of the hospital, whether he was well or not.

But she thought more about it and talked to her sister and to her sister's husband, Winston Jones. And he asked, "What about Carlos? How will he feel if you don't tell him?" She called Carlos that afternoon.

Because of the death, the doctors allowed him to make the trip home. His burns were completely covered now, and all the grafts were healing well. He would return to the hospital on December 30 for further treatment and evaluation. Then on January 5, 1970, he was released and placed on convalescent leave. On January 31, 1970, he reported back to Quantico,

Virginia, as a member of the Marine Corps Rifle Team.

Because of his burns, he could not compete: He could not stand the rigors of strapping himself into a shooting jacket and withstanding the pull and twist of the tight leather slings on the M-14 rifles that the team members shot. He could not take heat or cold. He could not even withstand the effect that sunlight had on his tender, burn-scarred body.

Hathcock wore long-sleeved shirts and utilities with the sleeves rolled down. He wore his wide-brimmed campaign hat. And he wore white gloves. He avoided all exposure to direct sunlight. The only job he could perform was that of coach.

During that first year he made several trips to the hospitals at Portsmouth and at Quantico. His burns were healing but something else was wrong. He felt dizzy. He felt exhausted. He shook and lost control of his muscles. He walked with a straddle-legged gait. Something else was wrong—something that the doctors had missed. Something that had sent him to the hospital in Cherry Point when Sonny was born and plagued him in Vietnam.

But they found nothing. It was the burns, they told him. It was his body's inability to sweat and control his internal temperature. In cool weather he suffered hypothermia and in warm weather he suffered heat sickness. It was a condition from which he could never recover.

Hathcock was angry. In his soul he was still straight and strong, a champion. Had he cheated death, beaten the odds and survived burns that would kill most men, only to stand and watch others perform the activity—the sport—that had been the inspiration for his recovery?

The Marine Corps transferred him to the 2nd Marine Division at Camp Lejeune, North Carolina, on February 13, 1972. There he gained the reputation as one of the finest rifle-team coaches ever in the Marine Corps. No one could come near his teams in the High Power, Long Range competitions—he owned the six hundred- and thousand-yard lines. But still, within his heart, he wanted to shoot. He rarely smiled anymore. And the shaking and dizziness grew worse.

On September 20, 1973, after nineteen months of coaching and teaching marksmanship at the rifle ranges near Sneed's

Ferry and Topsail Island, after nineteen months of trying to regain his long-lost steady control and unmatched long-range marksmanship prowess, Carlos received another set of orders. Orders away from rifle ranges and gun powder and the sweet smell of Hoppe's Number 9 powder solvent. Orders away from the greatest love of his life outside his wife and son.

October 16, 1973. Richard Milhous Nixon felt the pressures of Watergate slowly pushing him out of office. On this October day the Army of the Republic of Vietnam fought back the North Vietnamese without the aid of U. S. troops. The last American combat soldiers left there March 29, and the corruption within the ARVN forces that followed that departure would serve as a major factor in the eventual loss of the war in less than two more years. On this same day, while seats of power teetered in those troubled times, Carlos Hathcock stood at a shaky position of attention in front of the desk of Capt. Howard Lovingood, commanding officer of the Marine detachment aboard the USS *Simon Lake*, AS 33, a submarine tender out of Rota, Spain.

Captain Lovingood saw Hathcock's value in spite of his injured body, a body that certainly could not pass any physical fitness test the Marine Corps had ever devised. Lovingood saw the great benefit of the leadership and experience that Hathcock offered his Marines, and he confidently made him his detachment gunnery sergeant—his NCO in charge.

Hathcock performed outstandingly.

Lovingood transferred to the Amphibious Warfare School at Quantico, on July 22, 1974, and turned over command of the *Simon Lake* Marines to a stocky, square-jawed captain who wore a flat-top haircut and saw only Hathcock's limitations. Walter A. Peeples became the former sniper's adversary, rating him substandard on his fitness reports and succeeding in having Hathcock returned to the United States, and relieved from duty, with the recommendation that he be discharged.

In that spring of 1975, the Vietnam war came to a bitter end. The defense of Da Nang crumbled, and hundreds of thousands of Vietnamese fled south along Highway One, seeking refuge behind the collapsing ARVN line.

Marines from the 1st Marine Amphibious Brigade out of

Hawaii, bolstered by the 1st Marine Aircraft Wing and the 4th and the 9th Marine regiments, waited on the USS *Blue Ridge* and USS *Okinawa* and watched as the eight years of efforts by more than 8,744,000 Americans—of whom more than 47,322 died in combat and 10,700 died in support of that combat; of whom 163,303 survived wounds, and of whom 2,500 Americans remained missing in action—ended in bitter defeat.

As the tanks with the single star flags crashed through the gates of the American embassy in Saigon on April 29, 1975, Gunnery Sergeant Carlos Hathcock suffered his own brand of defeat on the USS *Simon Lake*. A month later, at the United States Naval Hospital at Portsmouth, Virginia, he began two months of tests and review by a medical board. On August 5, the verdict came in.

The final paragraph of the report stated: "The patient is limited only in that he cannot perform his physical training exercises as prescribed by the Marine Corps. He is fully able to perform all the other physical duties required of his position. In addition, the demyelinating disease has caused only mild ataxia and has in no way interfered with his ability to perform his job. However, because of the improving nature of his neurological deficit, it is the opinion of the board that the patient is not yet fit for full duty, but is fit for limited duty."

Although the report seemed uplifting, its findings actually were not. This demyelinating disease—what the physicians called his neurological deficit—was multiple sclerosis.

The doctor sat back in his leatherette chair and folded his arms. "Gunny. I've been around for a while, and I'm familiar with the ways of the Marine Corps. To be honest with you, I don't think you're going to make it on active duty. I think with what you have, the Office of Naval Disability Evaluation will give you a 60 percent disability retirement."

"I thought I was fit for duty?" Hathcock said.

"For six months . . . maybe a year? If you were in another branch of service, I could see it, but not in the Marine Corps. You need daily rest and no stress."

Hathcock's mind went immediately to the one place in the Marine Corps that operated at a different pace with a different breed of people, people who did not rush but were tranquil. Because they had to be. They could not hold a steady aim otherwise. Marksmanship Training Unit—the Marine Corps Rifle Team. It was his only hope.

Hathcock looked at the doctor and asked, "Sir. What if I could find a place in the Marine Corps where I could work my own set of hours. Rest when I needed. Where I could live and work and not have stress. What if I could find a place like that?"

"That might be a solution, Gunny, but there isn't any such place."

Hathcock smiled and asked to use the doctor's phone.

A few seconds later the voice of Lt. Col. Charles A. Reynolds, commanding officer of the Weapons Training Battalion at Quantico and the officer in charge of the Marine Corps' Marksmanship Training Unit came on the line.

Hathcock told the colonel the requirements that the doctor had placed on him and finally concluded by saying, "Sir, can you help me? I love the Marine Corps, and I don't ever want to leave it."

"Hathcock," Reynolds said firmly, "We will always want you! Just tell that doctor to sign your chit. You'll have a set of orders in two weeks."

20

The Legend and the Man

As THE SUMMER weather cooled to fall, the hardwood forests that surround the Quantico rifle ranges turned yellow and red and russet and gold. The breezes gave the world a mildness that made thirty-three year old Carlos Hathcock feel almost like his old self as he stood and sat and lay on the two hundred-, three hundred-, and six hundred-yard lines shooting hundreds of rounds. Making his aim true again. Getting ready for the 1976 season. He dreamed of coming back—being a champion again.

His happiness acted as an anesthetic to the pain he felt as he forced himself into the tight, contorted positions from which one must shoot. He could hold them all well since the shooting positions relied on bone support and muscle relaxation. He hit well at three hundred, six hundred, and a thousand yards, but when he had to take the sling off his arm and stand and shoot without the bone support, standing on his two trembling legs, he became frustrated. His off-hand* was horribly below what his average had been before his burns.

The Marines who shot beside him, however, were in awe. They saw the blood-soaked sweat shirt when he took off his heavy shooting jacket. They saw the white gloves with blood-

*Shooting standing without any sort of artificial support, such as a sling strapped to the arm, or the rifle against a solid object.

soaked palms when he took them off after pulling his share of targets in the butts—wrestling down the one hundred-pound steel and wood racks that hold the giant targets and shoving them back in the air after he marked the shot. The Marines who fired beside him admired the fact that he would not accept the assistance or substitutions usually offered a handicapped man.

It seemed as though he had just arrived at Quantico when Maj. David J. Willis confronted him in the parking lot outside the rifle range command post. Hathcock could not remember not knowing Willis. As long as he had been in the Marine Corps, Willis had always been there—a tobacco-chewing Marine who shaved his head and wore the two gold shooting badges of a marksman distinguished with both the rifle and the pistol, and who, like Hathcock, spoke reverently of John Wayne.

"I sent a letter to your medical board at Bethesda. You know they have to make a decision on your case soon. This copy is for your files."

The major put his arm over Hathcock's shoulder and gave him a friendly pat. Then he left Carlos alone, standing near his car, reading the short letter:

From: Operations Officer, Marksmanship Training Unit
To: Commanding Officer, National Naval Medical Center, Bethesda, Maryland 20014

Subj: GySgt C. N. Hathcock, 429 74 6238/0369, USMC

1. The physical capabilities and limitations of GySgt Hathcock have been of great interest to the members of this unit over a period of years. We have served with him through the good and the bad and always with great admiration.

2. He knows, we know, and his medical records indicate that he can no longer do certain tasks within his present capabilities and conditions. However, this does not mean he can not perform as a Marine and more specifically an assignment within this unit. He possesses an unusual, unique knowledge of Marksmanship that allows us to capi-

talize on his talents such as Ammunition Hand Loading, Weapons Repair, Training of Teams, Wind Reading, and Instructional abilities.

3. Probably there are very few Marines within the Corps capable of supporting the Marksmanship Program as well as GySgt Hathcock. Knowledge can only be acquired over a period of time and he has devoted many years to the establishment of his skills by actual participation vice reading material. The success of our teams largely depends on our coaches and he is one of the finest coaches we have. He has asked for no special favors and we have granted few. He is constantly called upon for advice and to perform in the interests of Basic Marksmanship and he has never failed us.

4. By his determination to overcome his physical disabilities, acquired while in combat, he is a constant inspiration not only to our younger Marines but to everyone he serves with.

5. Without any reservations we will continue to respectfully request that he not only stay on active duty but remain with the Marksmanship Training Unit. We are proud to serve with him.

The medical board did not vote on his case until June. Then they sent him the answer for which he had prayed. Yes, he could stay. The board placed him on Permanent Limited Duty—no physical training or physical fitness tests. He could not be transferred because the stipulations of his continued service required monthly visits to the National Naval Medical Center at Bethesda. And finally, to assure the best possible care for him, the chairman of the Department of Neurology, a captain in the Navy's Medical Corps named W. L. Brannon, Jr., assumed care of Hathcock as his doctor.

Hathcock would have been a happy man if the multiple sclerosis had not continued to advance.

July 1976 came hot at Quantico. On Range 4, the thousand-yard range that competitors from all services and NRA shooting clubs called Death Valley, Maj. David Willis lay strapped behind a 300 Winchester Magnum sighting down the powerful scope at the targets a thousand yards away. Carlos Hathcock lay on a shooting pad next to him, tightly wrapped in a shooting jacket and strapped hard to a rifle of similar design.

They practiced for the Interservice individual and team long-range rifle championship matches.

The temperature passed 95 degrees before noon and kept climbing. Willis had the shooters hang thermometers on their scope stands as a reminder to be on guard for heat stroke. The reflected heat sent the mirages boiling and waving so strongly that many of the shooters swore in frustration as they tried to see the targets.

Behind each pair of shooters, a coach sat with his eye fixed to the back of a gigantic, gray spotting scope made by the John Unertl Company.

Ron McAbee, now a gunnery sergeant, stood behind Hathcock, watching and listening to the coach call out the number of clicks to the two men in front of him. When he would call out a wind change, both men were to react by turning the windage adjustment knobs on their scopes and calling the numbers back to the coach.

"Come three right," he said.

"Three right," came a single voice from the right. Hathcock lay on the left.

"Hathcock!" the coach shouted. "Three right!"

Hathcock did not move.

Willis raised on his elbow and slipped the leather rifle sling off his arm.

Hathcock's cheek lay against the raised stock, his eye closed in position behind the scope. His jaw hung open and his breathing was faint.

The frantic Marines unstrapped Carlos from the rifle and began popping the buckles loose from his jacket. Blood dripped from its sleeves, and when they opened it, they saw his sweat shirt was soaked in blood. As the Mari........ .... Hathcock's burn-scarred body, they saw his injur.... bend in his body, his elbows and shoulders and ..... and chest, the skin had split open. They could ...... splits and the new splits, and knew that every ti....

shot, he bled, yet ignored the pain.

"Jesus Christ! Hathcock is gonna die on us! Get him to the reloading shed," Willis commanded. The small reloading shed at the end of the road that bisected Death Valley, just behind the 600 yard line, was the only building which had air conditioning. They took him there and soon after an ambulance arrived.

Major David Willis left Quantico in October of 1976 for a tour in Okinawa as the executive officer of 3rd Battalion, 9th Marines. And when he returned to Quantico's ranges a year later, Carlos was still trying to pull triggers. He still had not given up. But something else had begun in that year that took his mind off competition. Something attainable.

Major E. J. Land was now the Marine Corps' Marksmanship Coordinator, and he was based nearby at Headquarters Marine Corps. He visited Hathcock often during these new Quantico days and discussed a project that Colonel Reynolds was also involved in. It was a Marine Corps-wide sniper program.

There were independent sniper schools such as Colonel Dickman's 4th Recon Battalion school at San Antonio, but there was no organization that put the sniper schools and the sniper programs within the regular establishment of the Marine infantry battalions.

Land did the politicking within the Headquarters Marine Corps bureaucracy. He sold them with the Hathcock legend, with the idea of what the future could hold for battalions that each had squads of snipers. He sold them an exciting new idea that had been on the battlefields since Leonardo da Vinci defended the gates of Florence by sniping with a rifle of his own design, shooting the enemy from three hundred yards away.

But never before had anyone trained snipers during peacetime. It was against the conscience of most men, especially those from Western cultures, to "back shoot," to assassinate from a hide, to bush-whack like an outlaw. It was somehow cowardly to not give an opponent a "sporting" chance.

However, every Marine agreed that the snipers' effect on the Viet Cong and the North Vietnamese was dramatic. There the "Counter-Sniper" program had been applauded because it fought back at the sniper problem that the enemy unleashed on the U. S. forces.

Land and his colleagues pushed the idea of the program onto the commandant. And to sell this "unsportsmanlike" concept of war fighting, Carlos Hathcock became the key ingredient. He was their example of the effectiveness of the sniper in combat—their embodied concept of who the sniper is. And he was their expert, now stationed at Quantico, ready to put all his knowledge and experience and integrity into the foundation—the lesson plans and course structure and content—of the program.

In 1977, Gen. Louis H. Wilson approved the concept and established a program in which every Marine infantry battalion would have a team of eight snipers within a special platoon of scouts and snipers called the Surveillance and Target Acquisition (STA) Platoon.

The Marine Corps Scout/Sniper Instructor School was authorized to begin operation at Quantico. It's staff consisted of three Marines: an officer in charge, Capt. Jack Cuddy; a sniper instructor/armorer, Gunnery Sgt. Ron McAbee; and a senior sniper instructor—the Senior Sniper of the Marine Corps—Gunnery Sgt. Carlos Hathcock. The school would be part of the unit that Major Willis commanded.

In its first year of operation, the sniper school did not host any students. Hathcock and Cuddy and McAbee traveled to Canada, England, and the Netherlands, attending each nation's sniper and scout schools. They brought home ideas and innovations, things like the Ghillie Suit*—a uniform on which the sniper sews long and narrow strips of burlap in

---

*Ghillie Suit—developed from the camouflage suits worn by the gamekeepers and hunting guides in Scotland, called Ghillies, who use this camouflage technique to count game and watch for poachers. The Ghillie Suit was used by British snipers in World War I against the highly skilled German snipers. In 1960, Mrs. Ellie Land sewed together one of the first U. S. Marine Corps Ghillie Suits for her husband, E. J. Land, and his assistant, Chief Gunner (Chief Warrant Officer) Arthur Terry, when they organized the 1st Marine Brigade's scout/sniper school, from which Carlos Hathcock graduated.

various shades of green, brown, and gray. With this piece of gear, a sniper can lie in low grass, ten feet from a victim, and not be seen.

From the start Carlos Hathcock had been perhaps the school's greatest advantage. Men like Land and Reynolds had known they would have to find someone who could make quick decisions for them. How could they find someone who was a national long-range shooting champion, and also the best sniper around? In Hathcock they had him.

He allowed them to make rapid decisions by giving a sound opinion. They knew that if he said it would work, it most likely would, and if he saw trouble with a proposal, it more than likely would be a problem. They trusted his judgment, and that got the school off the ground.

With Hathcock's assistance, Capt. Jack Cuddy established what became the world's finest and most renowned school devoted to sniper training—the art and skill of solo combat. Today it provides training and expertise in areas as diverse as urban warfare, arctic and alpine skills, and counterterrorist tactics.

Hathcock gave all of himself to the program. When Major Willis reported to work at 5:30 each morning, he would look across the parking lot at the small, two-room structure that housed the sniper school. The lights would already be on.

"Carlos?" Willis called as he peeked through the door.

"Yes, Sir! Come on in! Have a cup of coffee!" Hathcock would answer. He had already been there long enough to boil the water for the coffee for the day and check through the lesson plans for his snipers.

The Marines Hathcock taught loved him, and they were in awe of him even before they met him. Captain Cuddy in his introductory presentation would tell them unbelievable stories of courage and cunning in combat—of how two men could hold off more than one hundred for five days, and of how one man could sneak inside an enemy commander's headquarters, kill him, and get away. Naturally they cheered and whistled and grunted and clapped when Cuddy then introduced the sniper who had done all those unbelievable things—Carlos Hathcock.

* * *

But Hathcock was pushing himself harder than he had ever pushed himself before, and his body was crumbling. He had become a man obsessed. He lived by his iron will, and it was strangling his inner peace. He was losing those qualities of patience and calm, steadiness and self-control that had made him a great sniper.

It was late in 1978, a pleasant afternoon out on the rifle range and Major Willis stood talking to Hathcock who was watching his sniper students shoot moving targets on Death Valley. Willis shelled peanuts and shared them with Hathcock.

Neither Marine felt the need for a jacket. Hathcock had the splotchy green sleeves of his camouflage shirt rolled down. His camouflage bush hat showed signs of fading, but still looked crisp, especially accented by his white feather.

Willis leaned against the fender of a pickup truck that was parked on the left side of the range. Hathcock stood near the front and watched the snipers shoot. The major did not see what set Hathcock off, but Hathcock began screaming at the snipers, "Don't you know better than that? You're about to graduate and you still make stupid mistakes like that? You dummies are gonna die if you ever get into combat!"

Hathcock slammed his fist on the hood of the pickup and continued to scream and swear at his men. It was the behavior not of an instructor but of a man falling apart. At that moment, Major Willis, Hathcock's commanding officer and his trusted friend, realized that the candle had burned short.

A few days later Willis spoke to Hathcock as a friend. The senior sniper had just finished a medical board and the news was worse. They contemplated retiring him and that worried Hathcock. He had to make twenty years.

"Hathcock, damn it, as far as I'm concerned, I'll bury your body on the six hundred-yard line. You can stay here with me as long as the good Lord allows us to stay on this earth, but in this command, you're gonna have to function."

"Sir," Hathcock said, leaning forward in the chair next to Willis's desk, beneath a statue of John Wayne and a giant, silver trophy cup filled with peanuts, "I gotta make twenty. That's only a few more months. Just until the end of June."

It was just before Christmas and Willis had strong doubts whether Hathcock could make those final few months, but he would not spoil a man's Christmas with a decision right now. However, he did plant a seed for Hathcock to consider.

"There are other things involved here," Willis told him. "You've had a long and illustrious career. You are a living legend. People respect you. All the snipers want to be Carlos Hathcock. They emulate your gesticulations, your voice, the way you go about things. Not only do they do what you say, but they want to be you. So you've got to watch what you do, because you can destroy what you've done here. And the destruction is not just that of a myth or a legend, but rather the sniper won't be as good as he should have been because he can't be you. You want to turn him into a top-notch sniper, but you want to do it within the Marine Corps order and within the means that we have available, not through total frustration and anger."

One day in January 1979, while he watched his snipers taking their final examination—trying to move across open terrain, camouflaged from sight, make it to their firing point, fire, and exit without either Hathcock or Captain Cuddy seeing them—Hathcock collapsed.

Doctor Brannon examined him, watched him for days, and read the tests. The inevitable conclusion occurred: It was time to quit.

He called Major Willis. When the major answered, Brannon began the conversation by simply saying, "No."

Willis knew immediately what the call was about.

"Look," Willis said, "I'll come up there and sit down and talk to you about it."

"No!"

"I know him. I've known him a long time."

"No," the doctor said. "I know him too, and I've counselled him and the answer is no. He has to get out."

It was hard for Willis as a commanding officer, and doubly hard as a friend, to hear that final verdict. And if he couldn't accept that no, then how could Hathcock?

On April 20, 1979, in Maj. David Willis's office, Gunnery Sgt. Carlos N. Hathcock II ended his Marine Corps career, transferred to the Disabled Retired List with 100 percent disability.

Hathcock had taught classes up to the day before his retirement. He told the snipers that afternoon, "Remember, the most deadly thing on the battlefield is one well-aimed shot." He turned, fighting back tears, walked out of the room, put on his bush hat with the white feather in its band, and went outside to be alone with his thoughts.

On that April afternoon when he stood before Major Willis and listened to the order transferring him to that retired list, he cried. Hathcock stood at attention and accepted a rifle from McAbee—a rifle built by the Marines from the Marksmanship Training Unit's armory. Carlos Hathcock had been involved in determining the requirements for this rifle and in testing it once it was made. The rifle was an M-40 A1 Sniper Rifle—a rifle made only for and by the Marines using a Remington Model 700, 7.62mm Rifle Receiver, fitting it with a "heavy" barrel made of stainless steel, free-floating it in a solid fiberglass stock, and then mounting a 10-power Unertl scope on it.

When Major Willis, fighting back tears, read the plaque— a bronzed Marine campaign cover mounted above a brass plate—the room stood silent. "There have been many Marines. There have been many Marksmen. But there has been only one Sniper—Gunnery Sergeant Carlos N. Hathcock. One Shot—One Kill."

Hathcock slumped low in the boat's front seat, holding his camouflage bush hat atop his head as the craft, with a stainless steel hull covered with metal-flake red and silver fiberglass, raced through the surf, sending salt spray across his face as the wind whipped over the green nylon jacket that he wore. His eyes focused on the yellow circle of letters on the jacket's left breast that spelled out U. S. Marine Corps Shooting Team. After six years of retirement, he still missed the Marine Corps.

The transition from active duty had been horrible for Hathcock. As he first saw it, the Marine Corps had cut him adrift, and he spent the rest of 1979 and much of 1980 sitting in a dark room in the rear of his Virginia Beach home—a room filled with Marine Corps relics and haunting memories—brooding. He called it the Bunker, and there he withered, saying nothing and asking for nothing. He anguished over the $610 a month pay that represented the sum of his nineteen years and ten months of active service and how that meager paycheck was all he could offer his family. He could not work for pay and collect a disability retirement too.

The feelings of rejection, inadequacy, and uselessness sent him spiraling into deepest depression. The flame that once blazed within his soul and kept him coming back again and again, faded and threatened to die.

Jo Hathcock saw her husband mourn the loss of his career and hoped that, as in death, the mourning would pass and Carlos would again discover life. But after more than a year, she packed her bags and angrily told him that she was through living with a dead man.

Her decision to leave aroused Hathcock's shrunken emotions, and he no longer thought of his past as his future smacked him head-on. He could not imagine life without Jo and Sonny. Hathcock rarely asked for help and never asked for consolation. But this time he did, and the significance of his plea convinced Jo to unpack.

Hathcock first sought life in yard work, but the heat and stress often left him unconscious on the lawn. It frightened the neighbors and presented little excitement for him. Thus he and Jo searched for something else.

As the boat sped from whitecap to whitecap, racing away from the Virginia Beach shore, sending cascades of spray skyward, Hathcock glanced at his friend, who controlled the craft with relaxed ease, and smiled.

Steve McCarver turned toward Hathcock and yelled above the wind's roar, "Hear anything from Sonny?"

"He's down at Jacksonville, Florida, going to another school," Hathcock said. He was proud of his son—now a Marine lance corporal stationed at Cherry Point, and had made the shooting team there—the same team on which Carlos had gone distinguished and won a national shooting title. Sonny had joined the Corps on his own, and that pleased Hathcock.

"He'll be home in a few weeks . . . gonna take leave."

"Be good to see him," Steve said as he turned his face back toward the rising sun.

Hathcock had first met Steve McCarver at the Bait Barn, one of the dozens of tackle shops near the inlet. He had picked one at random and walked in, hoping to find something that might help fill the emptiness that his Marine Corps career had left. Perhaps talk of fishing might spark something hiding in that void.

Several men sat and stood near the counter. Men who wore baseball caps with names of fishing line companies and boat companies and tobacco companies sewn on their fronts. The calloused-handed men talked of fishing, all right. Carlos had fished for bass and trout and brim, but these men, who dressed in short-sleeve shirts and khaki trousers and had tan, freckled arms and hard fingers, these men who laughed as they talked, spoke not of bass or brim or crappie or trout. They spoke of sharks.

Hathcock sat in a lawn chair and looked at the rods and giant hooks and nets and trays of lead sinkers and huge spools of line and shelves filled with boxes of giant lures. He looked at the ceiling and the walls clustered with long-handled dip nets and gaff hooks. And among the busy work of hardware and tackle—gear to catch every kind of fish that swam past the shallow Virginia Beach waters—he saw the shark tackle. He saw the hooks as big as his hand. He saw steel line and leader and huge reels and stiff rods. Hardware more than fishing gear, but weapons made to wage an individual battle of one man against one fish, each trying to end the other's life. These tools spoke adventure to him, and his heart soared.

A salty looking man stood next to the counter and leaned against it, resting one hand on his hip as he crossed one foot over the other. It was Steve, and he talked of an ordeal in the shallow water, just off the shores. He told of the shark that refused to quit fighting. And when he got his fifteen-foot motorboat near the dangerous fish, the shark threshed from the water, his jaws spread wide, and lunged up and over the boat's stern, engulfing the motor.

It was awesome, and Hathcock returned to this place of

tales nearly every day, where he watched and listened as the men hauled in their catches: giant lemons and tigers and makos and sand sharks. Sharks from the distant deep and from the shallow shoals where unknowing weekend anglers searched for other sport fish, unaware that gigantic lemon sharks, known to eat man, lurked there too.

It seemed like a game, this sport of teasing disaster—of dancing on the wings of doom, tempting death and tasting that special part of life that only the adventurer can know. And for Hathcock, it was only a matter of time before he too would be out in the shallows, tempting the sharks. It frightened Jo, but she knew her husband was again alive—again "The Man in the Arena," a paragraph that he had kept among his personal possessions for many years, and now turned yellow on his Bunker wall.

> It is not the critic who counts, not the one who points out how the strong man stumbled or how the doer of deeds might have done them better. The credit belongs to the man who is actually in the arena, whose face is marred with sweat and dust and blood; who strives valiantly; who errs and comes short again and again; who knows the great enthusiasms, the great devotions, and spends himself in a worthy cause; who, if he wins, knows the triumph of high achievement; and who, if he fails, at least fails while daring greatly, *so that his place shall never be with those cold and timid souls who know neither victory nor defeat* [emphasis added].

Virginia Beach now appeared small on the horizon as the silver and red boat slid to a gliding stop. Steve stood and dropped the anchor in the shallow water. "Let's get at it, Carlos. They'll swim right by us if we don't get at em."

As Hathcock worked his way up on his unsteady legs, he looked across the brown water and wondered what long and sleek body with his deadly jaws agape might be resting just below, awaiting his bait. The water seemed so calm, yet when the hook would set, it would boil and churn. It was like life, he thought, it's not always like it appears. His impression of the Marine Corps forsaking him had been like that.

It was only when life became more meaningful that Hathcock noticed that his beloved Marine Corps had been there all along. Marines wrote to him and called him and came to his home to visit all during the time that he hid in the Bunker. And they never stopped. These friends drove him to Quantico to the Distinguished Shooter's Association's annual banquet, and home again. The Marine Corps League named its marksmanship award in honor of Hathcock—a trophy that the Commandant of the Marine Corps presents to the enlisted Marine who had made the most outstanding contribution to marksmanship each year.

But the most significant event came in the spring of 1985. A capacity crowd jammed themselves elbow to elbow, standing along the walls and filling every seat on a steamy Virginia afternoon to watch the Marine Corps Scout/Sniper Instructor class graduate and to hear a legendary Marine speak.

On that sunny third day of May 1985, Carlos Hathcock stood just outside the door, unsteady in his spit-shined cowboy boots. With crooked and stiffened, burn-scarred hands, he pulled and readjusted the dark brown tie around the crisp, beige collar of the new shirt that he wore with his brown suit. Jo had gone to Pembroke Mall and bought both the shirt and tie for this special occasion. Moments earlier, he had joked with Lt. Col. David Willis about wearing a suit and tie. "You should have left the price tag on the tie," Willis told Hathcock, "that way, when you're through wearing it, you can go get your money back."

Finally, at one o'clock that afternoon, across from the firing ranges that surrounded him through most of his career, Carlos Hathcock stood before the graduating snipers and their families, trembling—unsure of what to do or say. But despite his nervousness, fatigue, and muscular pain he was extremely happy. He paused and looked at each man's face, and with an emotionally choked voice, he opened his mouth and spoke not from cards or a memorized speech, but from his heart.

After a short, but emotionally charged speech, Hathcock

swallowed an enormous lump in his throat and through cloudy eyes he looked across the room filled with Marines and Army Rangers and Navy Seals who sat in awe of this great sniper, a sniper who until today had not seemed human but a legend used by their instructors as the example of what one man can do. And as Hathcock cleared his voice and fought back the knotted feelings that now welled forth, these men and their families and Marines who were friends of his and came to see the event all sat hushed and in awe.

"I love you all." Hathcock said as his voice cracked with emotion.

The men and organization that he loved had not forgotten him. Today they honored him at the school that he helped create and where much of his soul still remained.

The small boat rocked with the waves that broke across the shallows offshore from Virginia Beach. Hathcock had helped scatter the "shark chum"—mackerel and tuna heads and chicken blood. Now he sat with a thick fishing rod staked in a steel fixture and waited for its gigantic reel to sing. He had become an old hand at this now, after making several trips out to hunt these great and dangerous fish.

His face no longer looked ashen and pale; it was dark and beading a light coat of sweat. He was after another big and deadly shark that he would tail-rope alongside the boat, like *The Old Man and the Sea*. Nearly like being a sniper again.

Hathcock had learned the sport quickly and demonstrated his rapidly improving skills by landing a 277-pound lemon shark on one of his first outings—a shark tournament. He won second place with that fish he caught in four feet of water.

"You look good," Steve said as he and Carlos sat rocking and bobbing in the red and silver hunting boat they named "Shark Buster."

"I feel good," Carlos said, tilting his eyes upward.

"I told you. I would either kill you or make you well," McCarver said.

"I am getting better," Hathcock said as he sat in the rocking and bobbing craft, his bush hat tilted back, and a soft breeze rustling the white feather tucked in his hatband. As he gazed at the sea-filled horizon, listening for the line to spool off the reel and sing to him, a broad smile beamed across his sun-tanned face. He felt alive again. Again in the arena.

BIBLIOGRAPHY

Books

Bartlett, Tom (editor). *Ambassadors in Green*. Washington, D.C.: Leatherneck Association Inc., 1971.

Lippard, Karl C. (Sergeant USMC). *The Warriors: The United States Marines*. Lancaster, Texas: Vietnam Marine Publications, 1983.

The Tactics Group. *Platoon Commander's Tactical Guide*. The Basic School, Marine Corps Development and Education Command, Quantico, Virginia: U.S. Marine Corps. 1983.

U.S. Army. *Scouting, Patrolling and Sniping* [FM 21-75]. Washington, D.C.: U.S. Government Printing Office, 1944.

U.S. Marine Corps. *Sniping* [FMFM 1-3B]. Washington, D.C.: U.S. Government Printing Office, 1969.

U.S. Marine Corps, *U.S. Marine Corps Essential Subjects*. Washington, D.C.: U.S. Government Printing Office, 1983.

Von Schell, Adolf (Captain, German Army Staff Corps). *Battle Leadership*. Columbus, Georgia: U.S. Army, *The Benning Herald*, Fort Benning, Georgia, 1933.

Interviews

Hathcock, Carlos Norman II. Personal interview (5 hours taped), Aug. 2-3, 1984, Virginia Beach, Virginia.

Hathcock, Carlos Norman II. Telephone interviews: Sept. 23, 1984; Oct. 7, 18, 20, 1984; Nov. 14, 28, 1984; Dec. 5, 7, 28, 1984; Feb. 18, 1985; April 22, 1985; May 1, 23, 1985, Virginia Beach, Virginia.

Hathcock, Carlos Norman II. Personal interview (4.5 hours taped), Jan. 13, 1985, Virginia Beach, Virginia.

Hathcock, Josephine Bryan. Personal interview (4 hours taped), Aug. 2-3, 1984, Virginia Beach, Virginia.

Holden, David C. Taped statement (1 hour taped), Dec. 15, 1984, Chicago, Illinois.

Land, Edward James, Sr. Personal interview (3 hours taped), Nov. 27, 1984, Triangle, Virginia.

McAbee, Ronald H. (Master Gunnery Sergeant USMC). Personal interview (4 hours taped), July 12, 1985, Quantico, Virginia.

Wight, D. E. (Major USMC) and Hathcock, Carlos Norman II (Sergeant USMC). USMC Oral History Interview (1.5 hours taped), Feb. 15, 1967, Hill 55, Da Nang TAOR, Vietnam.

Willis, David J. (Lieutenant Colonel USMC). Personal interview (3 hours taped), July 19, 1984, Quantico, Virginia.

Willis, David J. (Lieutenant Colonel USMC). Personal interview (3 hours taped), May 10, 1985, Quantico, Virginia.

Magazines

American Rifleman, The (National Rifle Association). "Snipers—Specialists in Warfare," by Frank G. McGuire. Washington, D.C., July 1967.

Amphibious Warfare Review. "Gunnery Sergeant Carlos N. Hathcock II Award," Marine Corps League, Washington, D.C., November 1984.

Gun World. "One Course Open: Slay!" by Jack Lewis. San Juan Capistrano, California, June 1967.

Time magazine. "Vietnam: Ten Years Later," New York, April 1985.

U.S. News and World Report. "Vietnam Letters: Echoes from a War Long Gone," by five American servicemen. Vietnam, November 1984.

Newspapers

Bonnett, Alice. "Hathcock Will Have a Family Christmas." San Antonio, Texas: *San Antonio Express*, November 13, 1969.

Childs, Jack (Gunnery Sergeant USMC). "VC Defector Unveils Elite Sniper Company." Da Nang, Vietnam: *Sea Tiger*, July 19, 1966.

Dahl, Carolyn (Lance Corporal USMC). "Making Long Shots Count." Quantico, Virginia: *The Quantico Sentry*, April 1, 1977.

"Gunnery Sergeant Carlos Hathcock Retires." Quantico, Virginia: *The Quantico Sentry*, April 23, 1979.

Hardie, Jim. "They Learn Cong Way of Killing." Miami, Florida: *Miami News*, December 6, 1965.

LaBell, Dan (Corporal USMC). "3D Mardiv Develops Counter-sniper Plan." Vietnam: *Sea Tiger*, February 1, 1967.

Martin, Bruce A. (Sergeant USMC). "4th Marines Snipe at 1,000 Yard Range." Hue/Phu Bai, Vietnam: *Sea Tiger*, July 26, 1966.

Martin, Bruce A. (Sergeant USMC). "Snipers Hit Targets 13 out of 28 Shots." Phu Bai, Vietnam: *Sea Tiger*, September 21, 1966.

Martinez, David (Sergeant USMC). "Marine Snipers Prove Their Combat Value." Phu Bai, Vietnam: *Sea Tiger*, May 31, 1968.

Richert, Dave (1st Lieutenant USMC). "Marine Snipers: Dedicated, Deadly." Dong Ha, Vietnam: *Sea Tiger*, January 17, 1969.

Selby, G. F. (Staff Sergeant USMC). "Sniper Platoon Kills 117 in First Five Months." Da Nang, Vietnam: *Sea Tiger*, July 28, 1967.

"Scout-Sniper." Raleigh, North Carolina: *Raleigh News and Observer*, February 11, 1967.

Stokey, M. II (Lance Corporal USMC). "$8 Bounty Offered for Marine Sniper." Vietnam: *Sea Tiger*, May 12, 1967.

Taylor, Ira L. (Sergeant USMC). "Snipers Kill 60 Since January: Task Force X-Ray." Chu Lai, Vietnam: *Sea Tiger*, May 5, 1967.

Weigh, W. H (Sergeant USMC). "Marine Snipers Pick Off VC." Vietnam: *The Observer*, April 16, 1966.

Wilson, G.E. (Master Sergeant USMC). "1st Division Scout-Snipers Killing Two VC a Day." Da Nang, Vietnam: *Sea Tiger*, February 1, 1967.

Official U.S. Marine Corps Records

MARINE COMMAND CHRONOLOGIES: Organizational data, narrative summary, sequential listing of significant events, supporting documents that include subordinate unit chronologies, messages, situation reports, after-action reports, frag orders, and operation orders.

May 25, 1966—1ST MARINE DIVISION COMMAND CHRONOLOGY, 1-30 APRIL 1966. Lewis J. Fields, Major General USMC, Commanding General. Chu Lai TAOR, Vietnam.

June 12, 1966—1ST MARINE DIVISION COMMAND CHRONOLOGY, 1-31 May 1966. Lewis J. Fields, Major General USMC, Commanding General. Chu Lai TAOR, Vietnam.

July 10, 1966—1ST MARINE DIVISION COMMAND CHRONOLOGY, 1-30 JUNE 1966. Lewis J. Fields, Major General USMC, Commanding General. Chu Lai TAOR, Vietnam.

August 13, 1966—1ST MARINE DIVISION COMMAND CHRONOLOGY, 1-31 JULY 1966. Lewis J. Fields, Major General USMC, Commanding General. Chu Lai TAOR, Vietnam.

September 12, 1966—1ST MARINE DIVISION COMMAND CHRONOLOGY, 1-31 AUGUST 1966. Lewis J. Fields, Major General USMC, Commanding General. Chu Lai TAOR, Vietnam.

October 9, 1966—1ST MARINE DIVISION COMMAND CHRONOLOGY, 1-30 SEPTEMBER 1966. Herman Nickerson, Jr., Major General USMC, Commanding General. Chu Lai TAOR, Vietnam.

December 7, 1966—1ST MARINE DIVISION COMMAND CHRONOLOGY, 1-30 OCTOBER 1966. Herman Nickerson, Jr., Major General USMC, Commanding General. Da Nang TAOR, Vietnam.

January 2, 1967—1ST MARINE DIVISION COMMAND CHRONOLOGY, 1-30 NOVEMBER 1966. Herman Nickerson, Jr., Major General USMC, Commanding General. Da Nang TAOR, Vietnam.

January 30, 1967—1ST MARINE DIVISION COMMAND CHRONOLOGY, 1-31 DECEMBER 1966. Herman Nickerson, Jr., Major General USMC, Commanding General. Da Nang TAOR, Vietnam.

February 16, 1967—1ST MARINE DIVISION COMMAND CHRONOLOGY, 1-31 JANUARY 1967. Herman Nickerson, Jr., Major General USMC, Commanding General. Da Nang TAOR, Vietnam.

April 4, 1967—1ST MARINE DIVISION COMMAND
CHRONOLOGY, 1-28 FEBRUARY 1967. Herman
Nickerson, Jr., Major General USMC, Commanding
General. Da Nang TAOR, Vietnam.

May 7, 1967—1ST MARINE DIVISION COMMAND
CHRONOLOGY, 1-31 MARCH 1967. Herman Nicker-
son, Jr., Major General USMC, Commanding General.
Da Nang TAOR, Vietnam.

June 6, 1967—1ST MARINE DIVISION COMMAND
CHRONOLOGY, 1-30 APRIL 1967. Herman Nicker-
son, Jr., Major General USMC, Commanding General.
Da Nang TAOR, Vietnam.

May 25, 1969—7TH MARINE REGIMENT COMMAND
CHRONOLOGY, 1-30 APRIL 1969. R. L. Nichols,
Colonel USMC, Commanding Officer, Hill 55, Da
Nang TAOR, Vietnam: includes Operation Order 1-69,
"Operation Oklahoma Hills."

June 23, 1969—7TH MARINE REGIMENT COMMAND
CHRONOLOGY, 1-31 MAY 1969. R. L. Nichols,
Colonel USMC, Commanding Officer, Hill 55, Da
Nang TAOR, Vietnam.

July 18, 1969—7TH MARINE REGIMENT COMMAND
CHRONOLOGY, 1-30 JUNE 1969. Gildo S. Codispoti,
Colonel USMC, Commanding Officer, Hill 55, Da
Nang TAOR, Vietnam.

August 17, 1969—7TH MARINE REGIMENT COM-
MAND CHRONOLOGY, 1-31 JULY 1969. Gildo S.
Codispoti, Colonel USMC, Commanding Officer, Hill
55, Da Nang TAOR, Vietnam.

September 13, 1969—7TH MARINE REGIMENT COM-
MAND CHRONOLOGY, 1-31 AUGUST 1969. Gildo
S. Codispoti, Colonel USMC, Commanding Officer,
LZ Baldy, Da Nang TAOR, Vietnam.

October 23, 1969—7TH MARINE REGIMENT COM-

MAND CHRONOLOGY, 1-30 SEPTEMBER 1969.
Gildo S. Codispoti, Colonel USMC, Commanding Officer, LZ Baldy, Da Nang TAOR, Vietnam.

November 12, 1940—"Equipping the American Sniper,"
George O. Van Orden and Calvin A. Lloyd. Marine
Corps Schools, Quantico, Virginia: Detailed report recommending equipment for the Marine sniper prior to
World War II (including Model 70 Winchester rifle, like
that which Hathcock used in 1966-67 in Vietnam).

March 12, 1968—NAVY CROSS CITATION. Posthumous
award of Navy Cross to Corporal John Roland Burke,
USMC, Killed in Action June 6, 1967, at Khe Sanh,
Vietnam, while a member of Headquarters and Service
Company, 1st Battalion, 26th Marine Regiment. Presented by Mr. Paul R. Ignatuis, Secretary of the Navy.

April 17, 1979—CARLOS N. HATHCOCK II SERVICE
RECORD BOOK: All of Carlos Hathcock's official military records from May 20, 1959, through April 17,
1979.

April 17, 1979—CARLOS N. HATHCOCK II OFFICIAL
MEDICAL RECORD: Complete history of Carlos
Hathcock from May 20, 1959, through April 17, 1979
(includes all recommendations, findings, and data from
all medical boards held).

June 21, 1985—NATIONAL POW/MIA RECOGNITION
DAY. Official U.S. Marine Corps Message from Commandant of the Marine Corps to ALMAR [All Marine Corps], Washington, D.C.: Contains all specific
numbers of servicemen who served in Vietnam;
numbers of those wounded, killed, or listed as Missing
in Action; numbers of those taken prisoner; breakdown
of statistics state by state; breakdown of all numbers
year by year; and milestone dates and significant events
through the span of the war.

July 20, 1985—INTERSERVICE RIFLE MATCH REC-
  ORDS. U.S. Marine Corps Marksmanship Training
  Unit, Quantico, Virginia: All-time record scores of all
  legs of the Interservice Rifle Matches.

Scholarly Papers and Other Documents

Technical Intelligence Bulletin. "The Soviet M1891/30
  7.62 x 54MM Mosin-Nagant Sniper Rifle." 11th Military Intelligence Battalion, Aberdeen Proving Ground,
  Maryland: Detailed technical description of the Mosin-
  Nagant Sniper Rifle. February 17, 1977.
Joiner, Charles A. "Vietnam." A cultural, historical, and
  economic account of Vietnam from ancient times
  through the various conflicts, including the Vietnam
  War that involved the United States between 1964 and
  1973, and into the current communist system of government. New York: McMillian Educational Corporation,
  1976.
Sharkey, John. "Vietnam War." A scholarly record of the
  Vietnam War from the beginnings during the Viet Minh
  rebellion of the early 1950s through the ouster of Diem
  and on through until the end of the war in 1975. New
  York: McMillian Educational Corporation, 1976.

G-SUIT

Meray Halperin & Aharon Lapidot

Over forty years of continuous combat have made the Israeli
Air Force into one of the most formidable fighting units
and the most sophisticated Air Force in the world. G-SUIT,
a series of combat reports from Israeli pilots, records the
evolution and the reaction of this airforce from its earliest
days to the present day: Israeli Meteor squadrons fighting
Arab Vampire units; the rise of the Mirage in action against
MiGs; Skyhawks vs. MiGs; the Six Day War; the first
Phantom squadrons; the air war against missiles and the
Yom Kippur War. G-SUIT also reveals details of the less
well-known aspects of the Israeli War as well as the recent
hazards of active missions over Beirut, F-15s vs. MiG 21s,
and F16s on strike missions against the Nuclear Reactor
in Baghdad.

0 7474 0466 6   War Non-Fiction

ECLIPSE

Alan Moorehead

The Allied Landings in Sicily; the battles of Anzio and Monte Cassino; D-Day and the Normandy beaches; the liberation of Paris and Brussels; the tragedy of Arnhem; the crossing of the Rhine – and the final capitulation of the German armies. These were milestones in the eclipse of Hitler's short-lived empire. From the red cliffs of Taormina to the balcony of Oslo's Grand Hotel on V.E. Day, journalist Alan Moorehead was with the fighting soldiers at all times. His account is both a moving personal record and a brilliantly sustained piece of war reporting.

0 7221 6185 9   War Non-Fiction

CHOPPER 5: RENEGADE MIAs

Jack Hawkins

MEN OF THE FIRST AIR CAV

They were the cowboys of the sky – the U.S. helicopter gunship soldiers who believed in what they fought for and laid their lives on the line.

NO TERMS FOR TRAITORS

As the Viet Cong move in on the Special Forces camp near Dong Tre, the First Air Cav lays down awesome firepower, blasting the enemy from the hills. In the heat of battle, Brody spots something that turns his guts to ice – a Viet Cong squad led by a couple of American GIs.

Brody and his men have their orders: track down the killers and waste them. Outnumbered, they attack the enemy camp and fight hand to hand until the First Air Cav explodes on the scene, turning the bright green hills of Dong Tre into a Viet Cong bloodbath. And when the smoke clears, there's no place to hide for the

RENEGADE MIAs

Also by Jack Hawkins in the CHOPPER series in Sphere Books:
BOOK 1: BLOOD TRAILS
BOOK 2: TUNNEL WARRIORS
BOOK 3: JUNGLE SWEEP
BOOK 4: RED RIVER

COMBAT CREW

John Comer

COMBAT CREW

At the height of the Allied bomber offensive between July 1943 and January 1944 when in many cases only one in twelve returned, John Comer flew 25 combat missions.

To survive six months was a miracle. To live through them was to endure constant danger, tension, fear – and excitement. With thrilling and horrifying immediacy he takes us back to those heady days of the fighter and flak infested skies over occupied Europe to witness the vital part played by the 381st Bomb Group in the relentless war of attrition against Nazi Germany.

0 7474 0424 0   War Non-Fiction/Autobiography

RULING THE WAVES

Dennis Barker

From the destruction of the Spanish Armada to the victory at Port Stanley, the Royal Navy has served as Britain's sword and shield for centuries. But what role does our noblest fighting force have now in the world of Star Wars, satellites, defence cuts and deterrence?

As well as conducting numerous interviews and an in-depth review of the Navy's fighting ships, Dennis Barker went to the Arctic Circle with the Royal Marines and trained in 40 degrees below zero; took part in mock battles in dense fog; talked to crews of Sea Harriers, and witnessed the electronic tactics of destroyers preparing for battle. This is a complete portrait of a modern fighting force and its dedicated officers and ratings – the definitive account of the Senior Service today.

0 7474 0060 1   War Non-Fiction

A LETHAL VINTAGE

Martin Sylvester

William Warner, wine merchant and *bon viveur*, takes the murder of his wife's suspected lover rather seriously. Not least because he strongly suspects the gun-toting motorcyclists were really after *him*.

With irrepressible enthusiasm and a healthy contempt for Chelsea CID's moribund Superintendent Priestly, William launches his own investigation via the underworld connections of his Wapping warehouse manager. The bulldog breed don't give up, and whether floundering in Bavaria with the delectable Eva or almost floundering on the rocks of his marriage, he is unstoppable in pursuit of murder, mayhem, beautiful women and of course, a wine to drink with scrambled eggs . . .

Also by Martin Sylvester in Sphere Books:
A DANGEROUS AGE

0 7474 0053 9   CRIME   £3.50

THE OUTCAST

Philip Cornford

The first sign of a cover-up at Tindal air base comes by accident. But that's all Mackinnon needs. A top-notch investigative journalist with a zeal matched only by his recklessness, he digs with the tenacity of a man possessed.

For he has a very special reason for uncovering the truth. And his mole on the mysterious Monday Committee, as well as the notorious KGB hawk Yakov and the killer Maguire have their own sinister reasons for drawing him into their lethal web of subterfuge and violence. This time Mackinnon's deadline means exactly that . . .

0 7474 0138 1   THRILLER   £3.50

All Sphere Books are available at your bookshop or newsagent, or can be ordered from the following address: Sphere Books, Cash Sales Department, P.O. Box 11, Falmouth, Cornwall TR10 9EN.

Please send cheque or postal order (no currency), and allow 60p for postage and packing for the first book plus 25p for the second book and 15p for each additional book ordered up to a maximum charge of £1.90 in U.K.

B.F.P.O. customers please allow 60p for the first book, 25p for the second book plus 15p per copy for the next 7 books, thereafter 9p per book.

Overseas customers, including Eire, please allow £1.25 for postage and packing for the first book, 75p for the second book and 28p for each subsequent title ordered.